THE HORIZON BOOK OF THE
RENAISSANCE

THE

The
*c-*HORIZON
Book of

RENAISSANCE

By the Editors of
HORIZON MAGAZINE

Editor in Charge
RICHARD M. KETCHUM

Author
J. H. PLUMB

With biographical essays by
MORRIS BISHOP
GARRETT MATTINGLY
KENNETH CLARK
RALPH ROEDER
J. BRONOWSKI
IRIS ORIGO
H. R. TREVOR-ROPER
DENIS MACK SMITH
MARIA BELLONCI

Published by AMERICAN HERITAGE PUBLISHING CO., INC., NEW YORK

Book Trade Distribution by DOUBLEDAY & COMPANY, INC.

Horizon

PUBLISHER
James Parton

EDITOR
Joseph J. Thorndike, Jr.

MANAGING EDITOR
William Harlan Hale

Staff for this Book

EDITOR
Richard M. Ketchum

EDITORIAL ASSISTANTS
Martha House
Norman Kotker
Katharine H. McCagg
Mary Sherman Parsons

EUROPEAN BUREAU
Gertrudis Feliu, *Chief*
Timothy Green
Ann Natanson

COPY EDITOR
Margaret Robinson
Assistant: Sally Dreyfus Carr

ART DIRECTOR
Irwin Glusker

DESIGNER
Joel Szasz

HORIZON Magazine is published by
American Heritage Publishing Co., Inc.,
551 Fifth Avenue, New York 17, N.Y.

Above, an angel by the Florentine Filippino Lippi.
Title page: a detail from Cossa's Triumph of Venus.

CONTENTS

INTRODUCTION 6

THE DAWN OF THE RENAISSANCE 10
PETRARCH 24

THE PRINCE AND THE STATE 40
MACHIAVELLI 56

THE ARTS 88
THE YOUNG MICHELANGELO 104

FLORENCE: CRADLE OF HUMANISM 128
LORENZO DE' MEDICI 144

MILAN: CITY OF STRIFE 168
LEONARDO DA VINCI 184

ROME: SPLENDOR AND THE PAPACY 208
POPE PIUS II 224

VENICE: THE GOLDEN YEARS 256
DOGE FRANCESCO FOSCARI 272

THE IMAGES OF MAN 304
FEDERIGO DA MONTEFELTRO 320

WOMEN OF THE RENAISSANCE 344
BEATRICE AND ISABELLA D'ESTE 360

THE SPREAD OF THE RENAISSANCE 384

Acknowledgments and Index 417

INTRODUCTION

Man has an incurable habit of wanting to know where he has been and what he has done. This is his way of assessing the present and reassuring himself about the future, for he is heir to the best as well as the worst of his past—and, just possibly, history may repeat itself. There are few ages that make him so proud of the human achievement as the one called the Renaissance.

Curiously, there is no general agreement among scholars as to what this singularly complicated period was, or when it occurred. As a distinct historical period, its beginnings are blurred, its end unknown. Some historians date the Renaissance from the twelfth or thirteenth centuries, while others say the Middle Ages lasted until the seventeenth; another opinion holds that the Renaissance began with the fall of Constantinople in 1453, or with the introduction of printing from movable type in 1451 and its common usage fifty years later. As for what it was—one man calls it the birth of modern man, another a rebirth of interest in the classics, still others an emancipation from centuries of darkness, a period of transition from medieval to modern times, or simply an era of unusual creativity. There are even those who say it did not happen at all.

This last view is, of course, an exaggeration. So many novel forces and ideas came into the life of Western Europe in the fifteenth and sixteenth centuries, so many old forms and thoughts were abandoned, that it is impossible not to think of these years as a period of spiritual revolution. Before 1400 or thereabouts, no one thought of building a permanent theater and staging a secular play in it; by 1600 theaters were springing up in every important city, and accomplished playwrights were writing dramas for them. Before 1400 few artists would have dared paint a picture of a naked woman, unless perhaps she were a sinful Mother Eve; by 1500 Botticelli had not only painted one of the most beautiful nudes in the world, but had made it represent a pagan deity, Venus. In 1350 not a man in Western Europe could read a page of Greek; by 1500 there were thousands, and the Greek classics, lost for a millennium, were being reprinted and eagerly studied. During the Middle Ages, Aristotle (who was read in translation) was considered the ultimate authority in many fields of human thought; in 1536 Ramus took his doctorate with the daring thesis, "Everything said by Aristotle is wrong." Changes as potent as these operated in almost

every area of intellectual and social life; and many of the men who felt their power said they were living in a world born anew.

Yet if the word *Renaissance* has any general meaning to the average person, the chances are that it indicates a time of artistic achievement. The names Michelangelo and Leonardo da Vinci, Raphael and Botticelli, Donatello, Titian, and Cellini are familiar to all, and each conjures up its own image of some magnificent work of art. There is Renaissance painting and sculpture; music, architecture, and literature; fabrics, metalwork, jewelry, furniture—all the major and minor arts on a scale seldom approached before or since.

There is more, unknown or unsuspected. Today, when the French ambassador to the United States presents his credentials in Washington, he is carrying on a tradition of diplomacy that took shape in Renaissance Italy. An accountant in Dayton, Ohio, totting up corporate assets and liabilities, is following a system codified by a Franciscan monk in the fifteenth century. A scientist at Harkness Pavilion in New York, examining diseased cells in a piece of lung tissue, perpetuates a tradition of scientific observation outlined by Leonardo da Vinci; the arguments over what subjects American school children will or will not study are repercussions of an experiment in education begun in Mantua in the year 1423; the landscape architect who plots the placement of trees and shrubs in a formal garden is merely the modern exponent of an art developed in Italy five hundred years ago. Depending on the point of view, it is reassuring or dismaying to discover that women of that distant time bleached their hair, wore heels so high they had to be helped along the street by servants, and spent their husbands' money on jewelry and high fashion. To this day, the social life of Western Europe is subtly molded by concepts adopted by Italians of the Renaissance, in their fusion of aristocratic and bourgeois societies. So it goes; in countless ways we are products of that age.

In the nineteenth century, Jakob Burckhardt advanced the thesis that the Renaissance was nothing less than the discovery of the world and of man himself, and for decades his view of the period as a unique, self-generating epoch held. Then, during the past fifty years, scholars demonstrated that the Renaissance did not burst upon the world full-blown, out of some medieval desert. Rather, there were beginnings, ideas and institutions which had taken root and endured, developing gradually through the centuries. The appreciation of arts and letters and the understanding of their relation to life, which was humanism, had existed during the Middle Ages; a body of literature had been present and had been recognized since classical times. The Renaissance was more properly part of a continuing, ever-widening stream.

What made this extraordinary century and a half in Italy possible was a remarkable coincidence of genius with circumstance. The times into which men are born affect how they are able to use their talents and energies. For arts to develop fully, there must be substantial wealth, patronage wisely disbursed. There must, in other words, be inducements for artists, for it is not enough for genius or creativity simply to be present; like a plant, they need proper soil and care, an atmosphere that is friendly and invigorating.

By 1400 the bases of the Italian Renaissance had been laid. For financial support, there was a burgeoning trade and industry, cities and individuals newly rich; politically, a new freedom and energy were abroad in the land. The prevailing mood was one of change, of improvement; old moral restraints and medieval dogmas were crumbling, and in their place was a zeal for recovering the classics of ancient Greece and Rome, for building upon them to create a civilization better than any man had known. And finally there was rivalry: between cities, between merchant princes, between artists, all vying to be best, to do better than anyone else could do, whether they were planning an ideal state, building a church, or striking a medal. It was at once the richest and most menacing age Europe had ever known; Italy possessed the greatest concentration of gifted individuals that the Western world had seen for a thousand years; and the conjunction of men and the times produced an outbursting of energy that was like a volcano in sudden eruption.

The Renaissance was not exclusively an Italian phenomenon. Yet it began there and developed there, and while similar stirrings were heard in Northern Europe and in Burgundy, nowhere else was the scale of endeavor so large, nowhere did the roots range so wide or deep. The Italians were pioneers on a frontier which would be explored by French, Spanish, English, Dutch, and other Europeans during the sixteenth and seventeenth centuries. They opened the windows on a wide, new world which Western man has been exploring ever since.

The Editors

Francisci petrarce poete laureati quozunda clarissimoz herou epithomatis/ad generosissi —
mu patrum dominu iclitu francisci de camria Rubrice.

¶ de Romulo pmo Romanoz rege.
¶ de numa popilio secudo romanoz rege.
¶ de Tullo hostilio tcio romanoz rege.
¶ de Ancho matio quato romanoz rege.
¶ de Junio bruto pmo romanoz cosule.
¶ de horatio cocle.
¶ de lucio quitio acinato.
¶ de marco furio camillo.
¶ de Tito manlio torquato.
¶ de publio decio.
¶ de lucio papirio cursore.
¶ de marco curio dentato.

¶ de fabricio lucilio.
¶ de Alexandro macedone.
¶ de pirro epirotau rege.
¶ de hanibale cathaginensiu duce.
¶ de quito fabio maximo dictatore.
¶ de marco claudio marcello.
¶ de claudio nerone et liuio salinatore.
¶ de publio concho Scipioe africano maiore.
¶ de marco potio catone censorino.
¶ de baio Julio Cesare.

¶ de marco valerio coruino.

Petrarch's likeness, by a friend, appears in a manuscript of his last work.

Petrarch

by MORRIS BISHOP

"I was born to this world," says Petrarch, "in the Via dell' Orto of the city of Arezzo, just at dawn on Monday, July 20, in the thirteen hundred and fourth year of this latest age which takes its name from Jesus Christ, fountain and author of all my hope." The house of his birth still stands at the town's top, across from the cathedral. Houses occupied by great ghosts live long.

He was christened Francesco Petracco, a slightly inelegant name which he Latinized to Petrarca, which we have Anglicized to Petrarch.

He was an Aretine only by circumstance. His father, Ser Petracco, was an office-holding notary, or attorney, in Florence, living on the edge of poverty. He belonged to the bourgeois party of the Whites; and in the revolution of 1302 he was banished, together with Dante and many others, and took refuge in Arezzo, some sixty miles away. But as Arezzo gave a chill welcome to plotting Florentine exiles, Ser Petracco had soon to seek his fortune afar. His wife, Eletta, and baby were permitted to return to the family house in Incisa, on Florentine territory.

According to a dear family story, Francesco, seven months old, was transported to Incisa in a sort of sling depending from a stout stick borne over a mounted servant's shoulder. In fording the flooded Arno, the horse slipped and fell; the servant nearly lost his life in saving that of the child. This is the kind of incident that has made Fortune a deity.

In Incisa was born, in 1307, Francesco's brother Gherardo, the product of a furtive visit of Ser Petracco. In 1310 or 1311 the family was reunited for a year in Pisa, and there, or possibly in Genoa, Ser Petracco was visited by his old friend and fellow exile Dante. By this time Ser Petracco found a post in the papal court, which had removed from Rome to Avignon. There, in 1312, his wife and sons joined the exile.

Avignon was a town of some five thousand inhabitants. The arrival of the papal court affected it as would the establishment of the United Nations in a rural American county seat. Cardinals' trains were billeted in citizens' homes, petitioners and office seekers camped in the streets, on the walls, in cemeteries. Signora Petracco and the boys found lodgings in the town of Carpentras, fifteen miles away, and there they spent four happy years. Writing, years later, to Guido Sette, a schoolmate and a lifelong

ful self-distrust, *diffidentia*. To gain confidence and self-mastery, he surrendered to passion and ambition. But passion and ambition led him far from self-mastery; it was necessary to subdue them. Finally, recovering his liberty, he learned to scorn the world, and thus to gain possession of himself and to find at last peace and happiness. His was a lifelong process of self-culture, prompted by and ending in egotism.

His introspection did not prevent him from looking on the external world with delighted, observant eyes. His appreciation of scenic beauty and of country charm has no parallel in medieval literature. His realization of the beauty of mountains was not to reappear in recorded words until the end of the seventeenth century. (He describes, for instance, the blue waters of Como, with the snowy peaks of the Alps overhanging the lake, with forests hiding their heads in clouds, with the dark roaring of torrents pouring out of the heights, and everywhere the murmuring of brooks and the twitter of birds.) He loved flowers and country labors, and when asked his profession liked to reply, "gardener." On the other hand, he did not notice medieval architecture. He mentions only twice, I think, a church's beauty (the golden glitter of St. Mark's in Venice, and the rising Cathedral of Cologne, *pulcherrimum templum.*) The superb Palace of the Popes in Avignon was to him only a gloomy Tartarus. Nor had he much taste for art, though he had Simone Martini paint a small, portable portrait of Laura to sigh over, and though he knew Giotto personally and left in his will one of Giotto's paintings to a friend. ("The ignorant do not understand the beauty of this panel, but the masters of art are stunned by it.") Music, however, he loved; a good concert made him cease to envy the gods their privilege of listening to the music of the spheres.

His sense of beauty awakens occasionally corresponding chords within us. Frequently in his poems, often in his prose, a phrase or set of phrases will leap out as a personal communication over all the years that separate us.

One stormy night in Venice he sat writing late, in his study overlooking the Riva degli Schiavoni. He heard a great shouting below and ran to look down from his highest window. *Deus bone, quod spectaculum!* A number of ships were casting off from the marble quay below. "Their masts considerably overtopped the two corner towers of my palazzo. And at this moment, with all the stars hidden by clouds, as my walls and roofs were shaken by the wind, as the sea roared hellishly below, the ships cast loose from the quay and set forth on their journey. One, perhaps, was bound for the river Don, with passengers for the Ganges, the Caucasus, the Indies, and the Eastern Ocean. My heart bled for these unhappy men. And when I could no longer follow the ships with my eyes, moved and stirred I picked up my pen again, exclaiming: 'Oh, how dear to men is life, and how little account they take of it!' "

Again, he writes: "I had got thus far, and was thinking of what to say next, and as my habit is, I was pricking the paper idly with my pen. And I thought how, between one dip of the pen and the next, time goes on, and I hurry, drive myself, and speed toward death. We are always dying. I while I write, you while you read, and others while they listen or stop their ears, they are all dying."

These are expressions of a modern sensibility, with its awareness of the mystery and marvel of common experience. Petrarch helped to form and define the modern sensibility, which is, indeed, an eternal sensibility. Petrarch is frequently termed the first modern man. I would go farther; I would call him one of the eternal men. As he turned back to find his companions in the great past, we too may turn back, to find in Petrarch a companion and a friend.

PRECURSORS

"Giotto alone," Vasari proclaimed, "in a rude and inept age, when all good methods of art had long been lost, dead and buried in the ruins of war, set art upon the path that may be called the true one." For a century after Giotto's death, painters imitated his naturalism and his revolutionary use of space and light, proudly signing themselves "disciple of Giotto, the good master." One contemporary, the sculptor Andrea Pisano, also had managed to free his style from the Byzantine rigidity which dominated Italian art. Approaching medieval themes with a new realism, he and Giotto collaborated on bas-reliefs for the newly built campanile at Florence. The panels on this page show Icarus flying, Adam and Eve laboring, and, at bottom, a woman at her loom. Above her, a horse and rider, infused with a vitality new to art, symbolize man's unbounded energy, which was soon to abandon medieval ideals and inaugurate a proud new era.

When a papal emissary asked Giotto for a sample of his work, the painter drew a perfect circle with one stroke of his brush and told him to send it back to Rome. All Italy sought out this artist, who became so famous that, according to one legend, even Dante came to watch him paint. For Florence, Giotto designed the cathedral's campanile, the most beautiful Gothic tower in Italy. In Assisi he decorated the Basilica of St. Francis, and at Padua, in a chapel built to atone for the sins of a man so avaricious that Dante had assigned him to the seventh circle of hell, he painted his masterpieces—scenes from the life of Christ. Above, in the Pietà, weeping angels hover over the entombment. Opposite is the kiss of Judas.

THE
PRINCE
AND THE
STATE

"Horror waits on princes," wrote Webster, the Elizabethan dramatist for whom the bloodstained annals of Italy had a compulsive fascination. Certainly, the way to power was strewn with corpses; men murdered their wives, wives poisoned their husbands, brother slaughtered brother, family raged against family, city sacked city. In 1402 the chief members of the ruling house of Lodi were burned alive on the public square; at Bologna in 1445 the people, enraged by the slaughter of their favorite family, the Bentivoglio, hunted down their enemies and nailed their steaming hearts to the doors of the Bentivoglio's palace, as a token of their love.

Yet Bologna was a tranquil city compared to many, and even bloodless when matched with Foligno; there a noble—Pietro Rasiglia—cuckolded by his prince, took his vengeance. He flung his faithless wife from the turrets of his castle and killed two brothers of the prince. Retribution rapidly followed. The whole Rasiglia clan, men, women, and children, were butchered and chopped up; their joints, hung like meat,

were paraded through the streets. Of course, the ghoulish chroniclers liked to heighten the horror, and their macabre imaginations rioted in sadistic fantasy. Yet all allowance made, politics became a murderous game in which death in bed came only to the skillful or the lucky. The savagery used by men in pursuit of power was due to the nature of society and the prizes which it offered.

The city-states of Italy had won their independence by playing off the two greatest powers of medieval Europe—the Papacy and the Empire. In theory, the Pope ruled men's souls, the Emperor their bodies; the facts accorded ill with theory. The Church had acquired property which no emperor or king could match; its real estate, its pecuniary rights—first fruits, Peter's pence, and the like—made it formidably rich, rich enough to challenge the Empire and to claim the supremacy of the spiritual over the temporal power. Yet bishops were princes as well as bishops; abbots and their monasteries owed feudal obligations on their lands. The great baronage of the

bo won so
ink of no
solve this
and wor-
dventurers
Piero di
he Sistine
e Roberto
yed above
is name as
e occasion
in a sack.

have survived but for the aid of Venice. It was too strong and too remote for Venice to absorb, yet its powerful princes were an excellent buffer against their common enemy, Milan. So the Venetians hired the Gonzaga as condottieri and, to pay them, ceded Lombard towns that were too weak to maintain their independence and too poor for Venice to covet. The Gonzaga were too clever to allow a tradition of dependence on Venice to develop, and from time to time they sold their skill to the rulers of Milan. The balance of power kept Mantua independent, and the needs of Venice or Milan made it rich. Violent though its history was, it enjoyed more peace and greater security than was the common lot of Italian cities. The unruly, battle-scarred Gonzaga were never mere condottieri; they governed as strongly as they fought. Under Lodovico Gonzaga, in spite of plague and pestilence and flood, trade in wool and silks flourished, and the population grew to forty thousand or more. Money from war and trade was spent not only to delight the eye, but also to train the

mind. Opportunities for pageantry proved frequent enough. Pius II called a council there in 1459 to declare a Crusade against the Turks. In 1474 the King of Denmark paid a state visit and found a royal welcome. Powerful neighbors—the Sforza from Milan, the Este from Ferrara—expected and received extravagant hospitality. The births and marriages and deaths of Gonzaga princes were celebrated with appropriate solemnity and expense. So were their triumphs: few public occasions matched the reception of Francesco Gonzaga, the first cardinal of his house, a prince of the Church at seventeen and a symbol of his family's greatness.

As became Renaissance princes, the Gonzaga sought a permanent expression for their wealth and power and destiny. Lodovico (1414–1478) was, perhaps, the most gifted of his family and possessed abundantly those wide-ranging tastes and abilities that were so much admired in his day. He embodied the skill and decision of a man of action with the sensitivity of a scholar. He proved himself ruthless in war,

loomed of a
yed him. This
early enough,
ndottieri were
nal armies re-
hery, for no
fighting men.
ly prolonged.
war and con-
tion and the

e Renaissance.
the equilib-
orthern states
pealed to the
oyed and be-
or were they
destruction of

In 1445 Sigismondo Malatesta asked his friend Leon Battista Alberti to redesign the church of San Francesco in Rimini. A miniature (opposite, at upper left) from the Hesperides, *a poem by Sigismondo's court poet, Basinio Basinii, shows the reconstruction taking place. Below it is the finished building as it looks today. Known as the Tempio Malatestiano, this is one of the finest examples of early Renaissance classical style. Inside are monuments in honor of Sigismondo, along with reliefs such as the example at left by Agostino di Duccio, which shows the zodiacal sign of Cancer protecting the town of Rimini. In the background are the mountains of San Marino. The young girl at right, painted by Pisanello, is thought to be Sigismondo's first wife, Ginevra d'Este, who died in 1440 at the age of twenty-two, quite possibly murdered by Sigismondo.*

adept in diplomacy, yet more generous toward his treacherous brother Carlo than was usual in a despot, a sign of that human warmth which infused his private life and his artistic sensibilities. By 1460 he had persuaded Andrea Mantegna to make Mantua his permanent home and to become his court painter. The result was a splendid series of frescoes that still adorn the Camera degli Sposi in the Castello of Mantua; other frescoes have been destroyed, and pictures that were painted for Lodovico dispersed, but what remains is one of the great achievements of the Renaissance. As with painting, so with architecture: for Lodovico's taste was sure. He employed Alberti—a man of universal genius and a leading Florentine figure in the Classical revival—to design his churches, and urged Mantuans to give generously so that plans for Sant' Andrea could become a reality, which, as Lodovico said, "from its vast size and noble simplicity should be superior to any building of the kind in the leading cities of Italy, and worthy to stand beside the magnificence of Rome herself."

Huge buildings, sumptuous palaces, brilliant paintings— these were the common extension of a prince's greatness. Lodovico, however, was a man of wider and deeper sympathies. He encouraged philosophers and poets to stay at his court. Pico della Mirandola, Platina, Poliziano, Ognibene, Guarino da Verona, and Filelfo all, at one time or another, brought distinction to the Mantuan court. Lodovico himself took a delight in books; he collected not only manuscripts of the classics, but also of Dante, Petrarch, and Boccaccio, and employed the most gifted craftsmen to illustrate their books.

The width of Lodovico's interests was due partly to his native genius and partly also to his education, for it was in the education of princes that Mantua made one of its most remarkable contributions to the Renaissance. Lodovico's father had established the great humanist Vittorino da Feltre at Mantua. Vittorino's ideas were to influence European education profoundly for centuries. He believed that education should concern itself with the body as well as the mind, with

the Baglioni, as condottieri, did not believe in half measures. And to give an additional taste of horror, the plague found in Perugia a happy playground—between 1424 and 1486 there were eight severe epidemics.

Violence and sickness, suffering and death, made the Perugians susceptible to the more evangelistic expressions of religious fervor. The slaughters by, or of, the Baglioni were usually followed by days of solemn ritual and purification. On one occasion the cathedral was washed with wine and reconsecrated; on another over thirty altars were erected in the Piazza, and Mass was continuously solemnized. It is not, therefore, surprising that the vivid preaching of Fra Bernardino of Siena found a fruitful soil in Perugia. The people of the city responded eagerly to his denunciations of the vanity of all earthly life. He condemned the crimes of its citizens, called them to repentance, reconciled enemies, and made a large bonfire of worldly delights in a great act of public repentance. The results of Bernardino proved as fleet-

ing as were the reconciliations of the Baglioni and the Oddi later in the century, yet this thread of religious revivalism, of sensational open-air preaching, of the sudden need for public repentance, was not an unusual theme in city life of fifteenth-century Italy—it was a common response to the insecurities created by war and pestilence and crime.

Although the constant strife proved inimical to trade, although the population declined, these things failed to kill the vigorous artistic life of Perugia. In the midst of the turmoils, paintings of exceptional beauty were produced: Perugino and Raphael shared the city with the Baglioni and the Oddi. Perugino's frescoes of quiet, ecstatic saints, and Bonfigli's charming, tender, personal vision of the merciful Madonna, provided the background for fratricidal slaughter in a piazza reeking with blood and festooned with the grotesque shapes of slaughtered youths and men. At no other place were the dark and the light of Renaissance life brought to a stranger contrast.

After the massacre of the Baglioni family of Perugia in 1500, the mother of one of the murdered men commissioned Raphael to paint his famed Deposition *in memory of her son. The artist's sketch for the painting that now hangs in the Borghese Gallery is seen at left. Above is a griffin, the emblem of Perugia, suckling the two great condottieri who were born there: Braccio da Montone, who at one time ravaged his own birthplace, and Niccolò Piccinino, who succeeded Braccio as leader of one of the two largest mercenary bands in Italy. Sano di Pietro painted the scene at right, which shows Saint Bernardino of Siena preaching in his crusade against factionalism and strife.*

Sensitive, thoughtful men realized that this was a world like to none other. They searched the histories of antiquity —Livy, Suetonius, Plutarch—looking for the keys that would unlock for them the problems of princes and of cities. What made men succeed? Or fail? Why did some cities grow great and rich only to dissipate it all in war and rebellion? Why did free citizens become the prey of professional thugs? What were the causes of tyranny? Was tyranny bad? Did cities have a natural life like men—youth, maturity, age? And were learning, art, and the practice of humanism bound up with the nature of institutions? Did philosophers make the best citizens? They ransacked antiquity, read again and again Plato and Aristotle and, above all, Cicero, who seemed to demonstrate more clearly than any other the virtues of a philosopher at large in civic life. What they did not turn to was theology, to Saint Thomas Aquinas, to Saint Ambrose, or to Saint Jerome. The theological way of thinking about men and events was as alien to them as a salon painting to

Picasso. The key to their problems they knew to be rooted in the lives and actions of men, not in universal mysteries or the attributes of God. Consequently, there is an astonishing freshness about the historians and the political philosophers of the Renaissance, and, as with the painters and sculptors, the greatest by far were the Florentines, and the greatest of the Florentines was Niccolò Machiavelli, whose speculations about the nature of men's political actions are as remote from the thinkers of the Middle Ages as Leonardo da Vinci's drawings are from the illuminations of missals. Yet Machiavelli is no isolated phenomenon—from Salutati to Guicciardini, men were following the same quest. What general rules can be derived from political experience? As history enshrines political experience, thinkers grew profoundly interested in the past. In the Middle Ages political philosophers were theologians, in the Renaissance they were historians. This change had been brought about by the conflict of cities, the problems of despotism, and the crisis of liberty.

Niccolò Machiavelli wears a slightly furtive expression in this portrait by Santi di Tito.

Machiavelli

by GARRETT MATTINGLY

For most of us, Renaissance statecraft is typified by a single man, Niccolò Machiavelli—or rather, by a single name, a reputation, an epithet. After all, not many people have any clear recollection of the life and character of the man Machiavelli (not many, even, of the relatively few who have ever bothered to read anything about him). But everyone knows what the name stands for: all the complicated deviltry, hypocrisy, intrigue, secret murders, and public treacheries which for four hundred years the Western world has held typical of the Italian Renaissance. Seventy-five years ago a learned Frenchman identified the whole high Renaissance—the last decades of the fifteenth century and the first ones of the sixteenth—as the Age of Machiavelli. Certainly he realized the incongruity of labeling that bustling time after the drab little servant of a third-rate state, a man whose name even those princes and prelates to whom he had bowed probably never knew or, unless they were Florentines themselves, promptly forgot. But Maulde la Clavière was writing about Renaissance politics, and the name imposed itself. It came as naturally as saying the Age of Augustus, or of Louis le Grand, or of Napoleon, and it carried, like those labels, its own connotations, its own peculiar and, in this case, definitely sinister aura.

In a way it was appropriate that Niccolò Machiavelli should have become the interpreter of Renaissance politics to subsequent ages. He was a Florentine of the Florentines, and the citizens of his city were the quintessence of the new spirit that was then stirring in Italy. Not at first, of course: in the years after the great Guelph victory, after the popes had broken the power of the Empire in Italy forever, Florence was only one of the vigorous, turbulent city republics with which northern and central Italy swarmed. Some of these paid a token allegiance to the Papacy, although the popes knew how little that really meant, and some professed a loyalty to the Holy Roman Emperor, since no Emperor could endanger their liberties any more, but in fact they had all torn clean away from the hierarchical system in which the rest of Christendom was enmeshed, and were engaged in an external struggle against all their neighbors and an internal one of faction against faction, in which the only reality was the naked fact of power.

At first most of these new states were republics. Then, as the bigger fish devoured the smaller, not only were there fewer independent cities, but fewer of the survivors were republics. Presently came the

anxious moment when on the Italian mainland only one republic was left, or only one that mattered. By force or guile the great Duke of Milan, Giangaleazzo Visconti, was building himself a kingdom. All Lombardy yielded to him from Piedmont to the Adriatic, and then Genoa and Pisa, Perugia and Siena, and finally proud Bologna. Guarded by its lagoons, the Republic of St. Mark turned its aristocratic back on Italy. Only Florence still held out.

Florence had had as checkered a political history as any of her neighbors. In the century since she had exiled her greatest poet, the bitter factional strife which Dante lamented so pathetically and joined in so energetically had never ceased and only occasionally diminished. In the moment of crisis there was, of course, a clique to say that it would be madness for Florence to pit her unaided strength against the wave of the future, that it would be better for Florentines to live as the subjects of a tyrant than to die as his victims. But the Florentines chose to resist. Apparently they preferred the uneasy vigilance which is the price of freedom to the smug lethargy of the Milanese, and were willing to risk death as free men rather than embrace life as slaves. They did not have to make so hard a choice. As he advanced against Florence, the plague struck down the tyrant, and his jerry-built kingdom fell into ruins. By resisting, the Florentines saved not just their own liberty but the liberties of Italy.

In a series of masterly studies Hans Baron has recently shown how the outcome of this crisis altered the whole tone of Florentine and so of Italian thought. Florence became the center from which spread a new humanism, a new appreciation of political liberty and civic virtue, a new attitude toward the place of man in society. It was this attitude which insured the independence of the major Italian states, and consequently that vigor and diversity of Italian artistic and cultural development which characterized the Renaissance. Now that the point has been made, it seems strange that we did not see it before, but even without Baron's fresh insight, Florentine civic humanism has long been recognized as characteristic of one aspect of the Italian Renaissance. Although he was himself no humanist, if we make that term include a polished mastery of Greek and Latin letters, Niccolò Machiavelli was soaked in the spirit of Florentine humanism.

He was soaked, too, in the Florentine obsession with politics. He came of a family which had played a great role in the political life of his city for more than two centuries. Ancestors of his had been honored, time and again, with the republic's highest offices, and if his father was too stiff-necked a republican to hold a place in a government which was becoming a more and more transparent mask for the boss rule of the Medici, we may be sure that papa Bernardo saw to it that son Niccolò was thoroughly imbued not only with the history of ancient republican Rome, but also with the great traditions of his own city. When he was forty-four, Niccolò wrote that politics was the passion of his life, that he could think and talk of nothing else, and we may guess that this began to be true when he was still young.

For fourteen years he had a chance to indulge his bent in action. When the French invaded Italy in 1494, the Florentines, who had begun to be restive under the scarcely disguised rule of Lorenzo the Magnificent and had become more so under Lorenzo's incompetent son, rose up to reclaim their ancient liberties and drove the Medici out of Florence. Niccolò was then twenty-five. We do not know whether he held any kind of post in the first years of the re-established republic, but when the revolutionary fanatics who were swayed by Savonarola's eloquence gave place to a solider, less hysterical government in 1498, Niccolò Machiavelli, just turned twenty-nine, was appointed second chancellor of the republic. Shortly afterward he was given the additional charge of secretary to the influential committee known as the *Dieci di Balia,* the Ten of Liberty and Peace as they were sometimes grandiloquently called, or, more realistically, the Ten of War.

War was the chief preoccupation of the restored republic. Foreign armies were tramping back and forth across Italy. Spaniards slowly tightened their grip on Naples; Frenchmen periodically invaded the kingdom and were periodically chased out of Milan; Switzers and Germans were in the field, fighting sometimes for foreign paymasters, sometimes for their own hands; around Rome, first the bastard son of the Borgia Pope and then that warlike old man who succeeded to the Papacy as Julius II were trying to unify the anarchic Papal States; and once all the warring powers put aside their quarrels in order to combine against the one powerful, independent Italian state, the Venetian republic. In the midst of these big wars Florence was busy with an interminable little war, trying to reconquer Pisa, which, in the confusion of the first French invasion, had slipped from

under the Florentine yoke. Since his nominal chief, the first chancellor, was more interested in Greek poetry than Italian politics, Machiavelli took a large part in these affairs. He was deep in the business of war and the diplomatic bickerings and hagglings which were the normal Renaissance accompaniments of war. Most of the correspondence of the republic passed through his hands. He wrote memoranda to inform and advise his masters on a variety of subjects, and the Signory sent him on numerous diplomatic missions in Italy, Germany, and France.

Early in his diplomatic career his path crossed that of the man who for most of us typifies the prince of the Age of Machiavelli, the typical prince of the Italian Renaissance—largely because he is the leading figure, the ostensible hero, of Machiavelli's famous little book. Actually, Cesare Borgia was not much more typical of the princes of Italy in his time than Caligula was a typical Roman emperor, or than Al Capone was a typical tax dodger of the Age of Herbert Hoover, but there is no denying that for a few years Cesare cut a wide swath and attracted a lot of attention, even eclipsing his notorious father.

Throughout his papacy, the whole family of Rodrigo Borgia, who ascended the papal throne as Alexander VI, was surrounded by a buzz of scandal. Gossiping about popes has always been a favorite Italian pastime, but probably no pope has ever afforded so much occasion for juicy gossip. Other popes had kept mistresses in the Vatican, and simony and immorality were no more rife in Rome under the Borgia Pope than they had been under his predecessors and would be under his successors. But there was a sort of childlike shamelessness about Alexander VI which invited comment. Other popes had auctioned off high ecclesiastical offices, doubled-crossed their associates and allies, and used their exalted position for the advancement of their families and for base personal ends, but usually they had pretended that they were doing something else. Rodrigo Borgia had either an honest scorn for hypocrisy or a naïve ignorance of the force of public opinion. Other popes had thrown wild parties at the Vatican, but no other pope had made the parties so flamboyant or so public. And no other pope had had a portrait of his official mistress, robed as the Virgin Mary, painted over the door of his bedchamber or, at the same time, given his official mistress so many transient but reasonably well publicized rivals. Temperate, even ascetic in most respects (in spite, or perhaps because of his gross

body, he drank little wine and ate sparingly of coarse food), Rodrigo Borgia was a great lover of women, and this alone was the source of innumerable stories which grew more outrageous with each retelling.

But neither his private conduct nor his carelessness of concealment can account for all the stories about the Borgia Pope. The trouble was that although far from a saint, he was a first-rate administrator, with enormous energy and a driving will. He tried to police not only the streets of Rome, but even the Roman *campagna*, he tried to control the disorderly Roman nobility, he tried to make sure that the papal treasury received its proper cut of all the sums which the swollen papal bureaucracy and their hangers-on extorted from suitors at his court. He tried, and in part he succeeded, and this made him very unpopular with the Romans. Besides, he tried to assert the rights of the Papacy and his jurisdiction over the Papal States wherever it was challenged, whether by the Duke of Milan or the republics of Venice or Florence, by the King of Naples or the anarchic Neapolitan barons, or by the petty tyrants of Umbria and the Romagna. This made him unpopular with the ruling classes throughout Italy. Worst of all, he was a foreigner, a Spaniard, and Italians have always resented a non-Italian pope. Hence another whole cluster of stories, different and more sinister.

Two of Rodrigo Borgia's children, his eldest son, the Duke of Gandia, and his daughter Lucrezia, were less than ideal targets for malicious gossip. Gandia, although he inherited to some extent his father's disposition to run after women, was otherwise a conventional and colorless type. Lucrezia, although she had a checkered and somewhat smirched history of successive marriages before she was out of her teens —a foundation on which Roman scandalmongers readily erected a towering superstructure—was really a bland, vapid creature with nothing remarkable about her except a cowlike disposition and long blonde hair. But the Pope's younger son Cesare was something else again. Even as a mere stripling, just turned seventeen and newly made a cardinal, he was already a spectacular figure, taller by a head than most tall men, with massive shoulders, a wasp waist, classically regular features, a leonine mane, and blazing blue eyes. It was said that he could leap into the saddle without touching pommel or stirrups, bend a silver *scudo* double between his fingers, or straighten the iron of a horseshoe with a twist of his

wrist. And he was a show-off. He dressed himself and his household with insolent magnificence, and he used to organize *corridas* in the Piazza Navona so that the Romans could watch him behead a bull with a single stroke of a broadsword. Before long he was trailing a legend gaudier and more lurid than that attached to his father.

It was said that he was his father's rival for his sister's incestuous bed. (Almost certainly false.) It was said that after the horrible sack of Capua he seized forty beautiful highborn maidens and added them to his personal harem. (Highly unlikely. Cesare does not seem to have shared his father's excessive appetite. The maidens were probably commandeered by Cesare's captains, though perhaps in his name.) It was said that he seduced that gallant youth Astorre Manfredi, and when he tired of him had him murdered. (Possible, but the motive for the murder was more probably purely political.) It was said that he had murdered his brother, the Duke of Gandia. (Probable. At least his father seems to have believed it.) And that he had his brother-in-law, Lucrezia's second husband, murdered. (Pretty certainly true.) But it was a dull week when one, at least, of the embassies in Rome did not chalk up another murder to Cesare's credit, sometimes by poison, sometimes by the hands of hired assassins, sometimes by his own dagger. Probably he really was responsible for a fair share of those bodies hauled out of the Tiber. Freed by his brother's death from his cardinalate, Cesare became Duke de Valentinois (Valentino, the Italians called him) and Gonfaloniere of the Church, cousin and ally of the King of France, and commander in chief of the papal army. As he marched through the anarchic Papal States, seizing one town after another, by bribery or trickery or the sheer terror of his name, his legend hung over him like a thundercloud.

When Machiavelli first encountered the Duke, the spell of the legend must have been already at work on him, and it must have been heightened by the manner in which Valentino received him and his chief, at night, by the light of a single flickering candle which showed only dimly the tall figure clad in black from head to foot without jewel or ornament, the still white features as regular as a Greek statue and as immobile. Perhaps the cold beauty of those marble features was already beginning to be marred by the pustules which led Valentino later on usually to wear a mask. Perhaps the

eyes, lost in shadow, already held that glare which another ambassador noted in them shortly afterward, the look of a savage beast at bay. And perhaps a shrewder observer might have reflected that there was the smell of comedy about these negotiations, the Duke endlessly repeating the same banalities about his eternal friendship for Florence and how wise the republic would be to employ the services of so good a friend, while his captains warned the Florentine envoys that the Duke's patience was growing short, that France would support him against Florence and the Venetians would not stir, that the army was poised to spring and could be at the city's gates before the news of its coming. It was really one of the cruder forms of blackmail, but something about the Duke's personality put the act over, and the Florentine envoys carried away the image of a great prince, subtle, inscrutable, dangerous.

Not long afterward Machiavelli had an opportunity to observe Cesare Borgia in action at the time of his greatest triumph. Cesare was not much of a general: he never learned the rudiments of tactics or strategy, logistics or supply. He was not even a good combat leader, and though he has been praised as a disciplinarian, the only available instance seems to be that once he quelled an incipient riot among some of his brawling soldiers by the terror of his presence. Similarly, if he ever gave any proof of ability as a statesman or ruler, no evidence survives. But he was a ruthless gangster and an expert confidence man, and the revolt of some of the smaller gangsters, his captains, gave him an opportunity to display his talents. Machiavelli watched, fascinated, while Cesare, all mildness and good will, lured his mutinous subordinates into a peace conference, lulled their fears, invited them to a banquet to celebrate their renewed friendship, and when they arrived unarmed and unescorted at a rendezvous where Cesare had hidden his bodyguards, had them seized and murdered. Machiavelli was delighted at the virtuosity of the performance and set it all down in detail for the edification of his countrymen and of posterity.

Machiavelli had a third opportunity to observe the Duke. He arrived in Rome on the business of the republic some months after the death of Alexander VI and just at the moment when Cesare, with incredible stupidity, had helped swing the election of his most implacable enemy. It was plain to see that Cesare was finished. Everything really had depended on his father's being Pope, and as soon as his father

died, his allies deserted him, his people rose against him, and his army fell apart as his captains scrambled for the service of some luckier master. Machiavelli assessed the emptiness of the man at a glance, avoided him when he could, wrote of him and no doubt looked at him with cold contempt. But later Machiavelli seems to have preferred to forget the cringing, whimpering, blustering, dithering creature his hero had become. The picture is spread out in detail in his dispatches, but Machiavelli never openly alluded to this aspect of Cesare again.

One thing Machiavelli admired about Cesare was that he raised his soldiers in his own domain instead of hiring foreign mercenaries. It was not, in fact, a great departure. The Romagna was the great source of mercenary troops, and for years its petty despots had enrolled their subjects and farmed them out to fight other people's wars. But Cesare's action was like a project very close to Machiavelli's heart, one which after years of urging he finally got the Florentine government to adopt. They not only adopted it, they put him in charge of it, so that for the last six years of the republic, he had added to his other duties most of those of minister of defense. Instead of the cut-rate mercenaries who had prolonged the Pisan war for twelve years (being a republic in which the taxpayers held the purse strings, Florence hired only the cheapest mercenaries), Machiavelli persuaded the government to raise a militia in its own territory. Since the militia were not Florentine citizens, but conscripts from the wretched peasants of the *contado*, a folk without political rights or any material stake in the success of their bourgeois masters, the scheme had an obvious weakness, but it did not work badly at first. In 1509 Pisa fell, and Machiavelli's militia could claim a share in the long-delayed triumph. Three years later the militia failed a harder test. When the veteran Spanish infantry moved in to attack Prato, the militia ran like rabbits, and the Medici epigoni came back behind a column of Spanish pikes to rule once more in Florence. Machiavelli's active career in politics was over. But not his interest in politics. The next year he wrote that he could think about, talk about, nothing else, and from then on until he died in 1527, only a few weeks after the Florentines had again expelled the Medici, most of the writings with which he sought to allay the boredom of his exclusion from office were concerned, one way and another, with statecraft. He also wrote some verses—pretty

wretched verses—and a not unamusing version of an old, smutty joke, and comedies, one of which is a masterpiece. But mostly he wrote about politics. Had he been asked to name his political writings in an ascending order of importance, surely the top three would have been his *History of Florence,* his *Art of War,* and his *Discourses on the First Ten Books of Livy.* Into these writings, and particularly into the last, Machiavelli had poured, or so he thought, all his practical experience of government and diplomacy and all his wide reading of ancient and modern history. However surprised some of the successful statesmen of his day might have been to find the little Florentine secretary the political spokesman of their age, Machiavelli himself would not have been too surprised. He would have regarded the reputation accrued as a poor compensation for the fame as a statesman which fate had denied him, but he had often said that he was the first modern man to look at politics with a clear and open eye, and he would certainly have taken the recognition of posterity as no more than due to the merit of his books.

Only, of course, the recognition of posterity has nothing to do with the books Machiavelli would have named. When people speak of the Age of Machiavelli, they are not thinking of any of them, but of one little pamphlet apparently dashed off at white heat in 1513 just after the fall of the Florentine republic. It is called *The Prince* and it bears only an ambiguous, tangential relationship to Machiavelli's big, serious works or, some people think, to the actual history of the time and place over which its fame casts such a lurid and sinister light. The discrepancy between the impression of Renaissance Italy to be gathered from *The Prince* and that given by the rest of Machiavelli's writings, to say nothing of the writings of his contemporaries, who often turn out to be more reliable about matters of fact, is sufficient to raise some doubts about the appropriateness of letting *The Prince* describe the political atmosphere of its time.

Perhaps our doubts about letting Machiavelli speak for the age which bears his name ought not to be increased by our knowledge of his private life. But among his contemporaries, surely Niccolò Machiavelli was one of the least Machiavellian. It is true that he often professed a preference for drastic methods and for sweeping all-or-nothing solutions, along with a contempt for delay and improvisation and compromise, a set of attitudes usually more characteristic of

pletely to understand the proposition that *The Prince* was a satire. As for the theory that Machiavelli was willing to accept a tyrant prince in order to effect the unification of Italy, there is not the faintest indication anywhere in his writings that he would have grasped the idea if anybody had put it to him. There is nothing about unifying Italy anywhere in *The Prince,* only about driving out the barbarians, a commonplace of Italian rhetoric from Petrarch to Paul IV. But Machiavelli the Italian patriot is a little easier to swallow than Machiavelli the dispassionate scientist, unless someone can explain how the scientific temper can accord with facts and generalizations equally distorted by emotion and prejudice.

It is probably hopeless to try to explain the whole puzzle of *The Prince.* How do you reconstruct the motives at a particular moment of a man more than four hundred years in his grave who has left only the scantiest and most ambiguous clues to what they might be? How do you tell, in the case of a man like Machiavelli, how much of the demonstrable distortion in *The Prince* was due to faulty observation (he was a passionate man), and how much to the deliberate irony which he certainly sometimes practiced? How do you probe the bitterness and agony of spirit which must certainly have been his on the collapse of all his hopes, and decide which wild statements come from anger, which from despair, and which from a calculated will to undermine his enemies by indirection?

Probably, like most insoluble problems about men of genius, this one has taken up more time and energy than it deserves. The real importance of Machiavelli, his claim to give his name to a whole period of history, lies elsewhere, not in the points in which *The Prince* differs from his other writings, but in those in which it agrees. Here the transformation of his legendary figure from a diabolist or a rebel, a spirit who says "No," to a major culture hero, offers the clue. What had happened, in almost three centuries between the time when Machiavelli was either praised as a daring rebel or denounced as an emissary of Satan and the time when he began to be acclaimed as a prophet, was that all Europe had become what Italy in Machiavelli's lifetime already was, a congeries of autonomous, purely temporal sovereign states, without any common end to bind them into a single society or any interest higher than their own egotistical drives for survival and expansion.

To pretend that the relations between such states were governed by Christian ethics seemed to Machiavelli a contemptible hypocrisy. Many Italians since Dante had lamented that the nearer one came to Rome the wider the gap between Christian teaching and Christian practice, and charged that the Papacy had corrupted the morals of Italy. Indeed, the major assumption of the stern reformers of what we call the Counter Reformation was not much different. But Machiavelli went further. He compared his own embittered picture of the degeneracy of his countrymen with Livy's of the virtues of republican Rome, and without asking how much exaggeration there might be in either, he leaped to one of his drastic all-or-nothing conclusions. Christianity, whatever its value as a guide in private life, was not a viable fountain for the good society. So for the religion of Christ he proposed to substitute the religion of patriotism. In politics the Christian ethic was worse than valueless, it was positively harmful. It might serve to keep the masses more law-abiding in their private lives, but when it came to public actions the only test of good or bad was what best served the safety and aggrandizement of the state. Since every state was an autonomous entity, recognizing no superior and no interest higher than its own, no rules of ethics whatever applied to relations between states. The only test was success. This was Machiavelli's consistent position. It appears in his earliest state papers and is as firmly held in his writings in praise of republics as it is in *The Prince.* In 1513 it was a desperate paradox. By 1813 it was an axiom of statecraft. By 1914 it was the tritest of platitudes. Machiavelli did not invent it. It was apparent in the behavior of the Italian states of his time and more or less openly acknowledged in the memoranda of statesmen and diplomats. But Niccolò Machiavelli first gave the fresh attitude of his age toward statecraft a permanent literary form, and the progress of history compelled general recognition of his insight. For that reason, perhaps he does deserve to be accepted as the voice of the Renaissance State. Perhaps his age should be called "The Age of Machiavelli."

Machiavelli's Statecraft

Machiavelli's fame rests on a code of conduct designed to teach ambitious princes the devious art of governing men. An age dominated by rulers and upstarts as fierce as the seasoned condottiere shown above in Leonardo da Vinci's drawing had made the art of war the paramount concern of a prince's life, and Machiavelli introduced an analysis of tactics and weapons, fortifications, and military history into most of his writings. But the astute prince never relied solely on arms; and Italy's despots acknowledged Machiavelli's bold advice on how to run a state, heeding such precepts as those which appear on the following two pages in a selection of quotations from *The Prince* and from the *Discourses on Livy*. Only when diplomacy or guile failed to control the tumultuous course of events did princes have recourse to warfare, now made more terrible by new advances in military technology.

"A great and monstrous Arabian engine for storming cities, filled with men, bridges, ladders and various instruments of war" (left) appeared in a treatise on warfare published in Verona in 1483. It shot immense arrows from its mouth, and used an enormous scaling ladder to claw abreast enemy fortifications. The same book displayed a revolving gun with eight barrels, which is shown at right. Although it could imperil friend and foe alike if a spark accidentally ignited all the barrels at once, it was actually seen in battle. So, for that matter, was a less fanciful version of the Arabian engine. Inventing such fantastic weapons as these failed to overtax the ingenuity of Renaissance men. Leonardo da Vinci, who planned the bombard shown below with projectiles which explode in mid-flight, was one of the most industrious of military engineers. His notebooks are filled with designs for immense crossbows and mechanisms for raining shot, with scythed chariots and armored cars, rock-throwing machines and assault bridges. Few were built, for new techniques of war forced inventors to concentrate instead on improvements in artillery. Machiavelli regretted the trend, and nostalgically praised the projectiles used by the ancients, which "although not so noisy as cannon, yet were equally effective in the killing of men." But for once the Florentine was proven wrong. Within his own lifetime, artillerymen and their new weapons came to dominate the battlefields of Italy and all Europe.

A CONTENTIOUS PENINSULA

The "canker'd hate" of Montagues for Capulets had its origins in an actual feud between the houses of Montecchi and Cappelletti in Verona, but Shakespeare might have found prototypes for his play in any other city of Renaissance Italy. Time and again, the Guelph-Ghibelline conflict was echoed in vendettas between Orsini and Colonna in Rome, Pazzi and Medici in Florence, Baglioni and Oddi in Perugia, with the blood feuds such, as Mercutio put it, that "Thou wilt quarrel with a man for cracking nuts, having no other reason but because thou hast hazel eyes." The fifteenth-century manuscript above, with a bellicose Mars presiding over a scene of battle, was symbolic of the continuous strife. Factionalism existed on every level of society, as family fights developed into wars between rulers, cities, guilds, or towns. With Italy a hotbed of warring factions, it became an easy prey for the increasingly powerful and grasping monarchs of Northern Europe.

The Gonzaga receive the keys to Mantua after downing the Bonacolsi, in a detail from Domenico Morone's painting (above).

THE
PRINCES
OF
MANTUA

In January of 1462, Lodovico Gonzaga, Marquis of Mantua, presided over one of his greatest triumphs —the welcoming home of his second son, Francesco, who had just been made a cardinal. It was not a chance appointment; Lodovico had quarreled with his own brother over the succession and purposely placed Francesco in the Church to avoid any such rivalry between his sons. It was a policy continued by later Gonzaga princes. Having wrested control over Mantua from the ruling house of Bonacolsi in 1328, the Gonzaga had maintained and strengthened it by election, legitimization (upon payment of a substantial fee to the Emperor), and wise rule. Lodovico, a skilled condottiere, as were most of his family, kept the city peaceful and free from the encroachments of Milan by taking service with the Milanese. But it was in internal rule that he excelled; he carefully nurtured Mantua's prime industry, the cloth trade; he built hospitals to combat the frequent epidemics of plague, and bridges to span the marshes surrounding the city; he reformed laws and ruled justly (a rare quality in those days); he patronized humanists and authorized one of the earliest printing presses in Mantua; and he invited Alberti, Mantegna, and other artists to adorn both the city and his court. With only meager funds, Lodovico managed to contract several brilliant marriages for his family and died in 1478 with the knowledge that his dynasty was loved and secure. Gonzaga relatives were married into most of the ruling houses of Italy, and Lodovico's grandson Francesco was engaged to a princess of Ferrara, Isabella d'Este, who was, in time, to bring Mantua to the zenith of its fame, influence, and prosperity.

Cardinal Francesco Gonzaga's triumphant return from Rome (right) was painted by Mantegna in a famous fresco in the Camera degli Sposi in Mantua. He is greeted by his father (left) and nephews (front). The elder nephew, also named Francesco, who later became marquis and married Isabella d'Este, appears again kneeling at the Virgin's feet in Mantegna's Madonna of Victory *(left). It was painted to commemorate his victory over the French King, Charles VIII, at Fornovo in 1495—a questionable triumph, since Charles escaped with most of his outnumbered army and sustained many fewer casualties.*

Orator nri in Curia

Nuy ve scriuemo le prite cum tanti amaritudine et affano del animo nro, chi veramente ne affirmamo esser al tuto Impossibile poteruelo explicare. Ma vuy pla prudentia vra Intenso el caso poterete comphendere pla natura delo gli la grandeza dela molestia nra. Sapete quanto sij Carmo a nuj el stato nro el nd jo baptista Caracul Capitaneo dele nre Fantarie da nuy ameto quanto may fusse alsu par suo, et ple sue digme condutione et pla sinsterata fede chi lha et ogni como piu dunostra verso le cose nre. Heli zorni prox passati ne fu p luy dimandata licentia de andar fina ad veuno p condur de qui la sua consorte et nue le robe sue. Nuy veramente hauendo bisogno dela psona sua ple Importantissime occorrentie di tempi priti lo confortassemo ad remaner luy et mandar el Canccllier cum altri di soy a tuor et arompagnar la dicta sua dona: la quale p vra Informatione e una dele notabile et formose done de Italia.

In the court scene at right, one of Carpaccio's eight canvases on the legend of Saint Ursula, two typical ambassadors make their departure while a third has a final word with a scribe. The document above directed the Venetian ambassador in Rome to complain about Cesare Borgia's kidnaping of the wife of a Venetian condottiere.

DIPLOMACY

As the risks and expenses of mercenary warfare mounted, the Italian states were forced to seek new avenues of advancing or safeguarding their interest. Most of them had merchants and traders traveling abroad, whose experience in bargaining suggested a means of obtaining information about enemy plans or resolving problems of state. Frequently business or banking interests paved the way for an exchange of envoys, and by 1500 resident embassies were established in most European capitals. The earliest ambassadors, equipped with little training and less money, were expected to gather and report information, entertain lavishly, make diplomatic contacts, and uphold the prestige of their states. They engaged in endless wrangles over precedence and were highly suspect (in Venice, the penalty for discussing politics with a foreigner was banishment), but in spite of such difficulties, diplomats were remarkably successful, and none more so than the Venetians, who set the pattern for diplomacy as we know it today. In her proud isolation, and with a relatively stable and legitimate government, Venice preserved her diplomatic records systematically, thus lending continuity to her policies. A Venetian humanist envoy, Ermolao Barbaro, first laid down the rules governing the duties of a resident ambassador; and Venice initiated the first triumph of the new diplomacy—the League of Lodi in 1454. This twenty-five-year nonaggression and defense pact between all the major states of Italy was grudgingly adhered to at first, and later blatantly ignored; but it was the foundation upon which Renaissance diplomacy grew.

and the fifth century there was a great gulf of barbarism.

And yet the art of the early fifteenth century was deeply entangled in its past. The scenes which painters were called upon to paint were the traditional scenes of Christian mythology—Nativities, Circumcisions, Crucifixions—the miracles of saints, the Stations of the Cross—and they were expected to execute them in traditional places, on the walls of churches and monasteries and on panels for altars. And skill in the control of perspective, or even a delight in the antique as absolute as Mantegna's, did not abolish the old symbols or the traditional iconography: four or five jagged rocks, realistically drawn, still represented mountains, as they had done for centuries in Byzantine art. The egg, hanging in the apse in Piero della Francesca's great picture of the Madonna and Child with saints, in the Brera, Milan, represents the four elements of the universe—a purely medieval symbol—as well as being a perfect conic section and the central point of a complex composition, requiring superlative skill in perspec-

tive. And although Uccello might gently mock the traditions of chivalry in his *Saint George and the Dragon,* nevertheless they absorbed his imagination; and Gozzoli's *Journey of the Magi* is as Gothic in feeling and intention as a fifteenth-century tapestry from Burgundy. Indeed, the new art of Donatello and Masaccio had no easy victory except in technique, for the Gothic feeling from the North seeped like an estuarine tide through the brushes and canvases of Italian artists of the fifteenth century: they were no more conscious of it than children playing with new toys in the sunshine, yet it caught them inexorably.

The other great triumphs of Renaissance art—the painting of landscape, the exploration of space and light through color, the full acceptance of the nude, and the development of the portrait—came only slowly.

And again they were partly due to foreign influence. Landscape in early Renaissance art was mainly the landscape of symbol, such as the paradisal gardens derived probably from

Leonardo da Vinci kept a room full of botanical specimens; Uccello collected sheaves of perspective drawings of the mazzocchio, *which was the turban-shaped headgear worn in Florence. Leonardo's drawings of the star-of-Bethlehem plant (right) and Uccello's* Saint George and the Dragon *(left) both transform the artist's scientific studies into masterpieces of grace. Although his battle is in a medieval setting, Saint George is fully a Renaissance creation, with sculptured armor, charging horse, and a lance tilted so as to add depth to the painting. Dated about 1455, Uccello's picture is an early example of a painting on canvas instead of wood.*

Persia—containing sometimes delicately observed flowers and plants and animals, but painted for their value as symbols, not to stir feeling, not to evoke mood deliberately, except in a formalized and quasi-theological sense—or the terrible mountains, rocks, and forests which were the age-old symbols of hell and horror. But as individuality began to creep out from traditional expression, and as the control of technique became more certain, painters and illustrators could not resist the challenge of the outward-seeing eye. In the *Très Riches Heures* of the Duc de Berry, ordinary life is revealed—peasants cut the crops, the children swim, the sheep feed on the mountain side. About the time that these were being painted by the Limbourg brothers, a Flemish artist, Jan van Eyck, began to give small background landscapes to his great altarpieces, which influenced Italian art as profoundly as his discovery of oil painting. Both his feeling for landscape and his knowledge of oils were taken back to Italy, where Antonello da Messina was one of the first to employ

the new technique. The exploration of color, of light and shade, of the intimate relation of man and nature, became dominant themes in Venetian art. Actually, Florentine artists had not been entirely indifferent to landscape; its study was partially involved in their preoccupation with perspective. Also, feeling inspired by natural objects was an integral part of their Neoplatonism. Brunelleschi made an optical device for viewing the city, and Alberti told how nature stirred him to tears and to joy. The intellectual problem of drawing figures against a distant background was bound to preoccupy Piero della Francesca, and he solved it about 1465, when he painted his great Urbino diptych. And realistic landscapes, particularly of the Val d'Arno, were painted shortly afterwards by Pollaiuolo. But neither painter responded with such a deep sense of personal discovery as did Giovanni Bellini, although the stimulus for his preoccupation may have come as much from della Francesca as from van Eyck. Bellini loved light, loved the first clear

light of morning that touches the mountaintops and leaves the plain in shadow, and the golden light of the last hours of day, the time that Leonardo was to love so deeply, a time that gives depth to shadow and softness and glow to color. Even the full light of midday in all its hardness and brilliance did not repel Bellini. He could drink in its heat and intensity, as his Saint Francis does with his outstretched arms, raised as much to the sun as to God. Although his delight in light and its effects on color passed into the Venetian tradition, his almost Brueghel-like concern with the detail of landscape did not.

Landscape was used by Giorgione, by Titian, by Tintoretto, to interpret mood, to reflect the emotion felt by the painter and to stimulate it in the beholder. In Giorgione and in the early works of Titian, landscape painting reached hallucinatory heights of feeling, reflecting mystery, horror, fear, tenderness, security, bliss, and love. As with perspective, so with landscape, a new world of artistic expression had been created.

The Venetians, of course, were not the only artists in the early sixteenth century to take delight in the painting of landscape. True, Michelangelo largely ignored it, and Botticelli used it merely as decoration or to emphasize his flowing, vibrant movement, but the Umbrian painters—Perugino and Pinturicchio—drew much from the tradition of Piero della Francesca; a tradition that was absorbed with masterful ease by Raphael. And, naturally, Leonardo da Vinci's sense of beauty as well as his avid curiosity were stirred by nature. The geological structure of mountains as well as their evocation of emotion caught his imagination, as did the turbulence of water as well as the mechanics of its flow; as did the flight of birds or the botany of flowers as well as their beauty; and, as in so many other aspects of Renaissance art, the scientific spirit and the delight in the eye were combined in one aesthetic pleasure, for in Leonardo the creative imagination was as multidimensional as geometry.

Throughout the Renaissance, artists were working for a

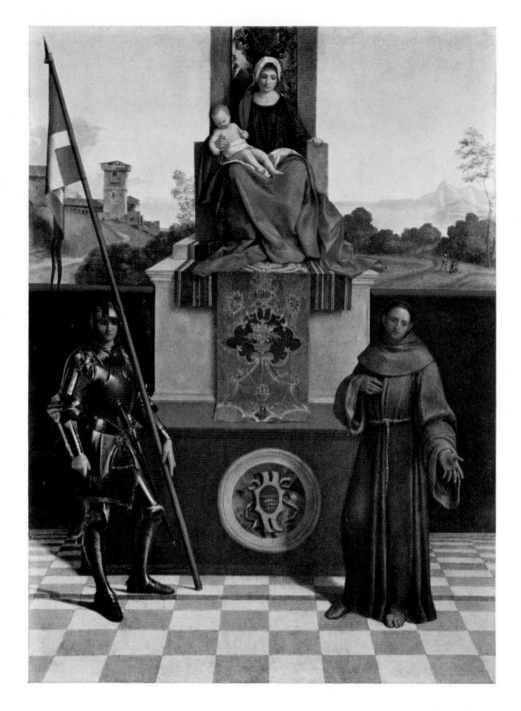

With the introduction of oil painting, at the time of Antonello da Messina, Italian art was revolutionized. The Sicilian artist copied the new technique from Flemish painters, whose characteristic style he imitated, too. Saint Jerome in His Study *(opposite) devotes meticulous attention to detail, with each shelf in the room displaying a miniature still life, and the whole set in a frame of Gothic architecture. Another revolution in Italian art, initiated by Giorgione, brought increased importance to landscape painting. Giorgione's* Castelfranco Madonna *utilizes an idyllic landscape on either side of the figure of Mary (right) to soften its symmetrical composition.*

small public. They were well known in their cities, they were familiar to popes and princes. The atmosphere in which they worked was intimate. Also, their art served a civic as well as a religious purpose. The Venetians realized early that narrative paintings about their heroic moments could have a public function, could impress both citizen and stranger with the republic's greatness. For the same reason, artists were paid to paint the vast pageants that gave drama and color and pomp to the Venetian year. In such pictures Venetians as well as Venice appeared, citizens as recognizable as the Piazzetta itself. The princes, too, helped to domesticate art. Their profiles had long adorned medals—indeed the only claim to fame of some of them is that Pisanello made a cast of their features. They hungered, as princes will, for eternity, and they needed not only to patronize painting or to construct huge palaces, but also to see themselves immortalized by one in order to adorn the other. They appeared, as the Medici did, in the retinue of kings making their offerings to the in-

fant Christ, or in symbolic pageant, as Federigo da Montefeltro and his wife, Battista, did in the Urbino diptych. And, of course, the preoccupation with the nature of man must of itself lead to the attempt to interpret character through portraiture; and for this the treatment of the face in profile was insufficient. Although there were brilliant portraits elsewhere—Pollaiuolo's *Portrait of a Man,* Botticelli's *Giovanni di Pierfrancesco de' Medici,* and many others—Venice was the true home of the portrait. A great series of doges, unhappily destroyed by fire in 1577, was painted by Bellini for the Doge's Palace. And the portrait rapidly became fashionable. Procurators and merchants quickly followed in the steps of the doges, and the walls of private palaces were adorned with the portraits of their owners, many of them masterpieces of human interpretation by Titian.

Through perspective, through the introduction of oils, through the exploitation of landscape and the human body, Renaissance Italy created the traditions of Western art, in

which it was to remain embedded for centuries. Sculpture and architecture had flourished in like manner. Donatello's *David* remained an isolated phenomenon only for a generation. Verrocchio, Leonardo, and, above all, Michelangelo created statues of a beauty that equaled the best that the ancient world had to offer; and Michelangelo infused his statues with an emotional force that none have equaled since. The tragic nature of man—his immense loneliness and his inevitable end—gripped him like a vise. His tension and suffering, generalized for mankind, passed into stone or paint. Social circumstance and technical change allowed such supreme artists to flourish. And the distance traveled in a little over a hundred years—from Lorenzo Monaco, Gentile da Fabriano, or Lorenzetti to Leonardo, Michelangelo, or Raphael—is stupendous. Such a leap was only possible because art had become the expression of complex social forces.

By the High Renaissance, art had come to pervade all aspects of life. From the arrangement of sweetmeats to the con-

struction of fortifications—all were matters of moment upon which an artist's opinion might be needed or offered. And most of the great artists, too, regarded themselves as Jacks-of-all-trades. Leonardo did not think it beneath his dignity to design the costumes for the masques which his patrons loved or to fix the heating for a duchess' bath. And most of the great figures of the Renaissance displayed exceptional versatility. Michelangelo felt himself to be a man wholly dedicated to sculpture, yet after his reluctance had been overcome, he could paint the frescoes of the Sistine Chapel. And of course, he could, and did, turn to architecture with equal facility and, when the mood was upon him, express his deepest feelings in poetry. The versatility of a Leonardo or a Michelangelo was far from being unusual. Princes and patrons wished their lives to be embellished richly, ostentatiously, beautifully, and they were willing to pour out their ducats and florins on all the arts and crafts that adorn the life of man. They pursued physical beauty like a drug. Their

In modeling the figure of Hercules (opposite), Pollaiuolo distributed muscular stresses as though he were solving a problem in physics, for unless artists studied science they remained mere artisans, linked with masons and bricklayers like the sculptor shown below. The distinction between art and artisanship remained vague in the Renaissance. The craftsman in the plate at left, painting portraits of a betrothed couple, might work in other arts, too. The highly developed craft of majolica (bust at right) was an inexpensive substitute for the fine arts.

heightened sensibilities, due to the sudden turns of chance which threaded their days with light and shadow, lusted for color, richness, wanton display. This aristocratic spirit at large in a world of bourgeois delights had no use for pewter dishes, sober costume, modest feasting, or chaste jewelry. It reveled in gold, in silver, in bronze, in gaudy dishes of majolica, and in silks, in satins, and in damasks, in cunningly wrought pearls, in sapphires, in rubies, and in emeralds. And the pageantry, the masquerades, the feasts, the dancing, and the music provided the background to this peacock world. This pride, this ostentation could find expression in the intellectual world as well as in the senses, and collections of antique bronzes, marble statues, splendidly illuminated manuscripts, beautifully bound books from the new presses, ancient rings and seals, became a prince as much as his palace or his pictures. The mania for collecting, as a reflection of social grandeur, emerges during the Renaissance. This delight in the eye, this desire to impress, created a constant demand for

the services of the great masters, even for the most trivial and most ephemeral commissions—the molding of pastry, the decoration of a table, the casting of a candlestick, the cutting of an intaglio, the design of a dagger—almost all of which have disappeared into limbo. The works of a few craftsmen of genius—the terracottas of della Robbia, the metalwork of Cellini, the bronzes of Riccio—survive. Those of nameless craftsmen who achieved high excellence are more plentiful. Their ornate *cassoni*, their haunting bronzes, their brightly patterned majolicas, and, above all, their exquisite jewelry, scattered about the museums of America and Western Europe, give a glimpse of the sumptuous world for which they worked.

This was the way, they thought, the great Romans had lived. They loved to act the parts of classical mythology, to be Jupiter or Hebe or Apollo or Diana for a day. And although, of course, they never gave up their Christian roots, they were drawn increasingly closer to the pretense of a

In collaboration with his pupil Titian, Giovanni Bellini painted The Feast of the Gods *(facing page), an involved allegory based on a tale taken from Ovid. The metamorphosis of Daphne was another of Ovid's stories; Pollaiuolo shows the nymph (left) fleeing from Apollo's advances. Sprouting branches in place of arms, Daphne turns into a laurel tree to elude the god's pursuit. Pollaiolo's mythological paintings were an early result of the revival of interest in the classics. By the time of Titian, the ideals of humanism had come to dominate all painting. Titian decorated one room at the court of Alfonso d'Este at Ferrara with three pictures tracing a favorite humanist theme, the evolution of love, and placed* The Feast of the Gods *on the fourth wall. One scholar has conjectured that the amorous couple sitting behind a bowl of fruit at the right center of Bellini's painting represents Lucrezia Borgia and her third husband, Alfonso d'Este.*

pagan world. It gave them what all aristocracies need, a sense of separateness, as certainly and as completely as chivalry and feudalism had given a sense of caste to the warrior knights of the Middle Ages. Classical mythology, Neoplatonism, the mysteries of the pagan world, became chic. The education of a gentleman took on the strong classical bias which it was not to lose until modern times. The popular philosophers—Ficino, Pico della Mirandola, the friends of painters as well as their patrons—encouraged the revival of these ancient allegories. But they were not to be shared with the vulgar. Taste, sensibility, were to be linked with esoteric, almost private, knowledge. Poets, philosophers, painters, should speak in the language of riddles, of mysteries, which the *cognoscenti* alone could read. Such an attitude bred a sense of singularity, of exclusiveness, which courts and courtiers found as seductive as sin. Even Leonardo jotted down in commonplace books the trivial riddles of the Sforza, and Pico boasted in a philosophical essay, "If I am not mistaken

it will be intelligible only to a few, for it is filled with many mysteries from the secret philosophies of the ancients." The esoteric, the mysterious, developed a fashionable cachet, and its cult opened the floodgates not only to much of the nonsense of late Neoplatonism, but also to astrology, to the language of emblems, and to the absurdities of late medieval bestiaries, and in the revival of learning was intermingled a great deal of hocus-pocus. Much, however, of this is germane to the image that Renaissance man created of himself and will be dealt with later, but this delight in an exclusive world of myth and mystery also influenced artistic expression profoundly. A naked Mars and Venus, tired but happy from their wanton sport, might shock the uninitiated, but the cultivated knew better. Mars, of course, was War, and Venus Love, so Love could conquer War and bring forth Peace. And if by chance Venus was wearing a bit of the armor, that merely illustrated that Love itself involved Strife. Such were simple allegories which even the fringe of the elite could

read, but the theology as well as the mythology of poetic virtue grew ever more complex in its expression. Bellini's *Feast of the Gods* is the subject of a monograph, and all the iconographic scholarship of the Western world has failed to probe the hidden meanings of Giorgione's *Tempest.* For those artists who felt keenly the mystery of things, the way of allegory often proved enriching. It enabled them to explore feeling, to describe atmosphere, to hint at hidden presences, and to still in one luminous moment the fever and the fret of life and give its transience significance. So the *Virgin of the Rocks,* or even the *Mona Lisa,* possesses a sense of depth, of the abiding value of individual life, of eternal knowledge, that is both nostalgic and humane.

Giorgione responded to this sense of awareness as well as to Leonardo's mastery of light and shade. In Giorgione's paintings, and in many of Titian's, the value of earthly life is increased and given a significance that is as remote from the Middle Ages as it is from China.

A great artist like Giorgione could give universality to a private and exclusive myth, indeed deepen his genius by indulging in it, but many lesser artists could not. In their hands the mysteries became hollow, the allegories obvious and banal. Also, this cult of a private language of art marks the drift of the tide. The great masterpieces of the Renaissance had been, and many of them even in the first quarter of the sixteenth century still were, great public performances, even if they were created for popes or princes. But increasingly the direction of art was toward private enjoyment, and its style both more aristocratic and more exclusive. This was bound to be, as the heroic age of the city-state waned; as power and wealth and the sense of opportunity passed to the sea-borne nations of the West. Yet the achievement was so fabulously great that the traditions created in four or five generations proved far too strong for the creative imagination to wither quickly, and for the next four hundred years the arts of Italy continued to entrance the mind of Europe.

The Young Michelangelo

by KENNETH CLARK

Michelangelo belongs to that small company of poets, artists, and musicians whose greatness has never been seriously questioned; but he differs from his companions—Dante, Shakespeare, Goethe, Titian, Mozart—in one important way. All of them have maintained this hold on our admiration by appealing to a wide range of human experience, so that each generation may extract from their works what suits it best. But Michelangelo has made his own terms with posterity, just as he did with his employers. He is the most concentrated and undeviating of great artists. We come to him for one particular revelation, communicated by one particular means. And the revelation is so important to us, and the mastery of means so absolute, that having once experienced it we, like his contemporaries, can never get it out of our systems. It makes everything else seem small and tame and worldly.

When we speak of an artist's greatness, as opposed to his talent or even his genius, we are usually referring to an aspect of his personality, and this is particularly true of Michelangelo. We know about him from many contemporary records, including the two *Lives* of Condivi and Vasari, men who knew him well, and every one of these records gives us the impression of an awe-inspiring character. Leaving aside the great religious teachers, I cannot think of any other man in history who has commanded such respect.

Our visual image of Michelangelo is of an old man, his face deeply marked by spiritual struggles. But there is a quantity of evidence that as a young man his force of character was equally apparent. The following episode recorded by Condivi will serve as an example. In 1506 Michelangelo had left Rome in a huff because he had been debarred from immediate access to Pope Julius II. Seven months later Michelangelo was brought into the papal presence. Julius asked him why he had walked out. Michelangelo answered, "Not from ill will, but from disdain" (*ma per isdegno*). A bishop who was present nervously intervened, "Pay no attention, Your Holiness; he speaks out of ignorance. Artists are all like that." But before the wretched bishop could finish his apology he was hustled out of the room with blows; and Michelangelo resumed his former relationship with the Pope. Julius was then the most formidable figure in Christendom; Michelangelo was thirty-two.

Michelangelo in later years, by one of his followers.

Michelangelo used this transcendent force of character, which was like the spiritual power of a medieval saint, to transform the physical perfection of antiquity. He appeared at the moment when Greco-Roman sculpture was a new and compelling discovery, accepted by artists and patrons alike as an ultimate model. But in fact the bland materialism of antique art could not alone have expressed the crisis of the human spirit which took place during the years between Luther and Galileo. Michelangelo, by changing and twisting the forms of antique sculpture, created an instrument through which the spiritual turmoil of the sixteenth century could be made visible.

He was born in Florentine territory on March 6, 1475, and was one of the very few artists to come of aristocratic stock, although by his time the family fortunes had declined. His father, who claimed descent from the counts of Canossa, strongly objected to his son becoming an artist, which at that date meant an artisan; and when Michelangelo was one of the most famous men in Italy, his father still regarded the whole affair with bewildered incredulity. He was, as Condivi says, "somewhat old-fashioned"; but Michelangelo treated him with patience and respect, asked for his prayers and sent him money, and often said that his sole aim in life had been to help the family regain its former status.

From the very first no one had any doubt that he was supremely gifted in the arts of design. After a short apprenticeship with Ghirlandaio, the most successful Florentine painter of the period, he is said by his biographers to have joined the privileged youths who were drawing antiques in the Medici gardens of the Via Larga, under the direction of the sculptor Bertoldo, and where he attracted the attention of Lorenzo the Magnificent. I see no adequate reason for disbelieving this tradition, and Michelangelo's earliest carvings seem to confirm it, for they consist largely of imitations of the antique, of a kind which he would have learned only in this particular school. Bertoldo's own masterpiece was a bronze relief of a battle, done in imitation of an antique sarcophagus in Pisa; and Michelangelo's earliest carving is also an imitation of a battle sarcophagus, although the nominal subject is the *Rape of Dejanira*. Although it was surely begun in the Medicean academy (and was perhaps left unfinished on Lo-

renzo's death in 1492) it looks out of this enchanted garden, both backwards and forwards: back to the charged and passionate Last Judgments of the Pisani and forward to the achievements of Michelangelo's maturity. There is no more striking example of Proust's saying, *"Les grands artistes n'ont jamais fait qu'une seule oeuvre."* Michelangelo's first great carving foreshadows not only the classical style of his Florentine period, but the anticlassical expressiveness of his later works. In many respects it is closer to the *Last Judgment* of the Sistine than to the cartoon of the *Battle of Cascina*. And the affinity with the Dantesque spirit of Giovanni Pisano is also very revealing, for Michelangelo's heroic seriousness was, perhaps unconsciously, a reaction away from the daintiness of the *quattrocento*, back to the passion and gravity of the first founders of Tuscan art. His earliest drawings were copies of Giotto, and the poems of Dante were his continual inspiration.

But the Dejanira relief is exceptional. During his years in the garden of the Via Larga, and for some time afterward, Michelangelo's whole conscious effort was directed toward the imitation of the classical style, and he succeeded so well that one of his works, a sleeping cupid, was actually sold as an antique, having been buried in a vineyard by a Roman dealer. When the fraud was discovered, Michelangelo, unlike modern imitators of antiquity, derived nothing but credit for his skill, and the cupid was afterwards purchased by that most pedantic of collectors, Isabella d'Este. It has now disappeared, and the *Bacchus*, which survives from about the same epoch, suggests that the loss is not a serious one. For the *Bacchus* is an all too successful imitation of Hellenistic sculpture at its least attractive. The swaying, dreamy movement of the body and a certain Dionysiac beauty in the head do not compensate for the lack of tension in the modeling, and one is left wondering how Michelangelo, even in a technical exercise, has contrived to suppress his energy of hand.

The *Bacchus* was executed in Rome, soon after Michelangelo's arrival there in 1496. After the death of Lorenzo de' Medici in 1492 he had remained two years in Florence, and it was at this time that he is supposed to have begun a scientific study of anatomy, under the protection of the Prior of Santo Spirito. These were the years when Savona-

rola was the virtual ruler of Florence, and although Michelangelo was never a direct follower, he read Savonarola's books throughout his life, and told Condivi that he could still hear the *frate*'s voice ringing in his ears. So two essential ingredients of Michelangelo's art, a passion for anatomy and a consciousness of sin, were, so to say, poured into his mind at the same moment. But he was not happy in the Florence of Piero de' Medici; and in October, 1494, there occurred the first of those panic flights which were to be repeated three times in the course of his life. Psychologists have occupied themselves with the question why this man of immense moral courage, who was utterly indifferent to physical hardship, should have suffered from these recurrences of irrational fear; and perhaps it is true that continuous inner tension led to an occasional snapping of the spirit, which expressed itself in a sudden need to escape. Or perhaps in each case there really was some ground for running away, and Michelangelo, who recognized his own genius, felt that he must preserve his life at any cost. In 1494 he fled to Bologna, where, as usual, his gifts were immediately recognized and he was commissioned to work on the chief sculptural project of the town, the ark of Saint Dominic; but fifteenth-century Bologna offered no scope to a youth of Michelangelo's genius, and as soon as possible he returned to Florence, and thence to Rome.

He arrived in Rome in the summer of 1496, having a letter of introduction from Lorenzo di Pierfrancesco de' Medici, the pupil of Marsilio Ficino and friend of Botticelli; and a week after his arrival he wrote back to Lorenzo, "There are many beautiful things here." Medieval Rome, the city of vineyards and cow pastures, with its stranded basilicas and aggressive watch towers, was just beginning to give up its buried treasure; and Michelangelo's chief patron at this epoch, Jacopo Galli, had already a considerable collection of antiquities, amongst which Michelangelo's *Bacchus* was given a place of honor. However, the outstanding work during this first visit to Rome was of an entirely different character, the *Pietà* in St. Peter's. It was commissioned by a French cardinal, Jean Bilheres, and this may account for the fact that Michelangelo accepted a Gothic motif in which the full-grown Christ lies on Our Lady's knees. This was originally a wood-carving motif,

and the difficulty of adapting it to the crystalline character of marble has led Michelangelo to a marvelous feat of technical skill. This is the first work in which he shows that consummate mastery of his craft which his contemporaries, both artists and patrons, valued so highly. It has also involved a new stretch of the imagination, for he has achieved what theorists tell us is impossible, a perfect fusion of Gothic and Classic art. The motif and sentiment are northern, the physical beauty of the nude Christ is Greek; and Michelangelo has given the Virgin's head, so painfully distorted in Gothic Pietàs, a union of physical and spiritual beauty which is entirely his own. Ever since the *Pietà* was put in place, people have asked how the mother of a grown man, in the depths of grief, could appear so young and beautiful; and Michelangelo's reply is recorded in both Vasari and Condivi. It expresses in vivid, colloquial form the doctrines of Neoplatonism, which he had absorbed from the Medicean philosophers of his boyhood: that physical perfection is the mirror and emblem of a pure and noble spirit. This is the belief that had led his friend Lorenzo di Pierfrancesco to commission Botticelli's *Venus*; and we know, from Michelangelo's sonnets, that it justified to his mind his passionate admiration of the naked beauty of young men. Our scientific modern way of thinking, with its reliance on experience and psychology, may reject Neoplatonism as a compound of myth and self-deception. But there is no question of the sincerity with which Michelangelo believed (in Spenser's words) that "soule is form, and doth the bodie make."

In 1501 Michelangelo returned to Florence. These were the years in which the Florentine republic was able to assert some of the heroic virtues which had made it great a century before, and Michelangelo must have found the atmosphere of his native city a sharp contrast to the Medicean *douceur de vivre* of his youth, or the parasitic, antiquarian Rome of his more recent experience. It was an atmosphere which suited him perfectly, and he was immediately called upon by the city magistrates to carry out commissions which should express the pride, vigor, and austere idealism of their regime; and the results were the *David* and the cartoon of the *Battle of Cascina*.

The *David* was carved out of a gigantic block of marble from which, seventy years earlier, the sculp-

Two Sonnets by
MICHELANGELO

Although Michelangelo wrote his impassioned sonnets on art and love and his controversial verses against papal corruption only for circulation among his friends, after the artist's death his great-nephew published them in an expurgated version which smoothed out rough versification and censored any ideas which might be objectionable to the Church. In this translation by the nineteenth-century Renaissance scholar John Addington Symonds, the sonnets are restored to their original form.

ON THE PAINTING OF THE SISTINE CHAPEL

to Giovanni da Pistoia

I've grown a goiter by dwelling in this den—
As cats from stagnant streams in Lombardy,
Or in what other land they hap to be—
Which drives the belly close beneath the chin:
My beard turns up to heaven; my nape falls in,
Fixed on my spine: my breast-bone visibly
Grows like a harp: a rich embroidery
Bedews my face from brush-drops thick and thin.
My loins into my paunch like levers grind:
My buttock like a crupper bears my weight;
My feet unguided wander to and fro;
In front my skin grows loose and long; behind,
By bending it becomes more taut and strait;
Crosswise I strain me like a Syrian bow:
Whence false and quaint, I know,
Must be the fruit of squinting brain and eye;
For ill can aim the gun that bends awry.
Come then, Giovanni, try
To succor my dead pictures and my fame,
Since foul I fare and painting is my shame.

THE ARTIST AND HIS WORK

How can that be, lady, which all men learn
By long experience? Shapes that seem alive,
Wrought in hard mountain marble, will survive
Their maker, whom the years to dust return!
Thus to effect cause yields. Art hath her turn,
And triumphs over Nature. I, who strive
With Sculpture, know this well; her wonders live
In spite of time and death, those tyrants stern.
So I can give long life to both of us
In either way, by color or by stone,
Making the semblance of thy face and mine.
Centuries hence when both are buried, thus
Thy beauty and my sadness shall be shown,
And men shall say, "For her 'twas wise to pine."

A RENAISSANCE IN ART

Grieving over the disappearance of arts which had once flourished in antiquity, the architect Leon Battista Alberti came to Florence, and to his delight encountered there a new generation of artists with a "talent for every noble thing." They even surpassed the ancients, he decided, for with no models to imitate or teachers to follow, they had discovered "arts and sciences unheard of and never seen." Alberti caught their spirit; he codified new rules of perspective and determined harmonious proportions for his architecture by measuring musical intervals. Other Florentine artists invented ideal proportions for the human form, dissected corpses to learn anatomy, composed pictures upon mathematical formulas. The Venetian school soon rivaled Florence, and its richly painted nudes and sensitive landscapes established an enduring tradition in European art. But Florence produced Michelangelo, the supreme artist of the Renaissance. He found landscape painting trivial and portraiture almost as unsatisfactory; his great obsession was the human figure, which he employed as the expression of man in torment, struggling heroically, as in the red chalk drawings of Hercules reproduced above, against the forces of destiny.

113

THE PORTRAIT

The laws of antiquity, one Renaissance scholar stated, had forbidden artists to paint the portrait of anyone who was not a prince or a wise or virtuous man; but now, he complained, any low or infamous man could have his picture painted. The art of portraiture had been developed to glorify the great, and Pisanello's first portrait medal, a Byzantine emperor, continued an imperial Roman tradition which the Renaissance copied from ancient coins that had lately been unearthed. But soon petty princes, humanists, and even merchants began to commission their portraits on medals to send to friends as mementos. Florentine painters filled church frescoes with pictures of recognizable individuals, and sculptors modeled their work—statues of saints and of Plato himself—on the features of specific men. Scandalized preachers complained that these portraits served vanity, not religion, and painters soon realized that they distracted observers from the fresco itself.

The use of idealized images returned to fashion, and the taste for easel portraits spread as fresco portraiture waned. The sharply limned likenesses of the fifteenth century gave way to dramatic character studies, representing both the sitter's image and his inner nobility, propaganda portraits designed to satisfy the Renaissance thirst for individual glory.

Future generations, a court poet predicted, would praise the union of art and nature in Leonardo da Vinci's portrait (above) of Cecilia Gallerani, Lodovico Sforza's beautiful mistress. Leonardo had striven to reproduce far more than Cecilia's appearance: "Paint the face," he once recommended, "in such a way that it will be easy to understand what is going on in the mind." Earlier painters, like Pisanello, had ignored psychology, recording only the sitter's features. His medal of Leonello d'Este (right) posed the Marquis of Ferrara in a realistic but uncharitable profile, for in low relief a profile could be more precise than a full-face view. Botticelli balanced his own psychological insights with detailed description of the sitter; his glowing portrait (opposite) of Giovanni di Pierfrancesco de' Medici, who posed holding a medieval religious image, is idealized but highly suggestive of the young man's characteristics.

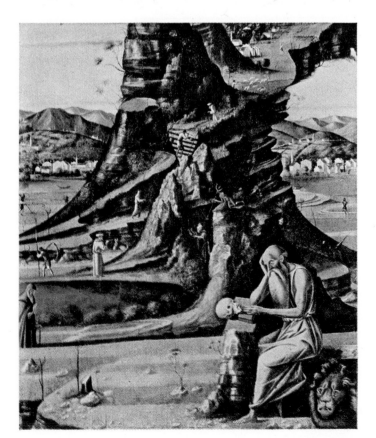

As ambitious princes cleared the highways of robbers and cultivated model farms according to agricultural precepts recommended by Virgil, the Italian countryside emerged as a new Arcadia. Fashionable poets, mooning over rural scenery, scribbled eclogues celebrating the joys of country life; painters followed their lead, cradling Holy Families and pensive saints in a hospitable landscape of gentle meadows and hills. Far behind was the stony wilderness of earlier paintings where hermits wandered through deserts to prove their saintliness, where jagged rocks, borrowed from Byzantine art, reflected nature's hostility to man. Now another tradition predominated. Man was completely at home in nature. Fantastic rocks, once merely emblems of mountains, were painted as realistic studies of natural formations. Portraits showed, beyond the sitter's shoulder, lovingly detailed views of the countryside; even in altar pieces and other religious paintings it was the custom to use the local landscape as the background for a Biblical event. Finally the landscape became important enough to dominate a picture. Florentine landscape painters were factual observers. The Venetian school began with a realism as exact but under Giorgione's lead soon transformed it, modeling precise details of the countryside into luminous idyls. The Venetian ideal—tranquil, poetic, and unified by light—eventually became traditional in European art.

Meticulous concern for the description of nature is evident in Giovanni Bellini's masterpiece, Saint Francis in Ecstasy *(right). But there were alternate ways of treating landscape. Giorgione idealized his pastoral scene (top left, a detail from* The Adoration of the Shepherds*). The painter of the* Thebaid *(center) used bleak conventional rock forms symbolically, to show the desert's hostility. Lazzaro Bastiani placed Saint Jerome (below) in a landscape of sheer fantasy, beside a rocky but optimistic highway to heaven.*

LANDSCAPE

ns for which
of the cathe-
. Among his
—Pico della
president of
ly that an old
Even. Lorenzo
s, had sought
rejected the
ring the fact
y in painting,
Of all Italian
naissance, but
rit of Savona-
ity of violent

Tuscan land-

The money changer (lower left) and wool merchants (whose emblem appears above) belonged to the greater guilds which controlled Florence's government. Most citizens, such as the silk reeler (below) and the market workers (left), were not in guilds.

scape, so rich, so fertile, so gentle in climate, bespeaks a pastoral, idyllic, Virgilian life in which the rhythms of living achieve a harmony with nature. Here, if anywhere, is a countryside made for a Giorgione or a Titian, yet Florence produced neither, nor indeed any painter who sought to immortalize the poetry of nature. The facts of Florentine life were brutal, not gentle. Rich and beautiful its situation might be; economically and strategically its position was always desperate. To the west, controlling its only outlet to the sea, lay Pisa, prosperous and powerful, linked by its commerce with the four corners of the Mediterranean world. Athwart the route to Pisa, Florence had an unbeatable enemy in Lucca. To the north, the peril was worse—Milan, ravenous for land and rich in men and money. To the south, almost on Florence's doorstep, Siena controlled the road to Rome, and the Sienese were as fiercely proud and warlike as the Florentines. To the east were the wolves, the ravagers, the petty tyrants of

the Papal Patrimony who lived by war and violence; for these despots the rich lands of Tuscany were sweet to plunder. To survive, therefore, let alone expand, Florence required from its citizens both courage and resourcefulness, a willingness to practice the arts of diplomacy as well as war. Both needed money, and, in the last analysis, wealth and wealth alone enabled Florence to survive and to triumph over the disadvantages of its geographical situation. The realities of Florentine life were the sword and the florin. The use of both was improved by skill in reading human nature, and it is not surprising that a preoccupation with man and his destiny lies at the heart of the Florentine Renaissance.

Despite all its perils, Florence triumphed. The prime source of its strength and wealth lay in its *arti*—the guilds which drew together its merchants and skilled craftsmen. One of the earliest to be organized was the *arte di Calimala,* and throughout the golden age of Florence it held its dominating

Brunelleschi's dome dominates Florence in a woodcut done about 1486. Feudal towers dot the city, but new mansions such as the Pitti palace, in the center of the walled section at far right, across the Arno from the cathedral, relieve the medieval appearance.

position. It was a company of merchants who traded with England, Flanders, and France, bringing undressed cloths to Florence, where they were reworked into fine materials and dyed in the splendid, vivid colors that the Renaissance painters have made so memorable—the blues and crimsons and reds in which they dressed their saints and madonnas. They exported the finished goods throughout Europe, and the stamp of the guild became a guarantee of worth and workmanship. The guild was meticulously ruled and its members subjected to a close discipline not only in their public, but also in their moral life. The *Calimala* became a model for the other great guilds that began to dominate Florentine economic and political life in the late twelfth and early thirteenth centuries. Including the *Calimala* there were seven of them—the wool merchants, the silk weavers, the bankers, the notaries, the druggists (Dante was a member of this guild, which also dealt in spices and precious stones), and

the furriers. These seven included all the great merchants of Florence, who formed the heart of its economic life. But Florence was a large town, and it served a populous hinterland, and its shopkeepers were numerous enough, and powerful enough, to form their own guilds, which were known as the lesser arts—the innkeepers, shoemakers, carpenters, blacksmiths, grocers, bakers, and the like—fourteen in all. Each guild had its officers of state—its consuls, its notaries, and its banner-bearer (*gonfaloniere*) who carried the heraldic symbols in the great processions which were held on the day of their patron saint. Each guild, too, had its church which it patronized and in which were held its special masses, for these merchants were as deeply steeped in religion as in trade. (At the head of each page of one of their surviving account books is the sign of the cross, made to make forgery hell-worthy.) The Florentine guilds were small worlds unto themselves, closely regulated, self-conscious, jealous of their

Reliefs on the façade of Giotto's campanile reflect Florence's devotion to humanist studies. The medallion at left represents logic, with portraits of Plato and Aristotle. The one below it shows a grammar lesson.

osophy, and in the countless arts and crafts that adorn the life of man. The change was as dramatic as water turning into ice.

After its failure by 1343 to secure dominion of Tuscany by force of arms, Florence had resolved to ally, whenever possible, with neighboring city-states, to protect rather than absorb. As Coluccio Salutati, the chancellor of Florence and one of its first great humanists, wrote, the Florentines who hated tyranny at home were willing to defend the liberties of others. The feeling was strong in the city's governing circles that Florentines were the true heirs of republican Rome: Salutati, Bruni, and Poggio studied Cicero in their leisure from running Florence's diplomacy and collecting its taxes. His ideas, which lie at the heart of humanism, struck them with the force of a new discovery, and they began to weave afresh the belief that the full life, indeed, the good life, could only be lived if a man dedicated himself to civic virtues. It was about

Rome, about Cicero, about Plato, that they talked when they lingered in the sun in the Piazza or gathered together in each other's houses. Nor did they disdain to discuss their ideas with the sculptors and artists—Ghiberti, Donatello, Brunelleschi—whom they and their friends patronized. And how right they seemed in their interpretation of the past and the present, when Florence withstood alone the might of Gian Galeazzo Visconti, who, in 1402, stood poised to overwhelm the city and so bring the whole of Lombardy and Tuscany under his sway. Then, as in some Athenian tragedy, the Fates took up their shears. Gian Galeazzo, in the prime of life, with the cup of success at his lips, sickened and died. So the threat to Florence passed, but, in passing, fused a mood into an attitude to life.

The Florentines did not consider themselves saved by chance. For them it was a triumph of civic virtue, of steadfast republicans thwarting tyrants. The ancient Roman virtues of

Beauty pervaded Florentine schoolbooks as well as religious tomes. Part of an arithmetic problem in the primer at right reads: "The King of France was routed in battle, with ¼ of his soldiers killed and ⅖ wounded and 1000 were taken prisoner and 6000 escaped." And the illustration almost makes its solving palatable. The high literacy of the populace inspired such humanists as Coluccio Salutati (above) to dream of Florence as the ideal city of man. An artist portrayed Saint Augustine writing The City of God *(left), and hopefully included Florence in the background of his illustration.*

which Cicero spoke and of which old Cato was the ideal, had been, they felt, reborn in Florence, which gave the city an identity with the past. The year 1402 represented a triumph and a liberation, and this sense of freedom renewed, of the breaking of the shackles of the immediate past, invigorated not only philosophy and history but also the plastic arts. It is not surpising that Masaccio's grave saints should wear their cloaks like togas.

Interest in classics, interest in ancient art, delight in new techniques of painting, sculpture, and architecture, existed before the cataclysmic struggle with Milan, but none can doubt that it gave an immense impetus to the peculiar qualities of the Florentine Renaissance. Symbolically, at the height of the struggle the city appointed Chrysoloras, the first and most deeply influential teacher of Greek, a public lecturer. A belief in the value of classical learning as the molder of a citizen's character, a conviction that great moral

value could be derived from a study of its philosophy, became as deeply embedded in the Florentine tradition as it did in nineteenth-century England. And when the Medici founded and encouraged a Platonic academy, and patronized handsomely the great philosophers—Ficino, Pico, and the rest—they were no innovators, and the purpose of their patronage was widely understood. It would strengthen an attitude to human life that was thought to be singularly Florentine. Although humanistic study had its roots in civic life, naturally it developed rapidly within the terms of its own disciplines and needs. Scholars dedicated themselves to the textual and philological problems inherent in the study of the classics—and as scholars will, became obsessed with their own techniques. Yet even if preoccupation with style, grammar, emendation, and the minutiae of criticism often took the place of creative imagination, there was nevertheless a great deal of fine poetry and fine prose, written in a Latin

ized Donatello for as long as he lived, and sculpture, as might be expected from so dedicated a Florentine, was his greatest passion after architecture. He preferred his sons to deal with mere painters and decorators, but *he* paid. And many superb frescoes of Fra Angelico, Filippo Lippi, and Benozzo Gozzoli were the fruits of Medicean gold, of their sense of the usurer's sin, of a need to return the riches that one man had acquired in beauty that all could enjoy.

Lorenzo the Magnificent, his grandson, amazed by the staggering sums that his grandfather had spent, preferred the cheaper patronage of philosophers. Nevertheless, he maintained the tradition of his ancestors, and the beauty and splendor of Florence steadily grew. The citizens were continuously regaled with pageants, tournaments, and carnivals. It proved to be a reckless world in which capital was too easily squandered on military maneuvers, diplomatic activity, and Lorenzo's anxiety to cut a figure in Italy whatever the cost.

As the fame of Florence reached new heights, so did its public debt (not that the debt worried the oligarchy overmuch, for they lent the money on excellent security and at a splendid interest). The world was a rich man's oyster: the tentacles of Florentine trade stretched from Cairo to the Cotswolds, and even the shocks and disasters in the eastern Mediterranean—the spread of the Ottoman Turks and the fall of Constantinople—seemed, for a time at least, to be turned to Florence's advantage by a benign Providence. The loss of Byzantine alum, so vital to the luxury cloth trade, was immediately countered by the discovery of huge deposits at Tolfa in the Papal States, for which, naturally, the Medici secured the concession. Wandering Greeks with manuscripts to sell and an ancient tongue to teach were welcome as a further adornment to a refined household. Secure and self-indulgent, the leaders of Florentine society tried to evade present disasters and future cataclysms, while the

Florentine government sought to survive by the use of mercenaries, diplomacy, subsidies, and bribes. The call to civic virtue, the mobilization of the city's wealth and the city's men, no longer appealed to a bourgeois aristocracy. Their exclusive world possessed too much delight to be foolishly risked. In the soft elegance of Lorenzo di Pierfrancesco de' Medici's villa, in the golden glow of the Tuscan evening, young men might listen to Ficino's subtle explanations of the hidden meanings in Botticelli's *Primavera,* which adorned its walls; for them the bales of wool, rolls of cloth, stacked hides, and piled spices were a necessity, not a way of life, and although they could use the dagger and the sword, they felt no compulsion to sweat in arms amid the horrors of war for the future of their city. All the authority, all the skill, of Lorenzo were used to avoid such bleak necessities. This elegant world was perched precariously, however, on the edge of turbulence, and it depended on the subtlety and statesmanship of

Lorenzo not only to prevent the system from collapsing in internecine strife, of which the Pazzi conspiracy was a clear enough warning, but also to still the dangerous antipathy of a restless population whose fears and hopes were already being played upon by a master demagogue, some years before Lorenzo's death.

The Florentine Renaissance has entranced generations of men by the astonishing range of its artistic and scholarly achievements—from the serene perfection of Leonardo to the tragic realism of Machiavelli—and all too often the endless toil of the laboring men and women, whose grievous lives made it possible, is forgotten. It was the tragic situation of the common man that stirred deeply the creative imagination not only of Michelangelo, but also of Botticelli, who reflected the bright elegance and exclusive charm of the Florentine world more faithfully than any other painter. The compulsive rantings of Savonarola haunted them both.

The last decades of the fifteenth century brought a sharp contraction of Florentine trade. Englishmen were beginning to make their own cloth, the Flemish were showing a more than Italian skill in dressing and dyeing it. In 1478 the London bank of the Medici was closed; in 1483 the Tolfa alum concession had to be abandoned; for a time the merchants of Florence even lost their traditional role as papal bankers. Trade with the eastern Mediterranean steadily wasted away. Renewed wars, with expensive alliances and even more costly condottieri, added further strain to an economy which had already accumulated far too many obligations. The Florentines had been dealing in futures for too many generations, and, skillful as their financiers were, they could not conjure increased wealth from diminishing trade. For centuries urban poverty had helped to breed epidemic diseases that raged with the ferocity of a prairie fire through the dirt-encrusted slums. Plagues, fevers, and consumption

made death a constant visitor at the houses of the poor, who, to exorcise horror, fortify their courage, and set their hopes on future blessedness, pleaded for the intercession of the Virgin and the saints. Religion—ecstatic, even apocalyptic—assuaged the wounds of their poverty and its pain. For them the elegant, exclusive domain of the scarlet-wearing burghers who exercised authority in their city was a bright, elusive world as impossible to understand as dreams in a language they could never comprehend. The sufferings of Christ and the pity of God lay closer to their knowledge, and in their lives the priest was as necessary as bread. This contradiction —poverty, suffering, and pain amid a world of profusion, extravagance, and delight—stirred the consciences of deeply sensitive men. It was this that made Pico della Mirandola seek the solace of Savonarola's mysticism, that led him, at his death, to adopt the habit of a Dominican; it was this that brought about that stranger conversion which drew Botticelli

To commemorate the Pazzi conspiracy, Lorenzo commissioned the medal below, showing his brother's assassination in the Cathedral of Florence. Giuliano's picture, seen above the choir enclosure, may have been copied from Botticelli's portrait of him which appears on the facing page. Pallas and the Centaur *(right) was painted by Botticelli as a tribute to Lorenzo. The goddess of wisdom, wreathed in olive branches and taming a centaur, has been thought to symbolize the Medici talent for ruling through suasion rather than force. But Lorenzo was not always gentle; when the Pazzi conspirators were hanged, heads down, Botticelli was asked to paint a picture of them.*

away from the gaieties and urbane moralities of the antique to an acceptance of Savonarola's prophecies; it was this that fused Michelangelo's tragic sense of human destiny with Savonarola's apocalyptic vision.

The story of Savonarola is a mixture of tragedy and hysteria, in which a genuine pity for man's condition became enraveled in hate and muddled by political intrigue. His denunciation of worldliness, his childish burning of vanities, his fiery condemnation of a lazy and corrupt clergy, were a part of the threnody of the life of Europe, frequently heard, frequently forgotten; but Savonarola spoke at a time when the young Piero de' Medici was displaying a singular lack of his family's genius. Behind Savonarola loomed the discontented poor, eager for a change, eager for secular as well as religious hope. Those families whom the Medici had excluded and despised knew how to manipulate this superlative demagogue, whose wild sermons could inflame a multitude. So what started in evangelism finished in political revolution.

The little people, the *piagnoni* (snivelers) as the old oligarchs called them, became a power in the land. *Popolo e Libertà* frequently echoed in the Piazza—a cry which Pisa promptly adopted as it threw aside the Florentine yoke and claimed the protection of the French, when invasion of Italy had triggered the revolution against Piero. Savonarola combined a dependence on the French that was quite unrealistic with a hatred of the Papacy that bordered on insanity. His loud denunciations of papal sins (interlarded from time to time with staggeringly sane bits of hardheaded diplomacy) grew more shrill as the French left him in the lurch. Alexander VI—aware of, and tolerantly amused by, his own shortcomings—bore with the fulminations so long as his diplomacy required it. Time, of course, favored the Pope. The French were content to use Florence, but naturally disinclined to save it from the consequences of its own folly, or to restore its

To replace the recently exiled Medici as protectors of Florence's liberty, Savonarola proclaimed Jesus Christ as the new ruler of the city. Shouting "Viva Cristo!" excited crowds roared their approval, for the friar's impassioned sermons had transformed Florence. From his cloister in the monastery of San Marco, shown in the photograph at right, Savonarola ruled the city. His preaching was so famous that even the Sultan of Turkey read translations of his sermons. A woodcut (right) taken from his Book of Revelations, shows him exhorting his flock. Savonarola castigated the Medici, the Pope, humanists, and painters, and found time to write a tract against astrologers. An illustration from the work appears above.

Tuscan empire. And in Florence itself, the oligarchs disliked both the rantings of Savonarola and the government of the people; in the wings lurked the exiled Medici—*they* were powerful in Rome. The inevitable end came: the rack and the fagot for Savonarola; the defeat of his *piagnoni*; and in the fullness of time, the return of the Medici.

The whole Savonarola episode is a curious mixture of idealism, ineptitude, and iniquity. Certainly Savonarola wanted a Florentine government that represented more fully the whole citizenship—the poor and the dispossessed as well as the rich and the powerful. He also hated life, grew drunk on his own megalomaniac visions, preferred prophecy to policy, and welcomed the disasters he had done so much to promote. Ignorance married to prejudice, blind hatred linked with a disgust for life, proved an unsatisfactory basis for statesmanship, even when practiced by a saint.

Never again was the republic the same; the power of Flor-

ence was greatly diminished. For a decade after the burning of Savonarola in 1498 for heresy, and after the failure of her mercenaries, Florence's blood and treasure were poured out in the Pisan war. In 1509 Pisa was captured, but the expense was far beyond the weakened resources of Florence's dwindling trade. Indeed, three years later a refusal to act in concert with the Papacy was treated by Julius II as an impertinence. His professional Spanish troops scattered the Florentine militia. The papal-inspired revolution followed, and the Medici returned. They lacked the ability of their ancestors, and proved little better than pawns in the hands of the Medici Pope Leo X, and it required further rebellions and plots, another brief republic haunted by the puritanism and religiosity of Savonarola, as well as the sack of Rome by Charles V, before Florence was finally subjected to the rule of the Medici as dukes of Tuscany. In the first three decades of the sixteenth century the greatness of Florence faded. Eco-

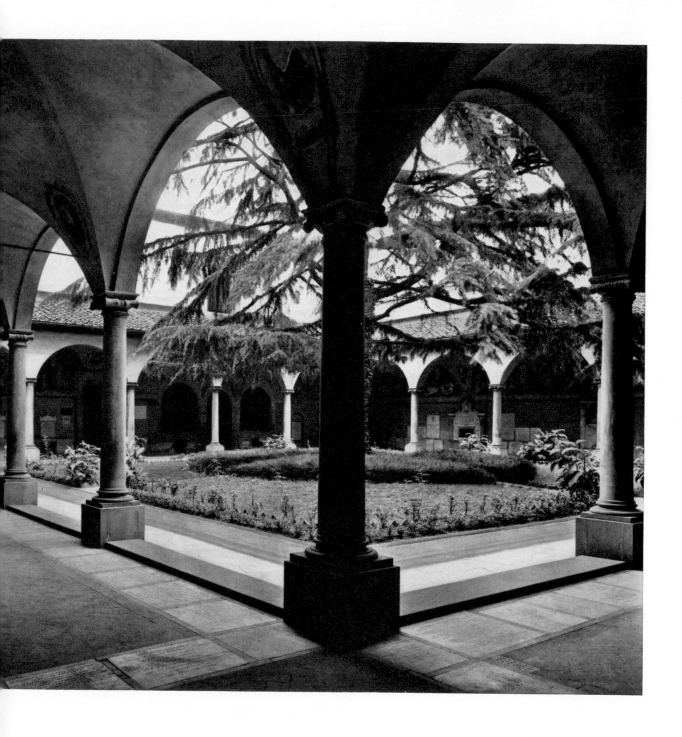

nomically—and the splendor of the Florentine Renaissance was based on its wealth—Florence lacked a future. The heart of its trade—cloth—was lost to England and to Flanders, and banking followed trade. Florence was far more vulnerable than Venice, or even Milan, to the great decline in Mediterranean prosperity which followed the discoveries of the New World and the sea-route to the Indies.

Artists lived uneasy lives in post-Medicean Florence, for patronage grew scarce. Art and humanism no longer reflected the civic virtues—these were adequately exercised by private prayer and public repentance. During the middle decades of the sixteenth century, the cult of sensitivity, of elegance, and of learning as the peculiar attributes of a gentleman had also narrowed the social basis of art and, to some extent, limited its appeal. In the wanderings of Leonardo and of Michelangelo, in the frustrations that marred their lives and marked their art, there is a reflection of the growing impotence and decay of the society in which they were born and grew to manhood.

Yet that tradition of individual destiny, of the worth of man, which the Florentines had cultivated so carefully in their heroic days, remained strong enough not only to sustain them in spite of the tribulations of their age, but also to buoy up a number of artists of lesser genius—Bronzino, Pontormo, del Sarto, and Fra Bartolommeo. And to one art, namely history, the decay of Florence provided a greater stimulus than its climb to greatness. The cataclysms of Florentine experience opened the same creative vistas for Machiavelli and Guicciardini as neuroses in individuals were to do for Dostoevsky or Proust. Indeed, even in its last, sad days, republican Florence still produced an astonishing array of genius, and no city of so small a compass has ever, before or since, made a greater contribution to art and letters within the brief span of a hundred and fifty years.

Lorenzo de' Medici

by RALPH ROEDER

Lorenzo de' Medici was, first and last, a financier; he was much more besides—politician, statesman, patron of art and letters—but these were merely functions of the financier developed by his forefathers, which he inherited together with the fortune of his family, and in each of these roles his performance was the consummation of theirs. His biography begins before he was born, and he sits for his portrait under his family tree.

His great-grandfather, Giovanni di Bicci de' Medici, was the first millionaire of the family. Of plebeian origin, the Medici had risen by prosperous trade to the front rank of the *nobili popolani*—the merchant princes of the major guilds—but they had not abandoned the class from which they sprang, and it served them steadily in their subsequent ascent to power. The banking business which Giovanni built up with branches in sixteen European capitals entitled him to a leading position among the eighty banking firms of Florence, and would have assured him a corresponding influence in the government had he chosen to claim it, since the bankers' guild supplied the capital and the connections for the enterprises of the state; but Giovanni was prudent and avoided politics. Retiring by nature, modest and unassuming, he spent his money on the construction of churches, the encouragement of art, and works of charity (the Foundling Hospital built for him by Brunelleschi, and the church of San Lorenzo rebuilt for him by the great architect as a family temple, were his monuments), and as long as he confined his public spirit to such modest activities, he passed for a safe man and honors came to him unsought. Summoned to the Signory, he revealed a different form of public spirit, however, by supporting against powerful opposition a tax reform, which substituted for the universal poll tax and the arbitrary assessments of the past a $1\frac{1}{2}\%$ levy on capital. This innovation was a boon for the poor, who reckoned it among his major charities; and since it was enacted when an unsuccessful war was about to be resumed and the tax rate raised, it won him high favor with the little people; but it incensed the rich. "Since the burden was to be distributed by law and not by men," Machiavelli, the official biographer of the family, observed, "it weighed heavily on the powerful citizens and was received with extreme displeasure by the mighty." Their anger rose and turned to alarm when the little people proposed to make the reform retroactive to compensate the losses they had suf-

ernment in his hands." The charge, old and familiar though it was, could no longer be ignored in the gloom of changing times, and it was followed by graver ones. Summoned to preach before the Signory, Savonarola said: "Tyrants are incorrigible because they are proud, because they love flattery, because they will not restore their ill-gotten gains. They allow bad officials to have their way; they yield to adulation; they neither heed the poor nor condemn the rich; they expect peasants and paupers to work for them gratis or they tolerate officials who do so; they farm out the taxes to aggravate the people more and more . . . The people are oppressed by taxes, and when they come to pay unbearable sums, the rich cry: Give me the rest . . . When widows come weeping, they are told: Go to sleep. When the poor complain, they are told: Pay, pay." The preacher was popular, his following grew, and in the Lent of 1491 he moved into the Duomo, where, before a congregation packed to the doors, he preached inflammatory sermons which terrified his hearers, predicting a coming calamity, ordained by divine wrath, which would sweep away the princes of Italy, including the Medici and all their iniquities. Lorenzo was tolerant, but he was troubled: what the Pazzi failed to accomplish, the prophet promised to perform. He made advances to mollify him, but he was rebuffed. He sent a delegation to reason with him. They hinted at banishment. "Tell Lorenzo to do penance for his sins," Savonarola replied, "for God will punish him and his. I do not fear your banishments. Though I am a stranger here and he a citizen, and the foremost in the city, I shall remain and he will go. I shall remain," he repeated proudly, "and he will go." And he foretold the death of Lorenzo within a year.

A year later Lorenzo lay dying in his villa at Careggi. He was in great pain, suffering from an abdominal disorder aggravated by his physicians, who fed him powdered pearls, and he sent for Savonarola to relieve his soul. Savonarola came. According to a popular but probably apocryphal account of the scene, the priest's price of salvation included the restoration of all ill-gotten gains and the restitution of liberty to Florence; to the first Lorenzo agreed, but he gave up the ghost and expired unabsolved before he could consent to the second.

Machiavelli was kinder. He acquitted Lorenzo of his political sins for the sake of the statesman whom Florence had lost, and acquitted him in a bountiful obituary. "Of Fortune and of God he was supremely loved, wherefore all his enterprises ended well and those of his enemies ill . . . All the citizens mourned his death and all the princes of Italy . . . and that they had good reason to grieve the result soon showed; for Italy being deprived of his counsels, none of those who remained found any means of curbing or satisfying the ambition of Lodovico Sforza, the governor of the Duke of Milan . . . as soon as Lorenzo died, all those bad seeds began to sprout which not long after, he who could quell them being no longer alive, ruined and are still ruining Italy."

And so it proved. Lorenzo was the pivot of Italian politics, and his eldest son, Piero, was born to be unfortunate—for himself, for his family, and for Florence. Two years after the death of Lorenzo, a revolt broke out, the Medici were driven into exile, and their palace sacked by a mob of vandals. Of Lorenzo nothing was left but the memory. The financier was a failure, the politician and the statesman were ephemeral, and of all the titles to fame which he left on deposit for posterity, only the patron of culture was remembered as Lorenzo the Magnificent.

FLORENCE OF
THE MEDICI

High and daring as the hopes of the city, the great dome, designed to astonish Italy, crowned the cathedral of Florence. Like the city's vaulting ambitions, it was based on the example of the ancients, but the new age's wealth and venturesome spirit provided a foundation even more solid. Spurred by the patronage and personal example of the Medici, Florence (shown above in a detail from di Michelino's *Allegory of the Divine Comedy*) welcomed art and learning, and under their rule became the cultural capital, the Athens, of Italy. As the center of taste and creativity, the city attracted artists from the entire peninsula and from all the countries of Europe. But with the death of Lorenzo the Magnificent in 1492, the Golden Age of Florence was no more.

The Medici established the foundation of their collection with masterpieces such as Donatello's Judith and Holofernes *(below) and* The Adoration of the Magi *(left) by Fra Angelico and Fra Lippo Lippi. Each generation continued the patronage of art. The humanist manuscript below the painting is a translation of Plotinus which was commissioned by Cosimo, dedicated to Lorenzo, and illuminated for Piero. Eventually Medici treasures, such as the medieval cup set in silver and enamel, were scattered; the rebel mobs which looted the palace in 1494 set up the statue of Judith slaying Holofernes in the public square as a warning to tyrants.*

THE MEDICI
AS PATRONS
OF THE ARTS

Afraid to defy the traditions of Florence, Cosimo chose a sober façade when he built the new Medici palace, but within its walls he freely indulged his own princely tastes. Donatello's *Judith and Holofernes* stood beside a courtyard fountain, and tapestries, designed in Italy and woven in Flanders, hung on the walls. Lavish commissions filled the rooms with pictures of saints and classical heroes, for merchant princes now shared the Church's role as patrons of the arts. Supported by Cosimo, Castagno experimented with the effects of light and shade, and each week Donatello called at the Medici bank to collect a regular stipend. Under Lorenzo the family even kept a court sculptor, Bertoldo, who watched over its collection of ancient art and tutored apprentices in the Medici garden. Promising artists, Michelangelo and Botticelli among them, were welcomed into Lorenzo's circle and were generously supported, for their work, like the Medici art collection, reflected glory on the family. Inventories of the Medici palace catalogued a rich assortment of antique busts and painted shields, goblets and haloed madonnas, an elephant's tooth and a serpent's tongue, each carefully described and valued. *The Adoration of the Magi* by Fra Angelico and Fra Lippo Lippi (opposite) was rated at a hundred florins, whereas a unicorn's horn set in gold was appraised for sixty times that. Most highly prized were ancient coins and cameos, over five thousand in all, which drew scholars and artists from all Italy to study the Medici treasures.

OVERLEAF: *On the chapel walls of the Medici palace Benozzo Gozzoli painted the story of the journey of the Magi. Leading the procession on a white horse is a handsome youth thought to be Lorenzo, in the golden robes and red hose he wore at an Oriental fete given in Florence in 1459. Cosimo, soberly dressed in blue, follows him, his mule plodding along beside a Negro page. Well back in the crowd between two bearded ancients is Gozzoli's self-portrait, with his name written along the rim of his red hat. The vivid fresco was commissioned by Piero de' Medici, who is seen in profile, riding on a spirited white horse behind his son Lorenzo.*

A boyhood spent writing Greek epigrams prepared Angelo Poliziano to tutor the Medici sons. Ghirlandaio's eloquent portrait shows him with Giuliano, a prince so gentle that his brother, Leo X, refused to let him govern Florence.

THE BATTLE
OF THE BOOKS

Accusing each other of debased morals or what was even worse—a degenerate Latin style—rival humanists squabbled furiously over the relative merits of obscure Roman authors. Invective was the favorite humanist pastime, and a good pen, the scholars boasted, could stab even a king. The Medici diluted the fighting spirit of Florentine humanists with generous patronage, but they failed to tame it. In the midst of the Pazzi troubles Lorenzo had to brave another violent battle, between his obstinate wife and his dearest friend, the humanist poet Angelo Poliziano. While teaching her son the Book of Psalms, Clarice was indignantly shouted down by Poliziano, who fiercely defended the purity of his pupil's classical education. In retaliation, she banished the scholar and confiscated his manuscripts, and it required months of negotiation by the patient Lorenzo to compose their quarrel. Poliziano continued his battles, but he confined them now to the field of scholarship, leading an attack against the group of humanists who tried to enthrone Cicero as sole dictator of a correct Latin style. But his polemics have been forgotten, and Poliziano is remembered best for his flowery and tranquil nature poetry. His lyrics written to match tunes the Medici women sang, and his poems celebrating the beauty of their rivals, the Florentine favorites of Lorenzo and Giuliano de' Medici, are among the undisputed classics of Italian poetry, and have made Poliziano the major poet of the Florentine Renaissance.

Platonic philosophy sought harmony everywhere, and the translator of Plato, Marsilio Ficino (far right in Ghirlandaio's group portrait of Florentine scholars, below), was the least pugnacious of humanists. His pupil, fourth generation of Medici scholar princes, was Pope Leo X, whose portrait by Raphael (detail above) lovingly displays a reading glass and illuminated manuscript, symbols of humanist learning.

MILAN

CITY OF STRIFE

Milan seemed singularly favored by nature; to the south, over an easy pass in the Apennines, lay the great seaport of Genoa, a city of such majesty that the Venetians feared its power and envied its wealth; to the west and north swept the great arc of the Alps, as natural a frontier as a statesman could wish for; the few mountain passes that led to France or southern Germany gave Milan control of the routes from the great Genoese emporium to the markets of the North. Seen spread across an atlas of physical geography, the great, fertile valley of the Po seems one of the more natural places in Europe for the development of a strong unified state. Between the fall of the Roman Empire and the unification of Italy in the nineteenth century this was achieved only once—by Napoleon. The history of the Lombard plain is a history of invasion and war. For more than a thousand years some of Europe's bloodiest battles were fought on it. If Florence belonged to Minerva, Milan belonged to Mars.

The trouble lay partly in the fertility of the alluvial plain: the great walls of the Alps and the Apennines gave it some of the forcing quality of a hothouse. Crops grew with ease; heavy crops meant a large and prosperous population; and the whole of Lombardy was studded with thriving cities—Turin, Pavia, Lodi, Brescia, Bergamo, Vicenza, Verona, Padua, Ferrara, Bologna, Mantua, Parma, Piacenza, and Alessandria, among others. Only in times of desperation were these cities capable of acting in unity, as when the Emperor Frederick Barbarossa attempted to extend his power over them: otherwise they were content to intrigue and plot and fight among themselves. From time to time a city or a family arose like a bubble in this boiling cauldron, and like a bubble burst. Furthermore, the Holy Roman Emperor often found it advantageous to strengthen his natural aristocratic allies at the expense of the communes, for the Emperor preserved the legal right of overlordship, even if he failed often enough to exercise it in fact. What he never failed to do, once he possessed the strength, was to angle for greater power in these

It took Milan's rulers more than a century to finish constructing the city's pinnacled cathedral, then the largest church in the world.

·MEDIOLANVS·

At the time of Constantine, Milan was second only to Rome among cities of the West, but in the centuries that followed, it was besieged 48 times and so ravaged that the 1472 map at left shows few Roman glories remaining in the city; instead, fortifications are prominent. At top is the Castello, built by Gian Galeazzo Visconti as an appendage to the high wall surrounding the city. A redoubt and strong towers protect each of Milan's seven gates; the streams that flow within the city connect with the canals of the Lombard plain. Filippo Maria Visconti constructed several of these, leading to his country palaces, for he preferred a journey by canal boat to risky overland travel.

troubled but fish-laden waters. In this he was not alone. The princes of Savoy found morsels of the Lombard plain far sweeter than the granite wastes of the Alps which their country bestrode. Beyond Savoy were the French, whose king was willing to try to hold Savoy in check—at a price—or urge him forward if they were unpaid. And naturally the two great parties, the Guelphs and the Ghibellines, which polarized so many ancient feuds, thought that they could manipulate the great European powers to their advantage.

Milan and its satellite cities had failed to do what Florence and the Tuscan towns had succeeded in doing—they had never subjected the feudal nobility to the authority of the merchant class. In this bull ring of Europe, it is not surprising that men harassed by invasion, ruined by petty strife, and hamstrung by vendettas should dream of a "natural" state in which princes—powerful, all-wise, and intensely patriotic—should succeed generation after generation, wielding an iron authority that brought peace and fame. At times the imagina-

tion of poet and panegyrist soared in a wilder flight and saw the princes of Milan, whether Visconti or Sforza, adding to the duchy of Lombardy the kingship of all Italy. There were three dukes of Milan—Gian Galeazzo Visconti, Francesco Sforza, and Lodovico Il Moro—who, for the brief periods of their rule, removed, at least, all absurdity from this vision, although they were far too realistic ever to indulge themselves in such fantasies. Nevertheless, they did between them what no other rulers did: they created a state equal in power and wealth to Florence and to Venice. Milan, which became the epitome of the Renaissance state, is best seen reflected in the lives of its three greatest dukes.

The Visconti's emblem was a viper, and they had needed all the serpent's cunning not only to survive the vicissitudes of a fickle and bloody fortune but also to grow in riches and in authority. By the time Gian Galeazzo Visconti was born in 1351, his family had played a leading part in Lombardic affairs for over two hundred years. They had resolutely de-

Gian Galeazzo Visconti, seen at left in Pisanello's drawing, ousted his uncle as lord of Milan, then, it was rumored, tried to poison him. Bernabò's bust, above, is part of a funeral monument fortunately commissioned while he was still in power.

fended the interests of the merchants, acquired increasing judicial authority from the Holy Roman Emperor to provide a legal basis for their power, and arranged their marriages with dynastic prudence. Nevertheless, his father had been forced to fight for his inheritance, for the death of a Visconti ruler, followed as it was by the division of his lands among his heirs, always provided an opening to rebels and exiles in the discontented cities on the fringes of their lands. Galeazzo II shared the Visconti territories with his brother Bernabò, who ruled in Milan, while he remained at Pavia. Bernabò struggled to regain Bologna, Galeazzo to push westward to the Alps; in so doing they aroused a hornets' nest, and in 1373 they were nearly overwhelmed. It was a typical story of treachery, turbulence, and violence that fed the darker side of Galeazzo's nature—his suspicion, his avarice, his hate. His son Gian Galeazzo, born of his diplomatic marriage with Blanche of Savoy, was turned as quickly as possible to dynastic ends. At the age of nine he was married off to Isabelle of

Valois, a princess of France, and by the time he was fourteen she had produced him a son. Both in battle and in diplomacy he proved equally precocious; but when he inherited his father's lands in 1378, his position was far from enviable. His uncle Bernabò, with a reputation for brutality and violence even in his own age, still ruled in Milan, and he had five sons, all ambitious, all land-hungry.

Gian Galeazzo was already known for his resource and cunning, but the latter got the better of his discretion. He suddenly made a wild bid for greatness. He secretly negotiated his own betrothal (his first wife had died at twenty-three) to the heiress of Sicily—a bargain that stood if he consummated the marriage within twelve months. The news outraged the particularist sentiments of the Italian princes, and they made certain that the bride never got within five hundred miles of her groom. And while Gian Galeazzo was wrestling with his strange problem of logistics, his uncle Bernabò extorted concession after concession from him, to

According to family tradition, the marriage of Venus and Anchises inaugurated the Visconti dynasty. The nuptial ceremony, performed by Jupiter himself, is illustrated at right; in line beneath the couple are their descendants, headed by Aeneas, a collateral ancestor of the Visconti. The lady at left displays a shield and a helmet crested with the suggestive family emblem, a serpent eating a man.

make certain that the Visconti of Pavia should never be linked with the power of Sicily to the discomfiture of the Visconti of Milan. When the year had passed, Gian Galeazzo found himself without a wife and tied dynastically far tighter than he had ever been to his uncle, for the latter insisted that, having failed with the heiress of Sicily, Gian Galeazzo's bride should be his daughter Caterina, and no obstruction was placed before the immediate consummation of this marriage.

Gian Galeazzo complied, and brooded. He cultivated his garden. He devoted his considerable intelligence and remarkable concentration to the problems of government. He reduced taxation, reformed administration, weeded out corruption, and what leisure he had from the cares of government he spent on the adornment of his palace, the conversation of scholars, and consultation with astrologers. Although he enjoyed a reputation for piety, he placed his trust in the efficacy of the zodiac rather than of prayer, and when the stars were truly propitious, he set out on a pilgrimage to the Madonna

del Monte at Varese. His timidity was known, and his entourage therefore surprised no one by its size; he hesitated (it was assumed through fear) to enter Milan, so his uncle and his cousins rode out to meet him. After an affectionate greeting they were taken prisoner, and Gian Galeazzo entered Milan to cries of "Long live the Count, and down with the taxes!" Gian Galeazzo's wife seems to have taken the destruction of her father and brothers with the phlegm usual in a Renaissance princess. The boldness of his enterprise was widely admired, and even Geoffrey Chaucer in far-off London turned a few verses on the event in his *Canterbury Tales*.

This success naturally gave Gian Galeazzo confidence, and since he was highly intelligent, he learned from it. More important than the timing of the plot, in the proper conjunction of the stars, was the fact that the Milanese did not close their gates but welcomed him as a liberator—a sentiment which he quickly turned to an article of faith by distributing some of Bernabò's treasure to the great financial relief of those whom

Seated on the lap of the Virgin Mary, the infant Christ welcomes Gian Galeazzo Visconti to heaven. This miniature and the family tree on the facing page are taken from a manuscript of the Duke's funeral eulogy.

he needed as allies. For the next seventeen years he exploited the paternalism of his government so that he might realize his almost insatiable dynastic ambitions. In order to impose his iron despotism, he posed as the liberator of cities and men. His success was the result of unwearying application, aided by good fortune and blended with a nice sense of contingencies. "He was wont," wrote his chronicler, Giovio, "to give himself up to meditation during solitary walks, to hold discussions with those who were most experienced in every branch of affairs, to quote instances from the annals of the past. He found relaxation for his mind in the conversation of scholars and in constant reading." Not for him, it would seem, "the delights of hunting or hawking, nor games of dice nor the allurements of women, nor the tales of buffoons and jesters." He thought, he planned, he acted. In two swift campaigns, having made certain that treachery was rife in the cities he wished to conquer, he had absorbed all of eastern Lombardy save Mantua and Ferrara.

The Florentines, of course, were deeply disturbed to see one tyrant control all the Alpine passes on which so much of their trade depended, and they used their powers of persuasion, of which the florin proved the most efficacious, to raise a league against Gian Galeazzo. This merely succeeded in enlarging Gian Galeazzo's ambitions, for he was quick to realize that his gains could never be consolidated so long as Florence remained unsubjected. To do this he proceeded with skill and caution; each city-state had its party that hated Florence or the powers that ruled it. He fought wars when he had to, but he adroitly avoided a head-on collision with the combined powers of Florence and Venice. By 1402 he had acquired control of Pisa, Siena, Perugia, and Bologna, and it was within his power to strangle Florence politically and economically. The foundation of a great northern Italian kingdom seemed within his grasp, when he caught a fever and died.

By that time Gian Galeazzo had done more than enlarge the boundaries of his dukedom, for he had created a state as

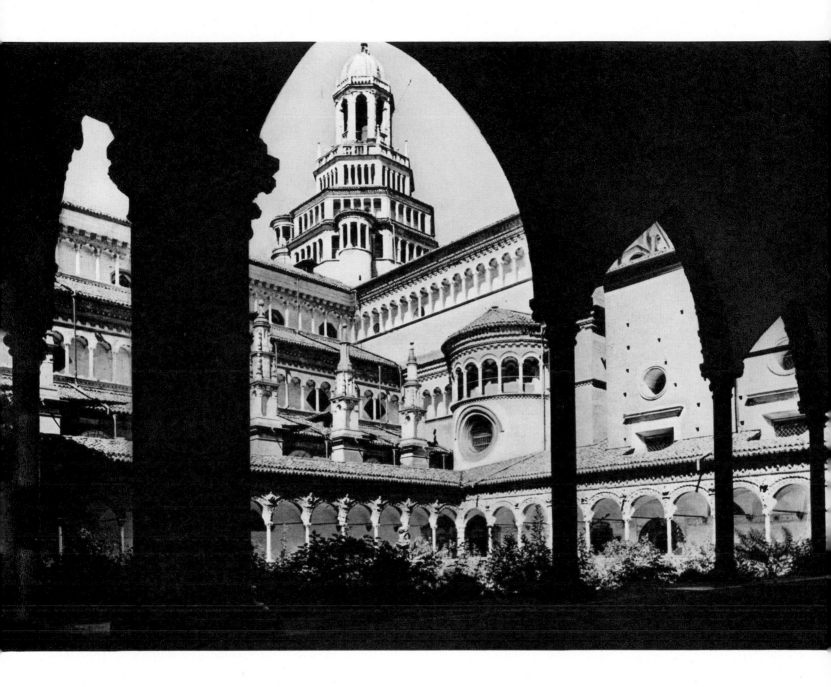

well as a despotism. He centralized government, reformed administration, and removed inequalities and special rights and privileges. Where possible he weakened the feudal nobility and encouraged the merchant class. He tried to fulfill the ideal which his humanists at Pavia had delineated—that of a "natural prince" whose state was serenely based on justice and equality. And by these means he had created the duchy of Milan, a coherent state that was to last until Napoleon swept it away. In many ways he is the prototype of the Renaissance prince—unscrupulous in diplomacy, yet deeply concerned for the welfare of the state; passionately ambitious for his dynasty, yet aware of the needs of his country; scholarly, remote, and dedicated to the pursuit of power.

Gian Galeazzo's death broke up his empire. His captains of war thought no opportunity better for taking their pickings; the Tuscan and Umbrian cities, mindful now of the power of Florence, threw off their allegiance. The Venetians' indifference to Gian Galeazzo's success turned to alarm; his

demise brought about a fundamental change in their policy. They decided to be a Lombard power—to secure territorial control of the Alpine passes which they needed for their trade, and of sufficient territory to give them ground for maneuver against a resurgent Milan. Once again the great feudal families whose power Gian Galeazzo had attempted to reduce flourished their standards. The Colleoni, Anguisola, Cavalcabò, and Correggio demanded their pounds of flesh, and the plain of Lombardy once more reeked of blood and slaughter, pillage and rape. In the midst of this desolation the Milanese core of the Visconti state held firm. It is a measure of Gian Galeazzo's success that it did so, for in some ways his heir was a greater disaster than the conflagrations of war that consumed Lombardy. Although it is certainly untrue that he fed his hounds on human flesh, such were his tyrannies that the Milanese had no difficulty in believing the story. His assassination in church in 1412 caused no surprise. Perhaps as a tribute to his brother's memory, his successor, Fi-

Upon the completion of the Certosa of Pavia (opposite), the income from its building endowment was supposed to revert to Pavia's poor. Citizens clamored for the work to end, but it took one hundred and fifty years before the poor finally enjoyed their revenue. Scholars were rewarded more promptly. When the humanist Filelfo, whose portrait medal appears at left, found his salary in arrears, his strident complaints soon elicited cash from Francesco Sforza. The Duke was awed by scholarship, and gave liberal support to the University of Pavia, a center of Italian legal studies. The relief below shows one of the lecturers at the university.

lippo Maria, had the murderers put to death by the most refined tortures. By nature Filippo Maria was not excessively cruel, merely neurotic. He was obese to the point of ridicule, and ugly to the point of embarrassment. His portrait was never painted, his marriage never consummated, and his appearance in public rare. Nevertheless, he ruled with skill if without panache. He maintained the machinery of the state and kept his head above the turbulent waters of Italian politics. Precluded by nature from the pursuit of martial glory, he was content to employ one of the best condottieri for this duty—Francesco Sforza—at least from time to time, for Filippo could never trust anyone for long.

Sforza, the son of one of the first great Italian condottieri —Muzio Sforza—came, as most condottieri did, from the Romagna, which had little to sell but the strength of its men. Sforza proved himself a great captain. His direct manner, tough physique, and aggressive nature made him an excellent general; his attention to detail, ferocious discipline, and deep personal loyalty gave him a band of soldiers of passionate devotion and exemplary technique. His personal magnetism was such that he won the enduring friendship of the two most outstanding men of his day—the highly sophisticated and cultivated banker Cosimo de' Medici, and the equally highly cultivated condottiere Federigo da Montefeltro. In the hard, tough school of war he won himself a vast reputation and a small territory, too small either for his purse or his ambition. And the situation in Milan was as clear to him as to his friends. Cosimo de' Medici did not relish the steady advance of Venetian power across the Lombard plain (the Alpine passes were vital to Florentine trade, and the Venetians were traders first and republicans second). A powerful, friendly Milan had become a necessity to Florence, so Cosimo provided Francesco with good advice and handsome loans. Federigo, as generous a condottiere as ever lived, admired Francesco's prowess as only a professional could, but he preferred, naturally enough, that Francesco should win his kingdom in

Filippo Maria Visconti, whose medal by Pisanello is at left, was so timid that he had double walls to shut the sound of thunder out of his chamber. The reverse, below, shows the Duke on horseback, attended by guards. Francesco Sforza (lower left) was bolder; he rode through Milan every day on his way to hunt, and exchanged greetings with the citizens. A predecessor, Bernabò Visconti, had been so fond of hunting that he kept 5,000 hounds and tortured anyone who interfered with them. Francesco, whose interest in the sport was more temperate, paid an authority to compose a treatise on it for him. On the facing page is an illustration from it, showing courtiers hunting waterfowl.

Lombardy and not on *his* doorstep in the Romagna, where the Sforza had their patrimony.

Filippo Maria did not need to be instructed in the drift of their thoughts, for he was as subtle as his father if less ambitious. It proved toil enough for him to weld together the Visconti lands, bring the recalcitrant nobles and cities to a proper subjection, and withstand the encroachments of Venice. For these projects he needed Francesco, and to stay alive for his natural span in his castle of Milan, it was necessary to keep Sforza both expectant and dependent. So Francesco rattled his sword, and Filippo Maria dangled his daughter—not a legitimate daughter, of course, but a mistress had been more skillful than a wife, and Bianca was the result. The long wrangle ended in a betrothal; a longer engagement ended in a wedding; the wedding ended in a son and heir. Before, however, his succession had been determined, Filippo died, when Francesco was away from Visconti territory.

The Milanese erupted with republican sentiment, abolished the dukedom, and created chaos. Neither Venice nor Florence was amused by the advent of a sister republic and gave no help as its troubles multiplied. Sforza moved cautiously until the republic crumbled, and when he finally entered Milan, the citizens went wild with delight, rushed him and his horse into the Duomo, and acclaimed him duke. For many years that was the sole right the Sforza had to their dukedom—that and the sharp edge of their swords—for the emperors refused to acknowledge them. The powers of Italy, however, lacked the prejudice of the Germans, and while Francesco consolidated his power with military precision, the Medici got a bank in Milan, and alliances were formed with France, Savoy, Naples, and Florence. The Sforza went bullheaded for peace and stability. Wars there could not fail to be, but Sforza wanted them local, petty, and circumscribed.

The dukes of Milan became an accepted fact in the major state-system of Italy as Francesco Sforza completed the work Gian Galeazzo Visconti had begun. No condottiere had won

such a prize as Francesco; and the tough captain who had once stood amazed by the luxury of Pavia and the splendor of its library now enjoyed the prosperity his sword had brought him. War or no war, the Milanese throve. Francesco settled his court at Milan, the heart of his dukedom, ruling his subjects until his death in 1466 as he had once led his troops—wisely, directly, decisively—always keeping within the limits of the possible. About him there was something of the inexorable single-mindedness of the long-distance runner. Unhappily, his children proved more devious, more extravagant, more brutal even than their Visconti ancestors. The Sforza brood would have done honor to the pages of the most bloodthirsty of Elizabethan dramatists. And the story of Milan and its Renaissance reaches a climax in the rule of Lodovico Sforza.

Francesco was a great warrior—in love as well as in war—and his brood of Sforza, legitimate and illegitimate (the difference in Renaissance Italy was scarcely remarked—Francesco himself was a bastard), numbered twenty. Lodovico was

number six (legitimate), so his prospects of the throne of Milan were remote enough. He possessed, however, one card, spurious perhaps, but not without value: he was the first legitimate child to be born *after* Francesco had been acclaimed Duke of Milan. Its use, however, lay in the future, for his brother Galeazzo Maria Sforza had every intention of enjoying to the full the power and the riches which his father had bequeathed him. Indeed, his court left no doubt that the Sforza had arrived, that the wealth of Milan was vast, that neither the Doge in Venice, the Pope in Rome, the Medici in Florence, nor the Aragonese kings in Naples could outvie them in magnificence. The great Castello Sforzesco, built like the Tower of London on the verge of the city—a convenience which fulfilled both the needs of strategy and sport—witnessed some of the most remarkable spectacles of the fifteenth century. Galeazzo loved shows. He made St. George's Day the great military spectacle of the year; tournaments, pageants, processions gave his mania full rein, and he thought nothing of

ordering a thousand or more special liveries in costly velvet to put on his servants' backs. A greater pleasure still was to take a visiting prince or ambassador to his jewel house, Galeazzo's special pride and joy, where rubies, emeralds, sapphires, and diamonds lay in heaps—a treasure which King Christian of Denmark somewhat churlishly called "unbefitting a true and generous prince." Galeazzo, however, possessed a taste for more refined delights: his interest in music led him to comb Flanders, let alone Italy, for the singers who were almost the dominating passion of his life. Almost, but not quite: undoubtedly Galeazzo's greatest pleasures were drawn from the enjoyment of his courtiers' wives and the exercise of his personal power; and neither endeared him to his subjects. The latter, in fact, was his undoing. Rumors of his cruelty were inflated to the heights of a Gothic fairy tale, and rendered just as macabre by the Duke's pious, almost morbid, insistence on the strictest observance of religious ritual. So perhaps it was not entirely unfitting that his

assassins should have dispatched him in church. They were a typical Renaissance bunch—a penniless noble adventurer, a cousin who resented the rape of his sister, an old, very disreputable master of rhetoric who had preached too ardently, and practiced too publicly, the Greek way of life, and a youthful republican intoxicated by the concept of tyrannicide, who, as he was slowly and carefully torn to pieces, murmured, *"Mors acerba fama perpetua est."*

Galeazzo's wife was deeply troubled that her husband, whom she knew so well, should have been dispatched unconfessed. She made a list of his sins and was appalled. He was, she wrote, "Versed in warfare, both lawful and unlawful; in pillage, robbery, and devastation of the country; in extortion of subjects; in negligence of justice; in injustice knowingly committed; in the imposition of new taxes which even included the clergy; in carnal vices; in notorious and scandalous simony and innumerable other crimes." Obviously the torments of Galeazzo in Purgatory would be long and grievous,

The impressive Castello Sforzesco, shown in a sixteenth-century engraving (opposite), was fortified by Francesco Sforza despite the advice of one Milanese citizen who reminded him that princes should rely solely on the love of their subjects for protection. Francesco could trust his people, but his son Galeazzo Maria, whose portrait by Pollaiuolo appears at left, was beyond protection after ten years of misrule. A woodcut below shows his assassination by conspirators who had spent days stabbing each other with sheathed daggers to rehearse their crime. Galeazzo unwisely ignored comets, ravens, and other omens foretelling his death, and imprisoned a priest who had warned him that he would not rule eleven years.

so the Duchess implored the aid of the Pope. The Pope, moved by the distress of the widow, granted absolution in return for a considerable subsidy for the papal army.

Galeazzo left a child and five brothers; so the years after his death proved dramatic enough for Milan and Italy. Conspiracies in Genoa and Parma linked themselves with greater conspiracies, engineered by the Pope and the King of Naples, in Florence. Lodovico tried his utmost to kidnap the child Duke, but he failed until the ructions in Florence gave him the backing of the Holy Father and King Ferrante. With luck and good judgment, aided by the silliness of the Duke's mother and the misguided cunning of her lover, Lodovico became regent of Milan. He imprisoned the Duchess, ousted her favorite, and chopped off the head of Cecco Simonetta, the brilliant ducal secretary who throughout his long life had devotedly served the Sforza, for the crime of attempting to secure an undivided inheritance for the legitimate heir. Fortunately for Lodovico, his most active and ambitious

brothers had died during the struggle for power, and his nephew proved so weak in intellect and character that it was unnecessary to dispatch him. As soon as this internecine struggle was over, Milan settled down to such spectacular festivities that they pushed the memories of Galeazzo's junketings to the commonplace. The child Duke was betrothed to Isabella of Aragon, and Lodovico himself took Beatrice d'Este, the daughter of the Duke of Ferrara and granddaughter of the King of Naples, for his bride. Although their marriages were long delayed, the festivities celebrating their nuptials provided the hired chroniclers of the court of Milan, long practiced in rhetoric and panegyric, a subject worthy of their hyperbole. Men and women were dressed, or rather undressed, as pagan gods and goddesses; fabulous animals were wondrously contrived; knights jousted in Moorish costumes; wild men, dressed by Leonardo da Vinci, scared the ladies; dwarfs, giants, hunchbacks provided robust fun; sycophantic poets produced verse by the ream to give a sense of immortal oc-

vading Naples. This seeming act of folly Lodovico encouraged; and in return for his benevolent neutrality Charles supported Lodovico's claim to the Emperor to be appointed Imperial Vicar of Milan—a legitimization of power never yet won by a Sforza. A further piece of luck—as no doubt the stars had foretold—took place. His nephew, the Duke, died. Lodovico proclaimed the infant Francesco duke. Not surprisingly, the Council would not have him; they begged Lodovico, at such a time of peril for the state, to assume the title with the power. Lodovico complied; the populace cheered. So Lodovico achieved his *coup d'état*—a bloodless one and timed to perfection. In his campaign against Naples, Charles VIII proved almost miraculously successful (as is common with military miracles, it was based on superior armament, particularly cannon). With Charles thus occupied and the imperial edict safe in his pocket, Lodovico suddenly changed sides, and when Charles began to withdraw from Italy, Sforza was one of those who harried and hurried him on his way. Then,

sensing the possible benefits, he seized the opportune moment to switch allegiance to Charles once again.

So Lodovico had his years of triumph. He could boast that the Pope was his chaplain, the Emperor his condottiere, Venice his chamberlain, and the King of France his courier. For a time Milan was prosperous, the court brilliant, the prince magnificent. And then death took a hand. Beatrice, who had done so much to bring Lodovico's subtleties to decisive action, died in childbed. Charles VIII of France also died; his successor, Louis XII, claimed Milan and regarded Charles VIII's failure to take it for him as a disgrace. Apart from Naples, which feared a fresh invasion, the powers of Italy leaped as rapidly as possible onto the French bandwagon (Venice alone bargaining hard for its ticket) and were overjoyed that the victim beneath the juggernaut's wheels should be Lodovico. The French won; Lodovico retreated to the Tirol; the French puppet outraged the Milanese; Lodovico returned; so did the French, and won again with consummate ease. This time they

Although his plumed helmet made him an easy target, the French King Francis I emerged unscathed from the Battle of Marignano in 1515 (opposite). His victory sent Massimiliano Sforza into exile and brought Milan under foreign rule for the third time in twenty years. In 1493 Sforza power had been at its zenith; Lodovico bribed the Holy Roman Emperor into marrying a Sforza princess, and capped the wedding celebration by exhibiting Leonardo da Vinci's monumental clay model of a horse, part of a statue planned in honor of Francesco Sforza. (At right is one of Leonardo's preliminary studies.) But by the time the huge horse was ready for casting, Lodovico could no longer afford the ten tons of bronze required for it.

packed Lodovico off to France, where his imprisonment was strict enough to titillate the most morbid humanist, obsessed with the fate of tyrants. He finally died in a tiny, lightless, underground cell in the dungeon of Loches.

It was not the end of the Sforza. They had become pawns in the battle between the great European powers who used Lombardy as their tilting ground. Sforza's son, Massimiliano, was brought back by the lances of the Swiss, and after a brief and extravagant career he was removed, after the Battle of Marignano, by Francis I and pensioned, not imprisoned, in France. These two wars, which devastated Milan, were soon followed by a third, when Charles V, who combined the formidable power of his Holy Roman Empire with that of Spain, decided to expel the French from Lombardy. This he did in 1525 outside the great Visconti capital of Pavia. It was a fitting place, for with that battle the last gleams of Milanese independence disappeared. The reason for this tale of blood is not far to seek. Although Milan possessed natural frontiers

and great wealth and an able ruling house, as a state it never acquired the stability of Florence or Venice or even Naples, simply because its class struggles went unresolved. The feudal nobility were never uprooted; they constantly quarreled with each other and provided a ready support for any adventurer, internal or external, who would favor their personal ambitions. This powerful aristocracy also thrived on the divisions and jealousies of the merchant class which hated it. Finally, Milan was hemmed about with cities almost as great as itself, all possessing rich, ambitious, jealous guilds of merchants who seesawed between wanting the stability which the leadership of Milan alone could bring and the gain that might accrue from its humiliation. In such an unstable world the abilities of the Visconti and the Sforza were largely wasted. The great horse designed by Leonardo for Lodovico in memory of his father seems curiously symbolic of their destiny—conceived in grandeur, executed in clay, never cast, ruined by the French, and destroyed by time.

183

THE BUILDERS OF MILAN

At one time a rumor went the rounds to the effect that Galeazzo Maria Sforza had caused Florence's church of Santo Spirito to catch fire by eating meat every day during Lent while on a state visit to that city. In truth, Milan's dukes traditionally fostered the building of churches. Gian Galeazzo Visconti endowed a fund to pay for the great Duomo, and nearby, in the ancient Lombard capital of Pavia, he established an immense Carthusian monastery, the Certosa, to serve the Visconti dynasty as family church and mausoleum. Work on both buildings progressed whenever Milan could spare money from its wars, but a century later, when Borgognone painted the Certosa (above) as a detail of *The Carthusians Following Christ,* its marble façade had not been completed. By then the last Visconti duke had been dead for fifty years, and Sforza power was at its height. Francesco Sforza inherited no money from the Visconti, but he carried on their tradition of building. On the site of one Visconti palace he commissioned a new hospital, shaped like a cross so that all the patients could hear Mass being sung in the central chapel. He continued work on the Certosa (the Visconti now shared it with their successors) and built a castle where his children held court above the ruins of an old Visconti fort. A tithe of the castle's cost went to finish the towering Duomo, where jubilant crowds had borne Francesco on horseback when he first became duke.

THE MAKING OF A DYNASTY

Surrounded by heroes of antiquity, with Julius Caesar on his right and Hannibal on his left (above), Francesco Sforza was enthroned by admiring contemporaries among the immortals of history. Chronicling his deeds, a well-paid humanist at the court of Milan turned out a twelve-thousand-line epic, *The Sforziad,* and the visionary court architect Filarete honored him with plans for Sforzinda, the ideal city of the future. *The Sforziad* failed to rival Homer, and Vasari called Filarete's treatise "perhaps the most stupid book ever written," but the court of Milan did not judge them for aesthetic value alone. The Duke found their propaganda useful in raising the status of the Sforza name. Francesco's father was a substantial peasant who got his start in life by running off with a band of wandering mercenaries; the conquest of Milan made Francesco's sons equal to princes and one of his grandsons later became a king. Marrying the daughter of the last Visconti duke was Francesco's wisest move, for it provided a secure dynastic foundation. With his own claim to Milan confirmed by his wife's title, Francesco shrewdly set about strengthening his family's hold on the duchy. He made his brother Bishop of Milan and one of his sons a cardinal. He sent another son to live in Cremona, and named his heir Count of Pavia. But the Sforza gained most from Francesco's carefully planned program of dynastic marriages.

His own marriage had set the stage; the Visconti were allied to English and French royalty,

Ranked among heroes, Sforza chats with Caesar.

and by mixing their blood with the less exalted Sforza strain, Francesco vastly enhanced his children's eligibility. He married one legitimate daughter to the future King of Naples. His heir, Galeazzo Maria, was wed to a sister of the Queen of France; she had no dowry, but her royal connections were enough for the *nouveaux riches* Sforza. According to their legitimacy or rank, Francesco's other offspring were pledged to less imposing mates—a duke's second daughter, a minor Italian noble, the son of an untitled condottiere who might make good. There was an occasional misalliance— one daughter, who wed Sigismondo Malatesta, may have been strangled by her violent husband —but most Sforza marriages had more positive results. The best match came after Francesco's death, when the family purchased an emperor for his granddaughter Bianca Maria. Her first fiancé, a prince of Savoy, died before she was old enough to marry, and her second lost his appeal by failing to inherit the crown of Hungary. Bianca's prospects improved with her dowry, however. Originally it had been three hundred thousand ducats, but then the Sforza added one hundred thousand more; that convinced Maximilian, ruler of the Holy Roman Empire, that it would not be beneath him to marry a Sforza once he gave his new in-laws legitimate title to the duchy of Milan.

Both of Milan's dynasties are portrayed on marble portals of the Certosa at Pavia. Opposite, Visconti and Sforza dukes; at right, Milan's duchesses.

JOHN XXIII (1410-1415) MARTIN V (1417-1431) EUGENIUS IV (1431-1447)

PAUL II (1464-1471) SIXTUS IV (1471-1484) INNOCENT VIII (1484-1492)

PIUS III (1503) JULIUS II (1503-1513) LEO X (1513-1521)

They terrorized the citizens, raped the nuns, robbed the monks, pillaged the churches. To compound confusion, from 1378 to 1429 there was an antipope as well as a pope, and in 1409 even three authentic successors of St. Peter—a glorious opportunity for rebellion, riot, and plunder. King Ladislas of Naples prowled about the broken-down streets of Rome, extorting what he could and decapitating whom he dared. Popes and kings hired the toughest, most brutal condottieri —including Braccio, who, according to a chronicler, enjoyed the sufferings of others, and for his pleasure would throw a few men from the highest towers in Rome or drop a prisoner into a boiling cauldron. After years of anarchy the Romans were willing to believe anything and nothing. When John XXIII, afterwards struck from the list of the popes and accused of a huge catalogue of crimes, the least important of which were incest, sodomy, and murder, swore that he would defend them to the death, they replied that they would rather eat their children than surrender to his enemies. During the

same night John XXIII flew under the cover of darkness, taking all the portable wealth he could lay his hands on, and the Romans opened their gates the next morning, their children undevoured. Such a kaleidoscope of brutality, such a cascade of violence, broke the government of the city in pieces and reduced it to a poverty and a misery it had not known since the barbarian invasions.

No one in 1425 could have foreseen that Rome was about to be reborn (not spiritually—the Renaissance popes were not to prove men of the spirit—but physically, artistically, and politically). St. Peter's, the Vatican, the churches, the tombs, the squares, the great palaces and gardens of Rome which now entrance the eye and delight the heart, were brought into being and gave an impetus to the pursuit of beauty that the stern moralities of the Counter Reformation could not stop. For two hundred years the beauty of Rome became the pride of the Papacy. The downward plunge into anarchy and destitution and poverty was checked by Martin

NICHOLAS V (1447-1455)

CALIXTUS III (1455-1458)

PIUS II (1458-1464)

ALEXANDER VI (1492-1503)

A GALLERY OF POPES

During the Great Schism, from 1378 to 1417, popes in Rome struggled with antipopes in France and, for a while, with a third claimant as well. Unity was finally restored under Martin V, but not until the advent of the "political popes" in 1471 were affairs in Rome fully under control. The temporal ambitions of Sixtus IV and his successors saw papal power and extravagance rise steadily, reaching a zenith during the golden age of Leo X, but that trend ended abruptly with the catastrophic sack of Rome in 1527, and papal magnificence never again approached the same grandiose scale.

ADRIAN VI (1522-1523)

CLEMENT VII (1523-1534)

PAUL III (1534-1549)

V, himself a Colonna and a Roman. During his pontificate (1417–1431) the dreadful split in the Church was cured, if not quite healed. Furthermore, he proved a good administrator and such a fearsome personality that he secured peace for the city. He checked the robberies, violence, and murder, and stimulated the city's trade. With the papal court back in Rome, back came the pilgrims and supplicants, back came the merchants, and back came the lifeblood—the papal tax harvest that was reaped from Europe's peasantry. And so the Roman soil was fertilized again, for without wealth no Renaissance was possible. The next pope, Eugenius IV, had to flee down the Tiber in a rowboat, disguised as a monk, and eluded capture only by a hair's breadth. For years he kept his court at Florence, where he patronized the humanists and bided his time, while he left Rome to be pacified by a ferocious bishop, Vitelleschi, who razed cities, hanged and decapitated barons, slaughtered right, left, and center, and probably met his own end by poison (possibly with Eugenius'

connivance). By such murderous methods were the popes reestablished. The calculated savageries of Cesare Borgia, that were to astound a later generation, were unusual only in the beauty and dexterity of their timing.

To be secure in Rome, the Papacy needed to control the States of the Church which stretched in a broad diagonal across the long leg of Italy. During its residence at Avignon and the Great Schism (1378 to 1417), men and cities had naturally usurped papal rights and privileges, and what they had won by force they would not yield by persuasion. Excommunication, interdict, or anathema left them unmoved. These had been flung about so wantonly by rival popes at each other that they had lost much of their force. Indeed, it seemed to the popes that the Church could only get back its own by acting like any other power in Italy. By alliance, by diplomacy, by war, the Church might wrest its possessions from alien hands. Its wealth permitted it to hire the ablest condottieri, including the great Francesco Sforza as well as Federigo da

Montefeltro. Having been a plaything of the great powers, the leaders of the Church wished to secure independence by giving the Church great temporal and political strength. That being so, they looked for a leader not among the saints nor usually among the scholars (Nicholas V and Pius II were exceptions) but among the administrators and natural politicians. They looked for worldly men, men of powerful personalities, tough fiber, and quick decision. And again, as the power of the Papacy steadily grew through temporal measures such as war and diplomacy, so did the need for such qualities in a pope seem ever more necessary. This is the explanation of what so many now find difficult to understand—of popes such as Alexander VI or Julius II. Alexander VI, whose lusts repelled even the tolerant age in which he lived, was a very hardheaded diplomat and excellent administrator, whose policy undeviatingly pursued what was thought to be a necessity for the Church—temporal power, expressed in the overlordship of central Italy. Julius II, even as pope, loved war, loved

to get on his horse, to feel the weight of his armor and hear the blood-call of battle.

So, by and large, the Renaissance popes were worldly men, pragmatic, tough, concerned with power. And like many hardheaded, ambitious men they did not wish to be outshone by their rivals in the symbolic display of wealth and greatness. They were determined to build vast churches, huge palaces, magnificent fountains; to employ the finest painters, sculptors, craftsmen; to collect the loveliest antiquities, the most resplendent jewels, the most remarkable books, the most exquisite manuscripts. These things, like their armies, were necessities of state, and the cost irrelevant. So hand in hand with the resurgent power of the Papacy went the artistic Renaissance in Rome; and because the popes controlled more wealth, the result was more splendid than anywhere else.

Rome was full of priests, monks, nuns, churches, monasteries, convents, holy relics, miraculous shrines, healing images. Every year thousands of pilgrims from all corners of

Jubilee years saw thousands of the faithful flocking to Rome to visit the city's shrines and take part in its religious ceremonies. A high point of the trip was a tour of the seven great pilgrimage basilicas, shown at left in a 1575 print by a Frenchman, Antoine Lafréry. Recent excavations under St. Peter's (it is in the foreground with the unfinished dome) have unearthed many ancient relics and treasures. One of them, the portrait at right of Pope John VII (705–707), was discovered in the upper grottoes. He is holding a model of the small chapel that he had built in honor of the Virgin, and the square halo indicates that he was still alive when the mosaic was made.

the Western world made their way to it in penitence and in hope. Most were simple people to whom the sight of a piece of the True Cross or a saint's leg justified the dangers and tribulations of their journey. They cared nothing for the whispered rumors of the Pope's children, of his poisonings, murders, or even the alarming sensualities of the Borgia. Twenty thousand of them reverenced Alexander VI in the great Jubilee year of 1500—unmindful of his lusts. For them the mounting grandeur of Rome was a wondrous thing, a visible proof of the glory of their Church. Humanist criticism of the Church's venality, corruption, immorality, and obscurantism fell on deaf ears. A Savonarola or a Bernardino of Siena might momentarily stir this multitude with a sense of the world's unrighteousness, but the vast mass of the Western world was locked in an accepting piety, and the luminous sins of the popes and cardinals were a matter for gossip but not for radical rage. Throughout the Renaissance, with its political and personal immorality and its intellectual skepticism,

Rome remained the center of the Western world's religion. From this atmosphere of worship no pope could escape, and it became subtly interwoven in the Renaissance in Rome.

There is no need to follow the twists and turns by which the Papacy gradually re-established its dominion over the Patrimony or to describe how from time to time this was endangered by popes trying to create hereditary dominions for their children (Cesare Borgia, for example), a tendency which scores of Orsini and Colonna died bloody deaths to prevent. The treaties, battles, and plots have faded to near-oblivion; there remain, however, in all their greatness, the treasures of the Vatican, its library, its antiquities, its sculptures, its paintings. And the Vatican is but a fragment of Renaissance Rome; the *Laocoön* and the *Apollo Belvedere* belong to it as much as St. Peter's or Via Giulia, for a reverence for her own past grew with her new delight in beauty.

The revival of Rome began, like the Renaissance itself, with literature. The Italian Papacy, at the time of the Schism,

of Atlas, of Perseus and Andromeda, the labors of Hercules were depicted life size on silver dishes. Castles made of sweetmeats and filled with eatables were sacked and then thrown from the loggia of the hall to the applauding crowd. Sailing vessels discharged their cargoes of sugared almonds . . ." By such means, perhaps, Sixtus obliterated the memories of his hungry youth, but many of his indulgences were less transitory. His taste in building was as simple and as austere as his delight in food was riotous and fantastic. He widened streets, constructed bridges, built hospitals, erected churches, gave land to all who would build houses and palaces. He encouraged his cardinals to foster the splendor of Rome: the market was expelled from the Piazza Navona and the building of its churches and palaces begun. There was scarcely a ward of the city that Sixtus did not improve or adorn, but his greatest glory is the chapel in the Vatican that bears his name. Utterly simple in design, it served merely as a frame for its adornment, and for this purpose Sixtus brought the best art-

ists in Italy to Rome—Signorelli, Botticelli, Perugino, Pinturicchio, Ghirlandaio, Rosselli. Later, in the pontificate of Julius II, who wished to complete his uncle's work, these frescoes were dwarfed by the superb ceiling by Michelangelo, for which the Sistine Chapel is so famous. Such, however, was the galaxy of painters in Rome in the 1470's that they founded their own guild, that of St. Luke, which afterwards developed into the famous academy. Although painters and sculptors and architects had been patronized by the popes long before Nicholas V and Sixtus IV (Giotto had created mosaics and painted frescoes for the old St. Peter's, and Fra Angelico had adorned many churches), yet with their pontificates papal patronage moved into a new dimension. It touched all aspects of art and learning. Possessing great wealth and sublime authority, many of the popes rose to the enormous visions of Nicholas V. The Basilica of St. Peter's—the work not of one but of a plethora of geniuses: Alberti, Bramante, Raphael, Michelangelo, Bernini—is the most impressive Christian

monument in the world, yet it is essentially a product of the Renaissance. The treasures of the Vatican Palace—paintings, sculpture, antiquities, ancient manuscripts, and rare books—are incomparable, yet in 1420 the Papacy possessed no more perhaps than three hundred books, and scarcely any antiquities or pictures or statues of merit. To the sensual, warlike, popes who ruled from 1471 to 1521 Rome owes a great deal of its present beauty.

What a strange gallery these popes make, yet essentially they are as much creatures of the Renaissance as Michelangelo's *Adam* or Donatello's *David*. The strangest of all is doubtless Alexander VI, whose name has become a byword for lust and cruelty. Certainly he was a man of strong, animal passions, driven remorselessly by his instincts. His attachment to his mistress, Vannozza, who bore him the terrible Borgia brood, was profound and life-lasting, no matter what other temporary indulgence he permitted himself. He loved his children to desperation, with a fierce physical passion. When

one son was stabbed and thrown into the Tiber, probably by another son, Cesare Borgia, his grief astounded the cardinals whom he called to a consistory in order to bewail the loss of his child. So deep was his grief that, in tears, he swore not only to reform his own life, but also the Church's. His animal spirits, however, soon reasserted themselves, and his slavish devotion to his son Cesare became the bane of Italy when he resolved to create for him a great Italian kingdom. After spectacular victories in which, with French aid, Cesare overcame the great, seemingly impregnable fortresses of the Romagna, as well as Urbino, he seemed to Machiavelli to be the destined ruler of Italy. Machiavelli admired the way Cesare welcomed his enemies as friends and then neatly strangled them. By such stratagems were the Orsini obliterated. The speed, the decision, the timing of Cesare had an almost physical perfection. Yet, as in some Greek tragedy, the fates kept a bitter end in store. Before Cesare could consolidate his power, his father died; at the time he himself was prostrated with a loathsome

Michelangelo crowned his huge statue of Moses (left) with the two horns symbolic of the prophet since the Hebrew word for "rays of light" was mistranslated as "horns" in the Vulgate. It was intended as a central figure of the massive tomb planned for Pope Julius II, but the monument was finally set up on a much diminished scale thirty-two years after the Pope's death, and the frustrated Michelangelo declared, "I lost all my youth in bondage to this tomb." The fierce stare of the statue is echoed in Raphael's portrait of Pope Julius, on the facing page. A detail from The Mass of Bolsena *in one of the Stanze, this was so realistic a portrait that Vasari said, "it seems alive."*

and debilitating sickness. Stripped of power, he became a pawn of popes, kept on sufferance, banished to prison in Spain, and finally was killed in a brawl in Navarre. The life of Alexander's daughter, Lucrezia, was marked by a similar irony of fate. The Pope loved her with an almost incestuous passion. He heaped wealth on her; no delight was too sumptuous or too lascivious to be denied her. No husband was worthy of her charms: one was declared impotent by Papal Bull; one was assassinated. But Lucrezia lived on long after her father's death, her life threaded with tragedy and stultified by a wearisome piety that mocked her past. The depth and ferocity of the Pope's passion for his children have made him an ogre of history, making men forget his astonishing dignity, his overwhelming physical charm, and the immense presence as well as that animal vitality which made him as unwearying at work as at pleasure, and the bull his proper emblem. His irresponsible virility was scarcely in keeping with the tiara, but his pontificate was far from disastrous for the Papacy. He

brought its temporal possessions more firmly under its control, and even though his intention to transfer these temporalities to his own family would, if realized, have ruined the Church, yet the possibility that this could be achieved was so remote that the success of Cesare merely redounded to the advantage of the Papacy.

That advantage was brilliantly exploited by Julius II. Sixty years old when he was elected pope, he possessed the strength and decision of a man half his years. He loved action, hated the French, loathed the great Roman families, not one member of which he elevated to the purple, and detested the tyrants of Perugia and Bologna who usurped the temporal power of his Church. Defeat merely increased his energy, and in all his dealings this tough, thickset priest was bold, decisive, and single-minded. His aim was the absolute independence of the Papacy from emperors, kings, or Romans, for without that temporal independence its claims to universality in a world of national states, he realized, would be meaning-

less. As in politics, so in art, Julius never vacillated. Nor did he play safe. Hearing of the abilities of the young Raphael, he sent for him from Florence, ordered him to obliterate paintings by Piero della Francesca, Signorelli, Perugino, Sodoma, and the rest and to cover the walls of the rooms now known as the Stanze of Raphael with subjects of his own choice. The result is one of the great glories of Renaissance Rome. In architecture Julius showed the same sweeping vision, the same decisive action. He patronized Bramante, a man whose dreams were as grandiose as Julius could wish, accepted his colossal plans with alacrity, and taxed the faithful. Nor was it in any way surprising that Julius, who always stared life directly in the eye, should contemplate death with the same robust realism. Michelangelo's designs for his tomb entranced him; after all, it was the largest and most ornate mausoleum conceived in Europe since Theodoric's, but he could not bridle his impatience with the sculptor's slow progress, his creative doubts and endless reconsiderations, which

drove the Pope to such furious quarrels that Michelangelo left Rome in anger and the project came to a standstill. Nor did reconciliation speed it forward—long after his death, a part of Julius' tomb went up in the little church of San Pietro in Vincoli; his bones lie in an undistinguished grave in the Vatican. Julius' furious spirit did not always meet such adamantine opposition.

The triumph of the Renaissance Papacy received its most splendid illustration in the coronation of Julius' successor—the young Giovanni de' Medici, son of Lorenzo, who became pope in 1513, at the age of thirty-seven. Bull-necked, pop-eyed, red-faced, he totally lacked the presence and ferocity of an Alexander VI or a Julius II. The cardinals in conclave had decided to avoid aggressive, virile temperaments. They had had enough of them. Leo X belied his name. Subtle, intuitive, sophisticated, he charmed with his generosity, affability, and sweetness of manner. Discretion veiled his private life, and his character and his education gave him a range of

intellectual interests and sympathies not matched by a pope since Nicholas V. Bred in riches and nurtured in luxury, he had no compunction in using the wealth of the Church in splendiferous pageantry. Since the days of the emperors the Romans had never witnessed a procession comparable to his, as it made its way from the Vatican to St. John Lateran. Cardinals and bankers vied with each other in the display of artistic treasures or the construction of ceremonial arches. Agostino Chigi erected an eight-column arch and festooned it with his best pictures and sculpture. Apollos, Ganymedes, Bacchuses, Minervas, Venuses, nymphs and dryads, emperors and princes, the best antiquities that Rome had to offer lined the Via Triumphalis, sharing it with the newly painted apostles and prophets of Christendom. The procession itself equaled its setting. Two hundred and fifty abbots, bishops, patriarchs, and cardinals were matched by the representatives of Italy's great families. The Gonzaga, Este, Sforza, Bentivoglio, Colonna, Orsini, Baglioni, nobles of Florence, patricians from

Venice, knights from the Romagna, the Duke of Urbino in black velvet, Lucrezia Borgia's husband released from excommunication for the occasion, and the rebel Cardinal, Alfonso Petrucci, whom Leo, four years later, was to have executed, were set like jewels amidst chamberlains, standard-bearers, guards, and acolytes. On that day passions were buried, no stones were hurled, no angry shouts drowned the plainsong, no daggers flashed in the cruel sun. All paid homage to the fat, perspiring, red-faced Pope, clad in white, sitting sidesaddle on his white palfrey. Eighty years earlier no pope could have risked his life and throne in such a spectacle.

Although Rome steadily increased in splendor, and the Pope's authority waxed majestic, violence, turmoil, and chicanery still threaded the papal annals with the scarlet of battle and murder. Enemies of papal power abounded: the French, the Spaniards, and the Milanese had found no resolution to their dynastic ambitions, and the Venetians had not given up their belief that security could only be achieved by

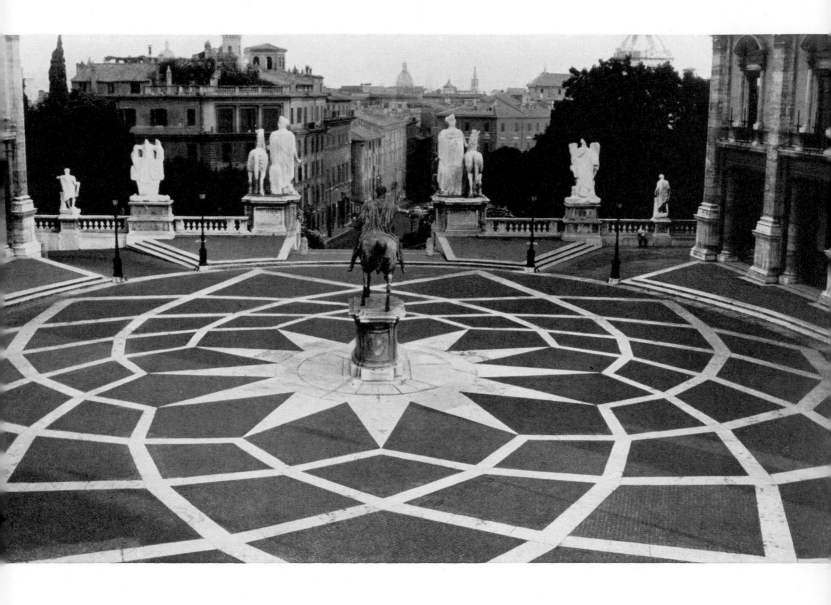

raping the Church of its northeastern temporalities. What was more, the wealth of the Church proved insufficient for its needs. Taxes grew grievous, the sale of indulgences more blatant. Across the Alps criticism of clerical worldliness, of monkish foolishness, of papal avarice, of Roman decadence, had often been sharp and prolonged. Under the stimulus of national needs, criticism developed a political and social purpose. And Luther, who might easily have met his end at the stake like another Savonarola, became the founder of a reformed Christianity that came to see the Pope as Antichrist and Rome as the whore of Babylon. The tribulations of the Reformation dimmed the luster of the Papacy; yet the heretic Germans were remote and their future uncertain, and it was a more immediate tragedy that jolted the Romans and the Church out of the gilded sweetness of Medicean rule into a sterner, harsher world. In 1527 the soldiers of the great Hapsburg ruler Charles V, whose dominions embraced the Spanish as well as the German Empire, sacked Rome effi-

ciently, brutally, completely. After the death of Clement VII, another Medici who succeeded Leo X, the growing rift with Protestantism and the shock left by the devastation of Rome bred a sterner spirit in the Church and Papacy. The more flamboyant aspects of the Renaissance were suppressed: speculation went out of fashion; dogma was more sharply defined at the great Council of Trent; the Holy Office and the Index maintained its purity; the new order of Jesuits soon dominated the school and the confessional, and men of ruthless will and unbending morality sat on the throne of Saint Peter, marshaling and leading the resurgent forces of Catholicism. They deplored paganism; repressed the licentiousness of the Romans, religious and secular; insisted on sacred subjects in art and clapped fig leaves on the statues of antiquity. So great, however, was the impetus of the Renaissance that they could not stop it. For centuries Rome continued to grow in beauty, and became, as no other city, the embodiment of the arts, if not the spirit, of the Renaissance.

perio comminuitur. Quid
nominis gloriam querimur
dulcedinem aliquam hau

Pope Pius II

by IRIS ORIGO

The road that winds up from the eleventh-century *pieve* of Corsignano—roughhewn in the golden stone of the region and containing the font in which Aeneas Silvius Piccolomini was christened—to the perfect little Renaissance city of Pienza—named after Pope Pius II—is a short one. But the ascent it symbolizes was one unusually swift and high even in a period in which able men quickly made their mark—the ascent which led a clever country boy from a humble secretary's desk to Peter's throne. A shrewd statesman, an elegant humanist, an inquiring traveler—keenly addicted to the learning of the past, but equally alive to any new ideas or discoveries of his own time—witty and urbane, skeptical and adaptable, he might be considered an entirely typical figure of the Renaissance, had he not, at the very summit of his career, devoted his last years to a vast and impracticable idea which was more closely in harmony with the spirit of an earlier age: the last Crusade. To carry out this plan, he cast aside every obstacle suggested by expediency or prudence and certainly hastened, though well knowing that his scheme had failed, his own death.

Aeneas Silvius Piccolomini, the son of an impoverished country nobleman who had been a soldier of fortune, was born in 1405 in the little Tuscan village of Corsignano, on the bare, dust-colored hills of the Val d'Orcia. A clever boy, he was sent by his father at the age of eighteen to Siena, the city which he called "sacred to Venus." There, while certainly not neglecting the charms of the beautiful Sienese women, he ardently pursued his legal studies with the celebrated jurist Sozzini, and later on continued his classical studies in Florence with Filelfo. Too poor to buy all the books he needed, he would sit up at night copying out long passages from the volumes lent to him by his friends—once even setting his nightcap on fire, as he nodded over his work. Cicero, Virgil, Livy, these were his first models, and among the moderns, when first he began to write verse, Petrarch. His first glimpse of the efficacy of eloquence, when he saw the whole congregation of Siena swept off their feet by the sermons of the famous popular preacher Saint Bernardino, excited him so much that he pursued him to Rome, to ask whether he, too, should not follow the same path. But Saint Bernardino firmly dissuaded him, telling the future Pope to return to the worldly pursuits for

altars were set up at street corners, branches of fragrant shrubs were set alight. "Any man who possessed paintings or a fine and lifelike statue displayed them in the portico before his door." Little stages were set up, on which children, dressed as angels, sang or played musical instruments.

Finally, on reaching St. Peter's, the Pope stood at the top of the marble stair before the church and displayed the head to the assembled crowd, renewing his own vow to the Apostle "to recover thy sheep and thy dwelling-place on earth," and calling upon God to deliver Christendom from the Turks. "Then there arose a great sound, like the murmur of many waters."

In the following spring, since the Turkish army was engaged in Bosnia, the Venetians, who had concluded an alliance with Hungary, decided that the moment was propitious to send off their own fleet to the Peloponnesus. "*We* are already at war," they declared. Pius had no illusions about the Venetian motives, but, as he pointed out to the Florentine envoys, even though the Venetians were "seeking the Peloponnesus and not Jesus. . . . if Venice is victorious, the Church will be victorious. . . . This war is our common war." Moreover, at just this moment, a most fortunate event had come to strengthen the Pope's hand. In the wooded hills of Tolfa, which were within the Patrimony, some mines of alum, the precious dye until then imported from Turkey, were discovered. This Pius declared to be a miracle, and at once set aside all its profits for the Crusade. On October 22, 1463, he issued the Bull *Ezechielis*, repeating his determination to lead the troops of Christendom himself. "In our spirit, old as it is, and in our sick body there is a determination to make war upon the Turks."

Already, however, he realized that many of his allies had failed him—in particular Francesco Sforza of Milan, Louis XI of France, and his vassal the Duke of Burgundy. The Venetian troops in the Peloponnesus had been swiftly defeated by the Turks, and their commander killed. The only troops to reach Ancona were a handful of unscrupulous adventurers, greedy for gain and loot. The Archbishop of Crete was appointed to weed them out, rejecting all those who had neither arms nor money.

Nevertheless, on June 14, 1464, in a solemn ceremony at St. Peter's, the Pope took the Cross, and four days later, so ill that he had to be carried onto his barge, he set forth. Turning back at the Ponte Molle for a last glimpse of Rome, he bade his city farewell, declaring, "You will never see me alive again." In all the history of the Crusades there are few episodes more pathetic than this journey of the dying Pope up the Tiber and across the Apennines—well aware that his enterprise was doomed. Often, as they drew near the coast, his attendants would draw the curtains of his litter, so that he might not see the bands of deserters who, scenting the prospect of defeat, were fleeing home before they had even begun to fight.

When the Pope reached Ancona, no Venetian ship was to be seen, and day after day, from the windows of the bishop's palace at the summit of the town, Pius scanned the Adriatic in vain for the galleys of Saint Mark. The city was now short of food and water and a pestilence had broken out, and the Pope himself was wasting away with dysentery.

When at last, on August 12, the Doge Cristoforo Moro sailed in with twelve ships, Pius was too ill to receive him. "Until now," he said, "it was a fleet that was lacking. Now the fleet has come, but I shall not be there." Two days later, feeling his end to be near, he summoned to his bedside the prelates who had come to Ancona with him, gave them his blessing, and told them that he was leaving them to finish what he had begun. Then, left alone with his nephew, his secretary, and his old friend Cardinal Ammanati, he once again exhorted the latter not to draw back. "Urge my brothers to go on with the Crusade . . . Woe befall you if you draw back from God's work." Asking for his friend's prayers, he lay back and died before the dawn.

On the next day his body was carried to the cathedral, where the Doge pronounced a long and insincere oration over it and then at once set sail for Venice, while the cardinals hurried back to Rome to elect a new pope. The last Crusade was over, with the death of the only man who had believed in it.

THE CITY OF POPES

Ninety years before Pius II became Pope, an exiled Florentine, Fazio degli Uberti, visited Rome. Inspired by its decaying grandeur, as were Dante and Petrarch before him, he wrote a poem eulogizing the ancient city. An illustration (above) from his manuscript personifies Rome as a widow forsaken by the popes in Avignon. Dressed in rags, she cries out her woe to the poet (upper left, with a friend), who listens as she points out the monuments of her past glories: the Colosseum lying at her feet; the equestrian statue of Marcus Aurelius partly hidden by an ancient aqueduct; the Baths of Diocletian (lower left) housing the cells of Carthusian monks; the Marble Horsemen standing on the Quirinal between the columns of Trajan and Marcus Aurelius; and the Pantheon (center), converted into a Christian church. All but forgotten during the reconstruction undertaken by the Renaissance popes, the aged ruins nevertheless affected nearly every artist from Alberti to Michelangelo, and humanists were inspired by their classical forms.

THE RESTORATION OF THE CITY

In 1377, when the Papacy returned from Avignon accompanied by its huge retinue of cardinals, courtiers, scholars, and artists, the glory of ancient Rome was slowly reborn. Spacious palaces were built amid the decaying ruins, churches rose in the ancient baths, gardens were laid out around the columns of the Palatine, and wide avenues swept over crumbling temples and arches. Much of the new building was at the expense of the old: Paul II used stone from the Colosseum to build the Palazzo San Marco; shops occupied the Theater of Marcellus; Sixtus IV destroyed the oldest bridge over the Tiber and built a new one in his name, using the old stone for cannon balls. Each pope strove to outdo his predecessors, and the coffered ceilings, collections of antiquities, magnificent paintings, and frescoes which adorned the interiors of the palaces made their handsome façades seem almost dull by comparison. The greatest monument of all, however, was the new Cathedral of St. Peter. The ancient basilica had been ordered destroyed by Pope Nicholas V, and in 1506 Julius II laid the cornerstone for a new church designed by Bramante. Successive popes poured money into the building as work progressed slowly under a series of architects, each with a new plan or addition. Finally the aging Michelangelo was put in charge. Ignoring the designs of Raphael and declaring that Antonio da Sangallo's plan would make the church so dark it would be dangerous for public morals, he returned to the original scheme, adding the great dome, which he modestly called "larger, but not more beautiful" than that of Brunelleschi in Florence. The master died before his work was complete, and later the plans were changed again, but the dome remained and rises today, the crowning achievement of the Roman Renaissance.

The anonymous sketch at left shows the huge dome beginning to rise over St. Peter's. Bramante's plan for the church, with two towers and a dome similar to that of the Pantheon, is on the bronze medal above.

wonder of Europe in the Middle Ages. Its two miles of forbidding fortifications enclosed the most formidable armory in the Renaissance world. Thousands of workmen toiled there, and a new galley was produced every hundred days. These ships could be commissioned with amazing alacrity. From the Arsenal to the lagoon the ships moved as on a conveyer-belt—masts, sails, oars, stores, and weapons were quickly loaded as the vessel slowly passed each storehouse. Most fittings on each galley were standardized, so that replacements could be stored in all Venetian warehouses, whether they might be in Southampton or Tyre; any crew could be moved to any ship without further training, or a fresh crew could be made up from survivors in battle. And every galley, whether used in commerce or in war, belonged to the state: no patrician, no matter what his wealth might be, could possess a Venetian galley. Such precise regimentation, such absolute control, gave Venice its pre-eminence over its rivals and

enabled it to ship a crusading army to the Holy Land without overstretching its resources. The other maritime powers of Italy hated the supremacy of Venice. Genoa ruined herself in a long and desperate war, which ranged from the Bosporus to the lagoon itself, in an attempt to crush Venice and despoil her of the riches which her great fleet carried for her merchants. By 1400 Venice had proved herself invincible; indeed, she had become the center of a sea-borne empire. Zara, Ragusa, Crete, and many Aegean Islands belonged to her absolutely; trading communities, enjoying extraterritorial privileges, had been established in Constantinople, Acre, Tyre, Sidon, Alexandria. Venetian merchants were as familiar with the Black Sea as the Adriatic; her ambassadors were to be found in Isfahan and in Cairo; her travelers, stimulated by the stories of Marco Polo, reached Sumatra and Ceylon long before Vasco da Gama rounded the Cape. And even though the Venetians never ventured to such far-flung

Jacopo de' Barbari's view of Venice in 1500 shows Neptune astride a porpoise, guarding the entrance to the Grand Canal. The Rialto b

...ses the S-shaped waterway. At the eastern end of the city (far right) are the Arsenal's drydocks, shipwrights' workshops, and boat basins.

places as the Genoese at the height of their greatness, their contacts with the East were more stable, more secure, and made up in volume for what they might lack in diversity.

By 1450 Venice was the only power in Italy, save for the Papacy, that was truly cosmopolitan, one whose interests required not only a great fleet but also a complex intelligence system. Venice needed to know the intentions of the Shah of Persia, the Count of Flanders, the Sultan of Cairo, the King of France, or the Duke of Ferrara. And every merchant, every priest was expected to spy for his country's good. The Signory knew at once the deepest secrets of the most carefully guarded conclaves of the Papacy, for the patriarchs of Venice put loyalty to the state higher than the command of the Church. The carefully, beautifully written, well-informed, judicious reports of the Venetian residents in London, Paris, or Bruges now form some of the most reliable sources not only for the history of Venice, but also for the history of England, France,

and the Netherlands. In the great building of the Archivio Centrale, next to the Frari church, is the greatest collection of archives ever accumulated by a single city. There are a quarter of a million books, documents, and parchments, which if placed end to end would circle the earth eleven times. For the fourteenth and fifteenth centuries there is a multitude of papers, a plethora of facts, a pyramid of accounts, still awaiting the toil of the historian. The reason for it all lies in the attitude and methods of the famous, or infamous, Council of Ten who, throughout the Renaissance, were the absolute rulers of the most highly organized state west of Byzantium.

The Council of Ten believed in knowledge, in facts: nothing was too trivial, too remote. They were as interested in the words and actions of a shopkeeper in the Campo di Santa Maria Formosa as in the gossip of the harem at Samarkand. So voracious was their desire to pry that, throughout Venice, they set up the famous Lions' Mouths by which Venetians

A decorated fourteenth-century trader's textbook includes insurance and cargo data and mathematics exercises. (Two merchants have met at the perennially problematical point between A and B.)

the timbers of his galley the night the Genoese defeated him, or the neatly folded skin of Admiral Bragadino, flayed from his living body by a sportive pasha. Such is the dulcet beauty of Venice, with its time-eroded buildings swathed in the opalescent light of the lagoon, that it is all too easy to forget the stern, unyielding, harsh, and dedicated spirit that inspired its rulers in their days of greatness.

Venice, however, was Janus-faced. Her commerce might be regimented, her aristocracy disciplined and controlled, her people subjected, yet she was cosmopolitan as no other city in Europe was. The crowded wharves of the Rialto and the Riva degli Schiavoni saw Gentile and Jew, Moslem and Greek, haggling over rich cargoes from the Orient. The Germans possessed a vast warehouse—decorated with frescoes by Giorgione—on the Grand Canal; the Turks, another, which had been the palace of the Pesaro family. Venice possessed the earliest ghetto in Europe, and the Armenians

followed their religion for centuries without fear of the Inquisition. All the nations of Europe mingled with the races of the Near East. They were brought together by the simple fact that Venice was the greatest market of the Western world. Anything could be bought and sold in Venice, but the principal commerce was in luxuries—in spices, slaves, gold, silver, glass, silks, damasks, jewels—cargoes that were small in bulk but huge in worth. Throughout the barbarian times, when Venice grew to greatness, Europe lacked the sophisticated skills and crafts that were commonplace in the Eastern Empire, or in Syria and Egypt; and in return for products from these places, Venice could offer the cheap raw materials that a primitive Europe produced—hides and tin from England, fine cloth from Flanders, raw silver from Bohemia, copper and steel from Germany. And there were the pilgrims. Decade after decade, century after century, in peace or in war, rich and devout Christians won their way

Venetian women developed an early form of lace by cutting away embroidery sewn on canvas (below), and Venice was famous for luxury fabrics, such as the velvet above, decorated with the Medici arms. But wool—an industry employing twenty thousand workers—was the city's most important textile product. The slave trade was of less economic value, since slaves worked mostly as domestic servants and were not used in industry. A sixteenth-century statuette carved of ambergris (right) shows an African girl at a moment of leisure, clothed only in fancy baubles.

to heaven via the Holy Places, to the great profit of the Venetians. For centuries the Crusaders warred in the eastern lands, and the Crusaders paid; paid for themselves, their armies, their horses, their necessities—and Venetians did not believe in bargains. In spite of their great wars—against the Genoese, the Greeks, the Turks—Venice waxed rich: rich on man's craving for luxury, for ostentation, for self-indulgence, on the pride of life and the lust of the eye. All the skills that she encouraged were luxury crafts rather than industries. The glass manufacture of Murano, based on secrets learned in the East, was guarded by the Council of Ten: for any workman with the knowledge of its manufacture to leave Venice was an act of treason. The Council hunted him down and killed him. Along with the monopoly in glass went another —the making of mosaic: this art, derived from Byzantium, was practiced only in Venice. Venetian jewelers had no rivals in the late Middle Ages, and emperors and kings sent there

for their crosses and scepters. Few Italian cities could rival Venice in the splendor of its silks, and none in the beauty of its lace. In Venice everything was for sale—love along with the rest. She boasted more courtesans than Rome. Their charges were carefully catalogued, and they were incomparable in skill as in price. They, too, had their rivals; the competition from homosexuals was so severe that the harlots complained loudly to the Council of Ten. As the wealth and prosperity of Europe lifted, so the riches of Venice soared.

On the threshold of the Renaissance, Venice possessed an unrivaled trade, and a stable and immensely powerful government firmly in the hands of its patricians. It was a city of hatchet-faced merchants. Jacopo Loredan entered in his great ledger: "The Doge Foscari: my debtor for the death of my father and uncle." After Foscari had been harried to death and his son killed, Loredan wrote on the opposite page, "Paid." In 1450 that was the spirit of Venice. By 1550

of the intimate enjoyment of physical love, yet whatever he might be painting there was warmth, and the reality that the Venetian knew. The huge *Paradise* of Tintoretto, the largest painting of its age, was peopled with Venetians. In Gentile Bellini's *Miracle of the Cross,* the canals, the gondolas, the roof tops and chimneys of Venice are all there. In Carpaccio's *Saint Ursula,* a Venetian girl sleeps in her bedroom; under the thin guise of a Christian story the rich, sensuous life pulsates, reflecting the splendor of the city.

Although the life of Venice was glorified in this way, individual men were not. An occasional doge, when dead, a patriarch or two, a brilliant condottiere, might be immortalized in a superb portrait or a statue—but the majority of portraits by Bellini or Titian have lost the names of their sitters, for they adorned the walls of those ordinary patricians who had no place in history—only the luck to be born in Venice at a time of artistic greatness. Yet how evocative are these

portraits, how infinite their variety, and how sharp the sense of the transience of living and loving men that broods over them. Nostalgia emanates from things Venetian like miasma from the lagoon; the streets of Venice echo with a sense of loss. The poetry of existence, the sadness that veils a sensual life, informs not only the best Venetian painting but also the writing of its one outstanding literary genius—Aretino. In him were mirrored the conflicting images of man—the cosmic and the noble, the moral and the obscene—that were to hypnotize the creative writers of Europe for generations.

Venice at the crossroads of her destiny created a society of exceptional complexity. It was still the city of hardheaded merchants, still the city of enterprise and ingenuity, still the city of the all-pervading, all-powerful state, of the swift and terrible justice. Its claim to dominion over the sea did not ring hollow: the hieratic splendor of the Doge had not been reduced to a quaint old-fashioned pageant. Yet the Renaissance settled

on Venice like a golden haze, sweetening life, softening the edges. Venice had lost the future; from the city of commerce she was becoming the city of carnival. And this feeling of the future lost was already pervading much of the attitude to life of Venetian men and women, drawing them to the luxurious life which they could so easily afford, to the new delights in painting, music, architecture, and letters that the Renaissance produced in such abundance. Rome itself could scarcely vie with Venice in the splendor of its new buildings both public and private. The splendid façades of Sansovino had given the Piazzetta its permanent face, and scattered about the canals and islands of the lagoon were the churches and monasteries of Palladio. Its artistic luxuries were incomparable (so many craftsmen possessing such an ancient tradition were bound to throw up genius after genius in the visual arts), and its gold and silver, armor, jewelry, bronzes, glass, lace, printing, and bookbinding—indeed all the arts and crafts that adorn the life of man—were practiced not only with the highest skill but also in a profusion that made Venice, both in its lagoon and on the mainland, the most affluent state of Italy. The splendor of its new palaces of white marble, porphyry, and serpentine overwhelmed generations of foreigners, while the profusion of its merchandise bewildered them. Philippe de Comines, nobleman of France, ambassador of its King, rich, sophisticated, much traveled, was as entranced by the Grand Canal—"la plus belle rue que je croy qui soit en tout le monde, et la mieulx maisonnée"—as the merry, uncouth joker Thomas Coryate of Somerset, who walked all the way there and gaped, openmouthed with amazement, believing himself in paradise. Other cities might possess nobler paintings, statues, buildings; the spirit of the Renaissance maintained in Florence a more heroic aspect, in Rome its expression was more grandiose. But nowhere did it permeate more thoroughly the daily life of a city and its people than in Venice.

271

Francesco Foscari, wearing the Doge's pointed cap.

Doge Francesco Foscari

by H. R. TREVOR-ROPER

In 1423 the old Doge of Venice, Tommaso Mocenigo, lay dying. The prosperity of the city was now at its height; this indeed was the golden age of the republic. But for a generation grave problems had clouded the city's future, threatening not only its security and its carefully nurtured wealth, but its very survival. Now it seemed at the parting of the ways: should it concentrate on its empire abroad or on its base at home? For both were threatened.

The empire abroad was centered in the Aegean Sea, although it extended to the factories in Constantinople and on the routes to the Middle and Far East. Here the threat came from the Ottoman Turks, now settled in Europe, with their capital at Adrianople, and pushing into the Balkans. All the efforts of Venice were needed to keep them out of the Aegean, and for years that had been the prime object of Venetian diplomacy.

The threat to the home base came from closer quarters: from new powers which were rising ominously in and around Italy. Hitherto, Venice had been able to build up its empire abroad because its neighbors at home had given little trouble. Bishoprics, communes, petty princes—they could not be ignored, but equally they offered no temptations compared with the huge profits of the Levant. So the republic had practiced a policy of the balance of power, involving the minimum of direct intervention. But now these petty neighbors were becoming part or projections of greater powers, and these greater powers were threatening the very life of Venice. The rulers of Hungary and Naples were closing in on its Adriatic lifeline. Above all, a menacing new state was pressing down the valley of the Po. For this was the time when the free republics of Italy were gradually being converted into despotic princely states; and the greatest of these states was the new duchy of Milan, under the Visconti family. Having crushed the liberties of Milan, the Visconti were creating around it an even larger hinterland or *retroterra*. In the south they had absorbed the great mercantile republic of Genoa, which, being confined between the Ligurian Alps and the sea, lacked such a *retroterra* in which to fight. In the east the Visconti were pushing toward another great mercantile republic, which was squeezed between the lagoons and the sea—Venice.

How could the republic ensure its survival? The

answer, according to some Venetians, was to enlarge its own *retroterra*, the Venetian *terraferma*—a process which had already begun, with the annexation of Padua, Vicenza, and Verona. But there were others who distrusted this policy. Land wars, they said, were costly; they distracted the city from its real task, in the East; they created a new class of landed nobility and made the city dependent on condottieri; and was it not precisely out of the landed nobility and condottieri that the powerful new group of princes, which threatened the liberties of all Italian cities, was rising?

The Doge Mocenigo was one who argued thus. As he lay dying he summoned to his bed the ducal councilors and there delivered a famous speech. The war for the *terraferma*, he said, had shattered the finances of the republic. It could not be continued. The wealth of Venice lay in manufacture, trade, and shipping: only by keeping to these pursuits, and to peace, would the city master the wealth of Christendom. Therefore they must be careful to appoint a sound successor to himself. Then he went down the list of the possible candidates. Bembo, Loredan, Mocenigo, Contarini—the political members of the great mercantile families who formed the closed aristocracy of Venice—there was something to be said for them all. But at the end he warned them explicitly against one man: Francesco Foscari, he said, was proud, ambitious, unscrupulous. If he were Doge, it would mean war, war, war . . .

To us there may seem something unbalanced in such a warning. Already by that time the republic had achieved its perfect aristocratic form—a form which was to be final (in all essentials) for centuries. Gone were the days when the people had power of election; since 1297 the Greater Council, the legislature and electorate of the republic, had been "closed"—that is, confined to the nobility, who in turn kept careful control over their own membership. Gone, too, were the days when the Doge, however elected, had exercised personal power. By now successive "ducal promises"—the conditions which the nobility, after observing the faults of each Doge, imposed upon his successor—had reduced the Doge to a mere figurehead. If offered the dogeship, a Venetian nobleman was unable by law to refuse it. Once elected, his power was narrowly circumscribed. He was unable to travel outside Venice. Neither he nor his sons could marry foreigners without permission. Neither his sons nor his personal officers could hold public positions under him (except as ambassadors or naval commanders, in which jobs they could not make trouble at home), and his official councilors, without whom he could do nothing, not even open a formal letter, could not be chosen by him. His income was fixed and his expenses limited, lest he should raise a party by bribery. His authority over the citizens was reduced, lest he should raise a mob in his support. He was not even allowed to give himself social airs. He could not set up his escutcheons in public places, nor answer to honorific titles. To foreigners, as representative of the greatest, richest republic in Italy, he might be *Serenissimo Principe;* at home, in that republic, he was only *Messer lo Doge.* And finally, he could not even lay down his office at will: except with the consent of his six councilors, ratified by the approval of the Greater Council, he could not even abdicate. Why then should an ambitious man want to be doge, and what could an ambitious man do, even if he were doge?

Nevertheless, Mocenigo's warning cannot have been entirely groundless. The Venetian constitution may have been completely aristocratic, and its aristocratic character may have been jealously preserved by a perpetual subdivision of authority, indirect elections, and a complex tissue of checks and balances. But even the most perfect constitution is operated by men with human passions, and the more complex a constitution is, the more certainly it falls into the hands of skillful politicians; and skilled politicians, even with the old rules, may play a new game. In the fifteenth century a new game was being played in all the republics of Italy. Faced by new problems, their old constitutions were crumbling, and new men —sometimes patricians rising out of their midst, sometimes condottieri in their service—were building up despotic rule. This had already happened in Milan, with the Visconti; it would happen again, with the Sforza. Soon it would happen in Florence, too. Cosimo de' Medici might begin as *pater patriae,* "the first citizen" of the republic. He would end by founding a dynasty that would last for centuries. Remembering this, no one can assume that even the Venetian constitution was proof against overthrow from above by an ambitious doge who, as a war leader, might build up a new form of patronage and

power. Such at least may have been the fear which inspired the Doge Mocenigo to warn his fellow noblemen against electing, as his successor, Francesco Foscari.

Who was the man who aroused these fears? The great Venetian aristocrats are always somewhat impersonal figures. The very system, with its intense jealousy of individual power, tended to depersonalize them. For it was the essential character of the Venetian republic that all personality was ruthlessly subordinated to the state. Instead of the cutthroat private enterprise of Genoa, or the brilliant individualism of Florence, here we see only an impersonal state capitalism, an implacable reason of state, an official state culture entirely hostile to "the cult of personality." So the official records of Venice do not bring to life even a controversial personality like Foscari. And yet he certainly was a controversial character. His whole reign shows it—a fact which is demonstrated, first of all, by the battle over his election.

Foscari, it is clear, was determined to be doge. Moreover, from the point of view of Mocenigo and his friends, he was an outsider. That was why they so feared him. He was also young (at fifty he was the youngest of the candidates); he was regarded as poor by the great "nabob" families, although he had enriched himself by marriage; he was experienced (after sharing his father's exile in Egypt, he had held most of the great elective offices of the state); and above all—and this was what Venice particularly distrusted—he was ambitious and the head of a party. Moreover, this party was particularly suspicious to the great mercantile aristocracy, like the Mocenigo, that customarily ruled Venice, for it was a party of "the poor nobles," the lesser noblemen, the radicals, the "Westerners" who favored war by land—as distinct from the "Easterners" with their Levantine interests. We are told that, as Procurator of St. Mark's, Foscari had used the large cash balances in his hands to create his following; he had relieved the wants of poor noblemen, given portions to their daughters, and made himself dangerous by their support. No doubt he had won other support by his merits, too. And finally, as was soon to be shown, he was a consummate election manager.

When the forty-one electors met, Foscari was not the favorite. He was too impulsive, too controversial, too committed to a policy. The favorite was Pietro Loredan, the admiral of the republic, who was also determined on office. But Loredan made the mistake of speaking confidently on his own behalf, which lost him votes. Foscari was much more prudent. Although his rivals did not know it, he had already nine ballots safely in his pocket. These voters acted as a bloc, but they did not reveal themselves until they had quietly contributed to the defeat of all the other candidates. Instead, they allowed it to appear that they, too, were opposed to Foscari. Then, suddenly, at the tenth ballot, they all plumped for the outsider and carried him into the ducal chair.

Thus began the longest ducal reign in the long history of the Venetian republic. Foscari, who always liked panache, hastened to celebrate his victory. For a whole year he dazzled the city with feasts and pageants. The new Sala del Maggior Consiglio—the Hall of the Great Council—was opened with splendid ceremony. He fetched his wife, the Dogaressa, in triumph to the Palace in the ducal galley, the *Bucentaur*, attended by the noblewomen of Venice. These spectacles, incidentally, were something of a sop to the non-noble citizens of Venice who in that year lost their last vestigial rights in the government of the republic; but it is doubtful if their personal emphasis pleased the aristocracy. Then the Doge settled down to the business of government.

The character of Foscari's reign can be described in three words—pageantry, war, and dissension. There were feasts and spectacles of unexampled magnificence. There was also—as Mocenigo had prophesied—constant war for the *terraferma*. And thirdly, there was the undying jealousy and hatred of those whom Foscari had defeated—particularly of the Loredan family, whom he had pipped to the post. The pageantry gave his reign its outward splendor; the war its real content; and the hatred of the Loredan brought it to a tragic end.

The outward splendor was shown in many ways. New palaces, public and private, rose by the Grand Canal and the lagoon. The Rialto bridge was rebuilt. Paolo Uccello worked on mosaics in St. Mark's, Antonio Vivarini painted in San Pantaleon. Famous visitors were received with ever greater pomp and show. In 1428 it was the Prince of Portugal whom the *Bucentaur*, escorted by a fleet of boats, fetched in

to a banquet attended by two hundred and fifty ladies dressed in cloth of gold and silk and jewels. In 1438 the Emperor of Byzantium himself, in his great time of trial with the Turks, condescended to come in person to Italy, with his brother the Despot of the Morea and the Patriarch of Constantinople, ready to accept the supremacy of the Roman Church in return for Western aid. When the *Bucentaur*, covered with red silk and golden emblems, carried the imperial party from the Lido, the whole lagoon was full of boats, flying banners and playing music, with oarsmen clad in cloth of gold. In 1452 even this event was eclipsed when the Holy Roman Emperor followed the Emperor of the East to Venice, and was drawn in triumph by the *Bucentaur* and the gaily colored boats up to the Grand Canal. By the next year the last Emperor of the East had perished in the sack of his capital, and the Doge Foscari would receive in Venice the fugitive scholars and salvaged treasures of Byzantium.

In Byzantine eyes, the fall of Byzantium was due to Venetian indifference. All through the reign of Foscari, it was said, the military resources of Venice had been turned too exclusively to the West. But this was hardly a fair judgment. The threat from the West was a real threat, as the fate of Genoa showed. And besides, in the first year of Foscari's reign there had been a great success in the East. In that year the Greek governor of Salonika, the emporium of Thessalian grain (Venice lived on imported grain) and the northern watchtower of the Aegean, gave or sold his city to Venice rather than lose it to the Turks. So the East, it seemed, was safe. Meanwhile, the republic had obtained an invaluable ally for war in the West. It happened that at this time the greatest condottiere in Italy, the man who had himself recreated the power of the Visconti in Milan, now, on some slight, deserted his master and offered his services to Venice. This was Francesco Bussone, known as Carmagnola. The Venetians could hardly resist such an opportunity. It was against a background of this double security provided by Salonika in the East and Carmagnola in the West that the republic, in 1425, made a league with Florence and declared war on the revived, aggressive power of the Visconti.

Thus, within three years of his accession, Foscari was carrying out the policy that had always been associated with him. There can be no doubt that it was

his policy: there exists the speech with which he persuaded the republic to make war. Of course, given the Venetian constitution, one can be sure it was not his policy alone, for he had only influence, not authority. Nevertheless, it seems that it was his influence, combined with circumstances, which weighted and held the scales. Even twelve years later, in 1437, that personal prestige was extraordinarily powerful. In that year the Doge sat, day after day, at the bedside of his son Domenico, who was dying of the plague. Foscari's supporters feared that he, too, would catch the infection, and then what would they do? The lives of many, they said, depended on his: if he were to fail, the fortune and the forward policy of the state would be in peril. Clearly, if men could say this, the Doge was no mere chairman. The forward policy of the state depended particularly on him in 1437, when those initial advantages which had made the western war popular a dozen years earlier had disappeared.

In fact neither Salonika nor Carmagnola lived up to their promise. Salonika was the first to go. In 1430 the Turks captured and sacked it; the slaughter was terrible, the loss final. From now on the Aegean Sea lay open to the Turks, with the wealth of Venice in it, scattered among subject islands whose Greek inhabitants preferred (or thought they preferred) Turkish conquest to Venetian exploitation. In the same year an attempt was made to assassinate the Doge. And as for Carmagnola, like so many condottieri, he proved thoroughly unsatisfactory. At the head of one of the greatest armies that had been seen in Italy, he somehow failed to be as victorious in Venetian as he had been in Milanese service, and he remained suspiciously familiar with his former employer and present enemy, the Duke of Milan. The Venetians offered to make him lord of Milan if he would only conquer it, but still he consumed time and money in mere parades or took cures at the baths of Abano. Finally the Venetians lost patience. With their usual circumspection, they did nothing rashly or openly, but invited Carmagnola to Venice to meet the Doge and discuss future strategy. He never saw the Doge. Instead, he was whisked from the palace to prison, tortured, tried, and condemned. When his sentence was discussed, the Doge voted for mercy, but was overruled, and Carmagnola was sentenced to death and beheaded. That was in 1432. After that the

republic employed other, less dangerous condottieri.

So by 1432 Foscari's policy was faced with difficulties on all fronts. He sensed the obstacles, and next year asked to resign his office. It is said that he asked again in 1442 and again in 1446, and this suggests that he was an impulsive man, impatient of obstruction, easily discouraged by defeat. But the Venetian aristocracy, or perhaps his supporters in it, would not allow him to give up his office. On each occasion they reminded him that, by the constitution, he could not resign except with the assent of the six councilors and the Greater Council. It was an answer which he was later to remember and to use against his enemies.

Meanwhile the forward policy continued. The war for the *terraferma* went on. It was very long, lasting, with brief interludes, for thirty years. It was also very costly; the first ten years alone cost seven million ducats. It had its dramatic incidents—among them the bringing of Venetian ships over the mountains from the river Adige to Lake Garda; it had its disappointments, too—the most bitter being the gradual slide of the Florentines, out of commercial rivalry, toward the side of Milan. But in the end the war was successful. It carried the westward frontier of the *terraferma* to its furthest and final limit, to incorporate the provinces of Brescia and Bergamo, and the Doge solemnly received them as imperial fiefs. He also obtained Ravenna as a papal fief. And before his death he inspired and signed a new treaty —a league with Florence and Milan, Rome and Naples, which was to preserve the liberty of Italy. It would have been a great triumph had it lasted: all we can say is that at least it outlasted Foscari.

So the pageants and the war went on. But meanwhile what of the third feature of Foscari's reign, the enmity of his rivals? This, too, was very long— long and bitter, as Venetian enmities always were. For if Venice, with its exaltation of state service, was free from the strife of parties which ruined every other Italian republic, it was enlivened, even more than the others, by fierce personal and family feuds. In particular, the Doge Foscari never escaped the bitter hatred of the Loredan family. He had defeated them in 1423. They remembered their defeat, and in after years, with their allies the Donà and the Barbarigo, mercilessly persecuted him at his weakest point—his family.

At the time of his election, one objection to Foscari had been his large family, whose members, it was suggested, would feed on the resources of the state. This danger did not materialize, for of his five sons, four died young of the plague. The last survivor, who alone had heirs, and to whom the Doge was devoted, was Jacopo, a young man of cultivated tastes—a Greek scholar and collector of manuscripts —but indiscreet ways. In 1441 his marriage to Lucrezia Contarini had been one of the most magnificent of the many spectacles which the Doge gave to the city. There had been boat races, feasts, and illuminations, with the city adorned in scarlet and cloth of gold, a great tournament before thirty thousand people in the Piazza San Marco, and two hundred and fifty horsemen had ridden in cavalcade over the Grand Canal on a specially built bridge of barges. But in 1445 Jacopo Foscari was secretly denounced for receiving gifts from Filippo Maria Visconti, the Duke of Milan. At that time Francesco Loredan, the nephew of the defeated candidate, was one of the three chiefs of the Council of Ten, the secret political police of the republic. His ally Ermolao Donà was another, and the Ten decided to act at once. They ordered the arrest of Jacopo and excluded the Doge and his kinsmen from all their deliberations on the matter. Then sentence was pronounced: Jacopo was exiled to Nauplia in Greece, and all his goods were confiscated. In vain the Dogaressa begged to see her son; the orders were given, and the name of the Doge himself was placed, with ruthless, impersonal irony, at their head. Before they could be executed there was a hitch, and then, on grounds of health, the place of exile was changed to Treviso, which was both nearer and more comfortable; but the humiliation to the Doge was no less. It was after this bitter defeat that Foscari made his third attempt to resign; but he was forced to remain in office and drink the dregs of the cup.

Before long, however, the Doge was able to score a point. In 1447 he made a moving appeal to the Ten, and the Ten consented, not on grounds of humanity but (a typically Venetian reason) "because it is necessary at this time to have a prince whose mind is free and serene, able to serve the republic," to remit the exile of Jacopo, now sick in body and mind. But the reunion of the Jacob and the Benjamin of the house of Foscari did not last long. In

A RESOLUTION CALLING FOR THE DOGE'S ABDICATION, VOTED BY THE COUNCIL OF TEN, THE PRIVY COUNCIL, AND THE GIUNTA, A BODY OF TWENTY-FIVE NOBLEMEN.

There is no one who does not thoroughly comprehend how useful and altogether how essential to our State and to our affairs is the presence of a Prince, without which, as becomes manifest from the results, the greatest inconvenience and detriment are apt to arise to our State which, since it has by the infinite clemency of our Creator been bequeathed to us by our forefathers hereditary and fair to look upon, we are bound to preserve with all our power and to hold dearer to us than our very life. And although this our city is furnished with holy laws and ordinances, it is of little avail if they be not executed, if the observance of the same be relaxed. The presence of the Prince besides in the councils, at audiences, in the transaction of affairs of state—how desirable it is, how glorious it is, it would be superfluous to point out. All are aware that our most illustrious Prince has vacated his dignity for a great length of time; and from his advanced age it is not at all to be expected that he will be able to return to the exercise of the functions appertaining thereto. How pernicious his absence and incompetence are is more easily understood than explained. Wherefore: it is proposed that by the authority of this most excellent Council and the Giunta the resolution be agreed to that the Privy councilors and the chiefs of the council shall repair to the presence of the most illustrious Prince and declare to him our opinion "that the government of our city and State (which as his Highness knows very well is excessively arduous) cannot be carried on without the constant presence and cooperation of a Prince; also considering how long his Excellency has for personal reasons renounced all share in this government, and that there is no hope that he will be able at any time hereafter to discharge his duties according to the exigencies of this state; and [considering] that his absence is threatening to involve consequences such as we are assured from his affectionate patriotism, he can never desire to witness;—on these grounds which his Excellency in his supreme wisdom will readily appreciate, we with the aforesaid council of Ten and the Giunta have decided upon exhorting and requesting his Serenity, for the evident and necessary welfare of our State—his native land—freely and spontaneously to abdicate, which on many accounts he ought to do as a good Prince and a true father of his country, and especially as we provide that he shall have for his support and proper maintenance from our Office of Salt 1,500 gold ducats a year for life as well as the residue of his salary due to the present day. Also that if it happen that the same most illustrious Prince, on this declaration being made known to him, shall demand time to consider, he may be told that we are content to wait for such answer till tomorrow at the hour of tierce."

1450 the Loredan family found another pretext, and resumed their attack.

That year one of Jacopo Foscari's judges, Ermolao Donà, was murdered, and Jacopo was at once suspected. Again the Doge's son was arrested; he was even tortured; and although nothing was proved and he was probably innocent (it is said that another man afterward confessed to the crime), the Ten, having gone so far, were afraid to go back. They sentenced him, without proof, to exile, and this time there were no second thoughts; he was carried off to Crete. Even in Crete his movements were watched, his indiscretions observed; and in 1456 it was reported to the Ten that he was planning, or at least discussing, revenge with foreign help. The Ten (of whom Jacopo Loredan was now one of the chiefs) immediately decided that the matter was "of the greatest importance"; and once again the Doge's son was fetched back for a trial.

Now began the final tragedy of the Doge's reign, the tragedy which Byron converted into his drama *The Two Foscari*. Before this third trial it was admitted that Jacopo's projects were entirely academic, and that being in Crete, he could do little or nothing to harm the republic; but that made no difference. He was tortured and judged guilty, and the remorseless Jacopo Loredan urged that he be publicly beheaded as a traitor between the columns of the Piazza. Even the Ten drew the line at this, and the prisoner was sentenced to renewed exile in Crete, this time in prison. Before returning to Crete, he was allowed to see his father, now eighty-four years old. He begged the Doge to intercede for him. "Jacopo," replied the old man, "go and obey your country's commands, and seek no more." But when his son had gone, he threw himself upon a chair, weeping and crying, *"O pietà grande!"* Within a few months he was shattered by the news that his last son was dead in Crete.

The Doge's distress was his enemies' opportunity, and they now decided to complete their victory. The Doge, they said, was too old; he was distracted by grief—the grief they had caused him; he could no longer attend to business. Therefore he must go. The Council of Ten met and decided to demand his abdication (*see* opposite). Their message was brought to the Doge by Jacopo Loredan. But now the old man had his revenge. He turned on them the argument they had used against him in the past: by the law, he said, he could not abdicate unless the councilors proposed and the Greater Council agreed. Here, too, he obeyed his country's laws. Baffled, the Ten consulted again, reinterpreted the law to suit their convenience, and told the Doge of their reinterpretation; but still he kept to the old interpretation and would not move. Finally they sent him an order: he was to resign and clear out of the ducal palace within eight days. If he did so, he would receive an adequate salary and a doge's burial; if not, he would be driven out and all his goods confiscated.

It was a completely illegal demand, but the Doge was powerless. He gave in. The ducal ring was taken from his finger and broken, the ducal cap from his head. He promised to leave the palace. Then, seeing pity in the eye of one of his visitors, he called to him and, taking his hand, said, "Whose son are you?" "I am the son of Messer Marin Memmo," was the reply. The Doge said, "He is my old friend. Ask him to come and visit me so that we may go in a boat for solace; we will visit the monasteries." The next day he left the palace. Wearing his old scarlet robe of state, he stepped forth, bent but unaided except by his staff. As he went to the stone steps leading down to the water his brother Marco urged him to go to his gondola by the covered stair. "No," replied the Doge, "I will go down by the same stair by which I came up to my dukedom." A week later he died— of rage, it was said, on hearing the bells announcing the election of his successor.

The people of Venice were indignant at the indecent deposition of the Doge who had reigned so long, who had enjoyed all the honors and prestige of government, whose figure and personality were so striking, whom the emperors of East and West had visited, and who had given them such splendid shows. There was much murmuring against the usurpation of the Ten, and even the Doge's enemies were now a little ashamed that they had not waited another week for a natural death. When Foscari was dead they gave him a splendid funeral, in spite of the protests of the former Dogaressa at this solemn humbug. He was buried in the church of the Frari, and a majestic Gothic-Renaissance monument commemorated his achievement—the conquest of the *terraferma*. Meanwhile the Ten withdrew from the invidious limelight, until the furore over their indecent treatment of the old Doge had abated some-

what. But there was no denying that they had won a notable victory. From now on the constitution was not only clearly oligarchical; it was also clear where the center of oligarchical power lay. It lay with that inner ring of self-elected councilors who could mobilize, even against the Doge, the Council of Ten.

Thus ended the long reign of Francesco Foscari. It ended, as it had begun, in bitter personal controversy, and even today historians dispute its significance. It has been said that it was Foscari who diverted the attention of Venice from East to West, sacrificing Salonika and Constantinople to Bergamo and Brescia. This diversion, it is added, led to disastrous consequences fifty years later, when the powers of Europe united against "the insatiable cupidity of the Venetians and their lust for power." And yet, one may answer, could any other doge really have acted differently? Before Foscari's time the dilemma had been there: if the land powers of Europe would not unite against the Turks, a sea power could not defeat them alone; and could Venice ignore the western threat, or the ominous example of Genoa? Other historians have dwelt on the fear of princely despotism; they have represented the Loredan as incorruptible republicans, Catos inexorable in the cause of the constitution. But is there in fact any evidence that Foscari ever entertained thoughts of altering the constitution? Perhaps in his early years he did (though we can only judge from the suspicion he inspired); but how seriously could an old man of eighty have threatened the established power of the oligarchy? In the end it was not he but his enemies who broke the constitution. He submitted to its most humiliating rules, malevolently applied; his foes broke through its last restraints in order to humble him.

Nevertheless it must be admitted that Foscari's reign was crucial in Venetian history. Whatever his personal aims, they were in the end subordinated and absorbed by the impersonal Venetian system. During his term in office the last Milanese republic was converted into the duchy of the Sforza, the great Florentine republic into the domain of the Medici, but the jealous republicans of Venice, whatever their motives, and whether they were right or wrong in their personal suspicions, positively strengthened their republic. They accepted the policy, and then crushed the personality, of the one man who might conceivably have recreated the old ducal power, so long undermined. And their victory over him was final. After 1457 the republic no longer feared the Doge. Before that date seven doges had been assassinated, nine had been blinded and exiled, twelve had abdicated, one had been sentenced to death and beheaded, two had been deposed. But after that date all is peace inside the republic. The Venetian constitution survived intact through the era of the native princes. It kept its independence when the other Italian states fell under foreign rule; it resisted the Papacy during the Counter Reformation; and it was to be praised, in the seventeenth century, as the most perfect model of government for any mercantile state which aspired to be free, effective, and independent.

VENICE OF THE DOGES

"Stupendissima!" exclaimed Beatrice d'Este when she was welcomed to Venice in 1493 by one of the colorful naval pageants with which the republic dazzled its distinguished guests. Venice was "the most triumphant city in the world," she declared, and the Venetians agreed with her completely. The city itself was the greatest spectacle of all, but its unique splendors were mirrored elsewhere, too—in the precious glass of Murano, in the villages and gardens of the Veneto, in official paintings commissioned to foster the worship of the state (above, a detail of Carpaccio's *Lion of St. Mark* shows the Doge's Palace and the domes and campanile of St. Mark's). But Venice did more than admire itself, for this was a city that faced outward. Its banner flew over thousands of ships, its traders were seen from Greenland to China. The republic's fate was intertwined with the life of Byzantium, a city almost a thousand miles away, where Venice not only borrowed traditions of government and art, but plundered treasures for the Cathedral of St. Mark. Venice inherited Byzantium's enemy, too, and the inexorable advance of Turkish power finally threatened to strangle her empire as it had ruined the empire of the Greeks.

A solemn Corpus Christi Procession, *by Gentile Bellini, crosses the Piazza in front of St. Mark's and the Doge's Palace (right rear).*

THE PIAZZA SAN MARCO

The center of Venetian life was the Piazza San Marco. In this spectacular setting, guilds and religious brotherhoods paraded before the Doge, bearing banners and jeweled reliquaries, and censers to perfume the salt air. Each new Doge celebrated his election there, scattering coins to the cheering crowd as he was carried past by a band of Arsenal workers. During the Renaissance, many of the Piazza's eyesores—the fish market opposite the Doge's Palace, and the barbers' and dentists' shops huddled around it—were cleared away, and a new border of colonnaded state buildings made the square a more splendid stage for Venetian pageantry. The focus of state ceremony was the eleventh-century domed Basilica of St. Mark, whose gold mosaics seemed to reflect the glory of Venice as much as the glory of God. It was the private chapel of the Doge and displayed, high above its central portal, the symbols of the state—four bronze horses stolen from Byzantium's ancient hippodrome, and the winged Lion of St. Mark.

THE RIALTO

Beside a great wall map painted to show the major routes of Venetian commerce, the merchants of Venice sat under the porticoes of the Rialto. Their wines, spices, and precious Eastern silks were displayed for sale in warehouses nearby, and along the quays before them, hucksters hawked fruit and fish. Overlooking the Rialto bridge (right) were Europe's busiest money market and its most celebrated bawdy house—both ready to service the hundreds of foreign merchants who lodged nearby.

The Rialto, where Venetians had first settled in the ninth century, was the hub of the republic's commercial life. Its merchants, like Shakespeare's Antonio, spread their risks carefully, prudently buying shares in several ventures to decrease the danger from shipwreck, pirates, or the Turks. The more daring bid at auction to rent one of the great state-owned galleys that sailed in fleets across the Mediterranean, for a shipload of luxury goods might return 40 per cent profit on a merchant's investment. At that rate, traders could afford to heed the warning written on the walls of the Rialto parish church: "Let the merchant's law be just, his weight true, his covenants faithful."

Under the careful supervision of the republic, commerce flourished. The government forced foreign ships, coming to pick up goods, to discharge two-thirds of their cargo at the port of Venice. It paid for provisioning Venetian merchant vessels, and granted warehouse space to foreign traders. Because trade depended on the city's naval superiority, the shipbuilding industry was guarded closely, and shipwrights required official permission to leave Venetian territory. Even closer attention was paid to smuggling. The lagoon was protected by regular patrols, and merchants who took on contraband cargo risked having their houses demolished.

On a loggia overlooking the Grand Canal, a priest armed with a piece of the True Cross exorcises a demon in Carpaccio's luminous painting, The Healing of the Demoniac. *A religious procession crosses the Rialto bridge, but the shaggy dog out for a gondola ride provides a secular note more typical of Venice.*

SCENES ALONG THE WATERWAYS

Preparing to attack each other with eggshells filled with perfumed water, masked carnival revelers (bottom right) walk past a pair of street jugglers. Like the peddlers fiddling to attract trade (left) and the dueling bravoes (below), they are from a souvenir book of Venetian scenes purchased in the sixteenth century by a honeymooning French couple and published here for the first time. On the facing page are other city sights: top, the Doge's Bucentaur, its figurehead bearing scales and a sword; below, hooded members of a religious fraternity and an aristocratic lady peering demurely from a sedan chair.

Dance pavilions floating on the Grand Canal, galleys decked with flowers, and regattas in which beautifully dressed women rowed were but a few of Venice's tourist attractions. A hundred thousand visitors came each May to attend the springtime trading fair and see the symbolic ceremony of the Doge marrying the Adriatic. Others came for the annual carnival, to stroll the streets in masks and watch harlequins perform in the piazzas. Masquerades were popular (maskmakers formed a separate branch of the painter's guild), and until the Senate restricted the use of disguise to carnival season, they were held throughout the year, with elaborate costumes copied from the dress worn by Venice's famous street actors, the forerunners of the Commedia dell'Arte. The actors in turn took Venetians as models; one of their stock characters, Pantaleone, caricatures a typical bearded merchant, such as the man (above right) whose bravoes defend him from robbers.

COUNTRY

LIFE

"Away with melancholy!" proclaimed one Venetian gentleman, preaching the joys of rural life. In the country, he said, the sun shines brighter, the sky is bluer, the stars are clearer, and bellyache is unknown. His fellow patricians agreed with him. In mainland villas, built in a classical style ordained by the architect Palladio, merchants devoted their leisure to hunting, concerts, card games, and to reading Latin poets who had inspired the fashion for country living. Frescoes on villa walls pictured their diversions, and gardens, sometimes designed by the same painters, provided a setting for their banquets and theatricals. Palladio had recommended that villas overlook the water, and the Venetians followed his advice as faithfully as their builders copied his models. Marshes were drained, farms irrigated, and a network of canals constructed throughout the Veneto. One river, the Brenta, with scores of luxurious villas built along its banks, became a mainland Grand Canal, crowded with boats carrying merchants in from the Rialto, and farm produce to city markets from the foothills of the Alps.

Rural life held simple pleasures, like the duck hunt (facing page) painted by Carpaccio, but in ornate mansions such as Villa Trissina (Palladio's plan for it appears below), luxury was usually unrestrained. A picnic could be as lavish as Pozzoserrato's Banquet of Epulon (below, left), and gardens elaborate as that of the Maggi family (left) were common, with mazes, banqueting loggias, and curiously clipped arbors. Attributed to Veronese's studio, the painting of the Maggi estate shows the rich merchant clan under a shower of jewelry and flowers, to symbolize the honors heaped on Carlo Maggi after his return to Venice from Turkish slavery.

With its two thousand workmen, the Arsenal of Venice was probably the largest industry in the sixteenth-century world. Its great sheds extended over sixty acres, and in them shipwrights could build and repair more than a hundred galleys at a time. Throughout the trading fleet, Arsenal standards prevailed, and even vessels constructed privately were identical with those built in the government shipyards. Thus every sailor (and all citizens were liable for naval service) knew his post on any galley in the fleet, and merchant vessels could be converted quickly to warships. Until 1500 galleys were the mainstay of the republic's navy. Equipped with both sails and oars, they were exceptionally swift, were never becalmed, and rarely ran aground. Their freight rates were high, but cargoes on them needed little insurance. But as cannon became more common, the galleys were gradually replaced with round ships, such as those that fought in the Battle of Zonchio (left), which could resist a cannon broadside and, with improved rigging, could maneuver just as well.

At the Battle of Zonchio in 1499 arrows, rocks, and cannon balls greeted Turks trying to board Venetian ships. But the Turkish leader Kemal Ali, or Chmali as the artist calls him at left center, still managed to capture one Venetian vessel (labeled "Nave del Armer" after its captain) and burn the Loredan ship ("Nave Lordana").

The republic's lucrative trade with Egypt was safeguarded by Venetian ambassadors in Cairo (painted by a follower of Gentile Bellini).

TRADE WITH
THE EAST

Venice faced eastward with both eyes open. She rented her fleet to the Crusaders once, at 85,000 marks a year; then persuaded them to leave her Saracen customers in peace and attack Constantinople instead. The Crusaders obliged, sacked the city during Holy Week, and gave a lion's share of the loot to the Cathedral of St. Mark. Venice grabbed the choicest quarter of Constantinople and the best ports of the empire; her merchants enjoyed trading privileges that even their Byzantine rivals did not have. The republic grew rich on Byzantine gold, and when Emperor John Palaeologus came to the Doge in 1369, pleading for help against Turkish attacks, Venice blandly imprisoned him for debt. This shortsighted, greedy action only helped the Turks, and the city soon faced a foe far stronger than Byzantium had been.

Traditionally, Venice's commerce depended on five great sea routes which her official trading convoys sailed each year; by 1517, when they conquered Egypt, the Turks controlled all but one. The republic remained strong enough to charge toll to every foreign vessel that sailed the Adriatic, but now she was subject to tribute herself, and had to pay 10,000 ducats yearly for the right to trade with ports under Turkish control.

Perched atop a galley, John Palaeologus (left, in a painting by a Florentine artist) sails to beg for Western aid. Venice refused help, and when Mohammed II seized Byzantium a century later, sent Gentile Bellini to portray him (opposite).

293

THE SPLENDORS
OF VENETIAN ART

Richly hued velvets and gleaming silks model the patrician figures of merchants and aristocrats in the immense gallery of portraits left by the Venetian artists. Nudes from the brush of Titian and Giorgione shimmer with all the subtle tones of the flesh; religious scenes that decorate the walls of churches and guildhalls are set in a blaze of luminous splendor. With their tastes molded by the treasury of Byzantine icons and mosaics displayed in the Basilica of St. Mark, Venetian artists became masters in the use of rich color. Foreigners, observing their work, were overwhelmed. If Titian had only drawn as well as he colored, Michelangelo proclaimed, "he would have produced works which none could surpass."

Venice's tradition of color was an ancient one. Early paintings had been encrusted with gold, in an attempt to imitate such Byzantine icons as the image of the Archangel Michael (opposite), guardian of the true Church, which had been stolen from the heretical Greeks in 1204 and deposited in Catholic Venice. Later painters never abandoned their love for lavish Eastern colors, but they muted their intensity, and transformed their predilection for painting with gold into a taste for hard cash which was well attuned to the atmosphere of Venetian society.

For the republic's painters achieved more than a mastery of color. Titian managed to garner pensions from the treasuries of Naples, Spain, and the German merchants trading at Venice. When a church which had commissioned a painting failed to meet his price of five hundred crowns, he judiciously presented the work to the Emperor Charles V instead, who gratefully gave him two thousand crowns for it. Giovanni Bellini reputedly put on a disguise and posed for a portrait in order to discover the lucrative secret of oil painting. His brother Gentile, repaying Venice's artistic debt to Constantinople, was sent as court painter to Mohammed II and there, despite the Koran's stern moral stand against painting, so gratified the Sultan with his erotic pictures that he returned to Venice with a golden chain around his neck and a patent of knighthood packed in his baggage.

Profits were high, but painters worked hard for their money. The Senate decreed that Giovanni Bellini and his assistant Carpaccio were to labor "continuously and every day" on their decorations for the Doge's Palace. Despite their prodigious output, artists sometimes spent years embellishing one building, covering acres of wall with paintings so immense that Carpaccio once advertised a picture as unequaled "not only for excellence and perfection, but also for size." Venice's concentration of great works of art was increased by the longevity of her artists. Giovanni Bellini lived to be eighty-six, and Titian was still painting industriously after he had passed ninety. The sea air eroded frescoes on palace walls, and frequent fires destroyed the vast murals of Venetian history in the Doge's Palace, so that each Renaissance generation had to do them over again, but the great body of work that remains in the city today constitutes one of the major monuments of Western art.

"The satisfaction of seeing the effigies of his ancestors," Vasari wrote, "is of the greatest value to any man and awakens in him the love of glory." Venetian artists were quick to take advantage of society's demand for portraits, and to quote Vasari again, there was "hardly a noble of high rank, scarcely a prince or a lady of great name whose portrait has not been painted by Titian." That artist portrayed the youthful Ranuccio Farnese (left) in a doublet of gleaming silk with a gold cross emblazoned on his cloak; he also painted the unknown woman above him, and the bearded nobleman at far left, whose ballooning blue sleeve rests on a parapet bearing Titian's initials. The sober Young Man in a Red Cap (right), attributed both to Carpaccio and Lorenzo Lotto, apparently did not possess such luxurious clothing, and other portraits of humbler folk were done occasionally. For example, Fra Teodoro posed for Giovanni Bellini as Saint Dominic (below), holding a lily and a book, the saint's sacred emblems. Bellini ignored traditional descriptions of Dominic, and, happily for posterity, decided to paint the monk exactly as he saw him.

Fresh from the studio of Giovanni Bellini, the young artist Giorgione rented a house near the Rialto and covered its outer walls with figures of musicians, poets, and cupids to advertise his genius. These pictures, like all of his frescoes, have now disappeared, for the south winds of Venice, as Vasari reported, "bear a most noxious saline humidity"; but they lasted long enough to win the artist an enviable commission to fresco Venice's newest trading warehouse. Giorgione covered the façade with allegorical figures which baffled his contemporaries, just as his surviving works have puzzled later generations. The meaning of the masterpiece at right, The Tempest, has never been clear, but the artist's feeling for the harmony between man and nature is evident in the relationship among the detached figures, the poetic landscape, and the approaching storm. It was begun as a picture of two women bathing; then the figure of the man in red was painted over one of them, and the fantasy grew as the work progressed. Like Giorgione's other canvases, this has the dramatic intensity, the evocative use of light, and the perceptive observation which set a standard for other artists to imitate. Titian, his friend and later his bitter rival, copied his style; his drawing of two figures in a landscape (above) integrates figures and scenery with a natural ease learned from Giorgione.

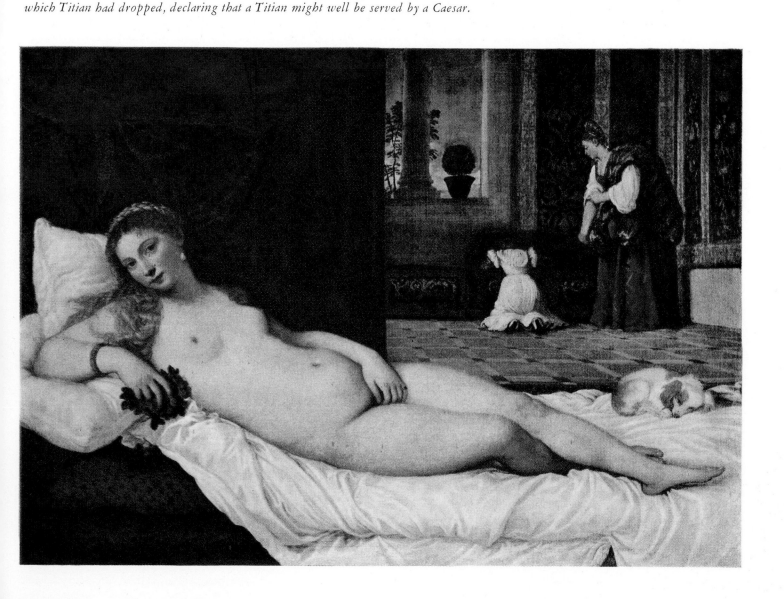

Newly risen from the sea, Titian's magnificent Venus Anadyomene *(opposite) wrings water from her flowing hair. This is probably an easel copy of a figure which the artist painted on the walls of the German merchants' warehouse near the Rialto in Venice. The theme was an ancient one (Emperor Augustus had placed a picture of the same subject in the temple of Julius Caesar), but Titian's treatment of it, with its spare and simple design, is unique. The reclining female nude, another motif which was to preoccupy painters for centuries, is represented by Titian's* Venus of Urbino *(below). Her pose was copied from Giorgione's painting of Venus in a landscape, which Titian completed after his colleague's death; but Titian placed his nude in a luxurious Renaissance room instead, with two servingmaids in the background rummaging through a clothes chest. To meet the new fashion for classical nudes, of which the anonymous sixteenth-century bronze dancer at right is an example in another medium, Titian painted a series of Dianas and Venuses. His best customer for them was Philip II of Spain. Philip's father had made Titian his court painter; he so admired the artist that he once stooped to pick up a paintbrush which Titian had dropped, declaring that a Titian might well be served by a Caesar.*

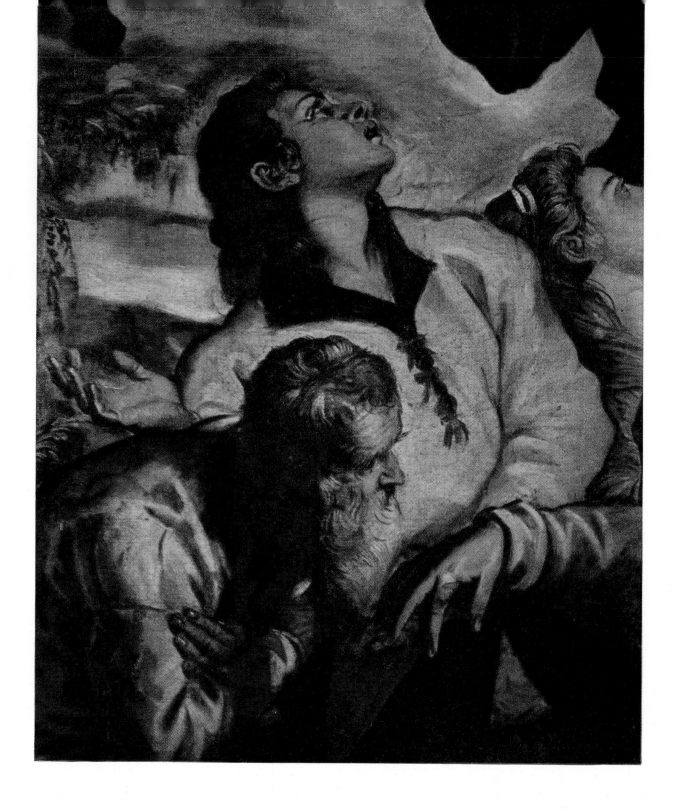

In 828, when patriotic Venetian merchants performed one of the proudest feats in the city's history by stealing Saint Mark's body from its sarcophagus at Alexandria, the saint himself, it was said, helped speed his departure by stirring up a tempest. Tintoretto, commissioned to paint the story for the School of St. Mark, one of Venice's five major charitable guilds, set the dramatic scene in a Renaissance piazza (left), under a stormy sky blazing with red light. Another charitable society, the School of St. Rocco, named after the patron saint of plague victims, also called on Tintoretto to decorate its guildhall, and promised him an annual pension of a hundred ducats in exchange for three pictures yearly. His masterpiece, a vast panorama of the Crucifixion, stretches for forty feet across the wall of one of their great assembly rooms; above is a detail from it, showing Nicodemus and the youthful Apostle John kneeling in grief before the Cross. Venetians rendered Saint Rocco the same compliment they had paid to Saint Mark. His remains, too, were stolen from their resting place in southern France and brought back to the city to serve as a talisman against the plagues which periodically attacked the Venetian republic.

THE IMAGES OF
MAN

Venice, Rome, Milan, and Florence were, physically speaking, new cities—cities in construction littered with scaffolding, scarred with half-realized plans. The villas, the taverns, the lounging places in the piazzas and gardens were filled with earnest argument about the new cathedrals and palaces. The statues that adorn the Piazza della Signoria at Florence gleamed with an almost raw whiteness. The Piazza San Marco at Venice shook itself free from the clutter of stalls, bakers' shops, and latrines to acquire the beauty that we see. In Milan the new citadel of the Sforza drew a wondering crowd of enthusiasts. In Mantua, Parma, Naples, Perugia, Viterbo, Genoa, indeed in all the towns of Italy, it was the same story —a new physical world was being built that buried or obscured the old barbarisms. In the churches and monasteries scarcely a year passed without a new masterpiece being painted on the walls. Today the blackened surface and faded pigments baffle the imagination and make it difficult to recapture

the sharp impact that these pictures had on the eyes that first saw them, and the same is true of statues and bronzes staled by centuries of reproduction and plagiarism. Impossible, too, to recapture the novelty of books, the miracle that it must have seemed to scholars to possess their own Virgil, their own Cicero, or to see their own poems and plays and familiar letters stacked by the hundreds in printers' shops. To this fresh, lavish, and splendid world were being added new horizons, and old certainties were dissolving as rapidly as the old scenes. Stories from Portugal and Spain, tales from Genoese sea captains, the gossip of the Venetian Cabots, told of a wondrous world of continents before undreamed of. Soon speculation became certainty, and the fables of Marco Polo and Mandeville gave way to the sober statements of mariners. The discoveries of Columbus, of the Cabots, of a whole generation of Portuguese in the Eastern Seas—"such great adventures as Fate had to no former age allowed"—confirmed

the belief, already held by many men and women, that the age to which they belonged was original and new, and that the immediate past was dead. Undoubtedly such convictions bred a sense of liberation and encouraged a belief in the unique quality of personal destiny. Men began to create new images of themselves—a habit as old as man himself, but always fresh and entrancing.

"Men," wrote Alberti, "are themselves the source of their own fortune and misfortune." "O supreme generosity of God the Father," apostrophized Pico della Mirandola, "O highest and marvelous felicity of man. To him it is granted to have whatever he chooses, to be whatever he wills." Man was heroic, destined by his own nature to greatness or to failure, but eternally alone, eternally himself. If born wise, then he might of course benefit by the wisdom of the past; if sensitive, he would gain from philosophy and religion; if apt, he could acquire the education of a gentleman. In the last resort,

however, all rested on himself—on his nature and on his luck, that curious personal destiny, controlled of course by God, but a mystery that could never be unlocked except by time. Portents and the conjunction or combustion of the stars might, as in a riddle, hint an answer, but essentially man was alone with fate. This attitude was deeply bound up with the growing capitalism of society, in which the merchant sought a profit by gambling on his own ingenuity, but there lay between these ideas a barrier of unawareness, like that which lies between the unconscious drives of a man's personality and his rational self. To the men who lived in the fifteenth century, this view of man—his individuality, his lonely destiny, his isolation—had nothing whatsoever to do with the active world or its expanding horizons. For them it was a new truth, self-evident, eternal, inescapable. As this attitude to man gathered momentum, it spread to places and communities that were unripe for its reception. Also it became entangled in the

strong, clinging, wayward tendrils of the past. Men were still priests, monks, scholars, soldiers, aristocrats, and merchants, and each profession, each community, each class possessed rules, regulations, beliefs, and attitudes already centuries old. On these the new conception of man worked, but, in working, suffered its own sea change.

Yet the concept of man, untrammeled, as a creature of destiny, but with his destiny provoked by his own self, enthralled most of the sensitive spirits of the Renaissance. Its fascination is beautifully illustrated in the growth and development of drama and the theater. Plays there had been in medieval Europe, but they were a looking glass of morality, not a mirror of man. They had concerned themselves, often in an intensely human way, with God, Christ, the Virgin, with the Creation or the Flood, or with personified moralities —vices like Lust and Sloth, virtues like Chastity and Humility. The humanists and their circle found these plays bar-

barous. They took delight in Plautus and in Terence, in the obscenities and the jokes, the brave declamations and fateful tragedies of individual men and women, crude as they were, two-dimensional as they might now seem; to us they are caricatures rather than living men, yet the change from the immediate past was very great. So, too, in history, the humanists looked for heroes, not men, looked for the individual life lived on a scale of intensity and drama beyond the range and experience of common mortals. And this spirit spread through literature like a dye. All aspects of a personal life—birth, love, marriage, ambition, defeat, senility—were blown up, endowed with an excess that in the hands of a genius, a Tasso or an Ariosto, acquired a heroic and universal significance. If the dramatists, poets, rhetoricians, and novelists were often second rate, if their creations now seem bombastic and ridiculous, they entranced their contemporaries. Nothing was more fashionable at any court than plays, masques, the declamation of

my fame. What do I need more? With a goose quill and a few sheets of paper I mock the universe." And he did, riotously, splendidly, until in his vigorous sixties he roared too vehemently at a bawdy joke, had apoplexy, and died. But what a life he had lived—shameless, selfish, magnificently free from humbug and splendidly creative.

Born the legitimate son of a poor shoemaker of Arezzo, Aretino passed himself off as the bastard of a gentleman until a fellow citizen, in a moment of rage, blew the *gaffe*; then Aretino boasted the truth as vehemently as he had paraded the lie. He received no serious education. He turned up for a time, in his late adolescence, at Perugia, probably living as a painter's apprentice. Already he had started to scribble sonnets. He next appears in the household of the great Roman banker Agostino Chigi (as a domestic servant, his enemies said, who was quickly dismissed for pinching the silver). Aretino claimed Chigi, however, as patron, not master. What-

ever his situation, Chigi's household gave him a lifelong taste for luxury, feasting, and pomp. Rome also offered him a golden opportunity for his natural literary genius.

At the corner of the Piazza Navona, a worn antique statue had become a curious sort of notice board. Learned lampoons of the Pope's government and the leading personalities of Rome were stuck to it. It was called Pasquino after a bitter-tongued schoolmaster. Later another statue in the Campus Martius was used in a similar way, and then the two statues took to having dialogues. These were known as pasquinades. Most of them were dull and pedantic, but risky in a mild way because of the freedom of their criticism. Aretino changed all that—his opportunity came on the death of Pope Leo X. To press the claims of his candidate, Cardinal Medici, afterward Clement VII, Aretino launched a series of unbridled lampoons against the cardinals. Every vice they may have practiced (and Aretino's imagination was rich), every dishon-

Titian painted numerous portraits of his friend Pietro Aretino, one of which appears at right. While working in the scullery of the banker Agostino Chigi, who is portrayed on the medal below, Aretino first gained notice for his libelous and obscene verses. As his fame mounted, he lampooned and pilloried all those who crossed him, and the medal on the opposite page shows him receiving gifts from men anxious to remain in his good graces. In later life Aretino boasted that "the alchemy of my pen has drawn more than 25,000 gold crowns from the entrails of various princes." The interest in the flesh whetted by Aretino is suggested by the carvings which decorate the ornate dagger and its scabbard shown on the facing page.

orable event in their own lives or their families', was widely and mercilessly pilloried. To make it worse, these verses were printed and sold as handbills. Rome rocked with laughter; princes asked their ambassadors for copies. No one believed that such impudence could go unpunished, but it did. Aretino demonstrated the power of the pen; he became the "scourge of princes." However, when an old Dutchman was elected Pope, Aretino thought he would cool his heels in Mantua. There the Gonzaga enjoyed his talents and boasted of his presence at their court, but with the election of Cardinal Medici as Clement VII, Aretino was summoned back to Rome to regale the papal court with his wit and license. At Rome he began to write his superb comedy *La Cortigiana;* of course in Italian, and with complete disregard for the models of Terence and Plautus that were thought sacrosanct. His reputation for wit and daring soared to new heights. His fancy, however, became powerfully stimulated by sixteen remarka-

bly obscene drawings by Giulio Romano that an enterprising publisher was about to have engraved. For each, Aretino provided a sonnet as explicit and as indecent as the picture. This did not endear him to his patron the Pope, who lacked the temperament and interests of the Borgia. At the same time Aretino was cuckolding as many husbands as he could. After a bad brawl in which he was nearly killed by an irate husband, the Pope's protection abruptly ceased. So off went Aretino to join the famous condottiere Giovanni delle Bande Nere. In that great captain, Aretino saw a mirror image—a man compelled like himself to follow his star, to fulfill his own life on his own terms, outside society, beyond custom, a man of destiny. With Giovanni he rejoiced in the freedom of military life, whose sweetness and pain were heightened by the dark presence of death. For a man of Aretino's powerful imagination and strong instincts, the grandeurs and miseries of war proved deeply enriching. The death of Giovanni acted

as a traumatic experience which Aretino described in one of the most remarkable letters that he ever wrote. In it he depicted, in language that was simple, grave, and noble, the last hours of a heroic man, triumphing over pain, accepting death, making his own terms with God as he had done with man. After Giovanni's death, Aretino felt more keenly his isolation from society; in his bitterness he poured his acid scorn on popes and princes. However, he had to live, and with his usual journalistic flair he brought out an almanac in which he flayed men and affairs by predicting the year's events. Its vast success enabled Aretino to settle in Venice—free, secure, rich from his pen: princes tumbled over themselves either to obtain a few flattering lines of prose from him or to avoid mention altogether; even the Pope forgave and pampered him; everything he wrote sold handsomely. He lived like a prince on the Grand Canal, his *palazzo* full of women and boys—the Aretines, he called them. There he of-

fered profuse hospitality, gargantuan banquets and feasts of love, orgies of literary gossip. Titian was drawn to him like a moth to a candle. He painted him over and over again, and in return Aretino pushed Titian's paintings on his patrons. They drank together, rioted together, lived the Bohemian life of the writer and artist that became one of the most seductive and compelling images of man, at once creative and destructive, and one that still had the power to hypnotize long after they were dead. Aretino's life gave great impetus to the idea that the artist was beyond morality, outside society, a spirit dedicated only to the compulsive needs of his art. At the same time he invested this image with a nobility, a certain grandeur, and the possibility of tragedy. The end of a free man could be brutal, harsh, and black with pain; in the midst of a riotous life those shadows were with him. Titian saw them in his face, and painted them.

Of course there were men who were alarmed by Aretino,

shocked by his life, disgusted by his writings, who condemned him roundly. Christian morality and the precepts of the Church were to the majority of men not shackles on the instinctive life but principles by which it should be lived. Yet in spite of themselves many were drawn to the image that Aretino or men like him presented. And some were honest enough to admit it. True, they tended, like Machiavelli, to discover man as a free agent more in princes and in captains of war, in the life of decision and action, than in writers and the writers' life. In war and politics, if anywhere, man was solitary, alone, without friends, and of necessity, they believed, without principle. To survive, to succeed, to kill before being killed, such were their destined lives. And this image artists evoked in painting as Machiavelli did in prose; the profiles, the faces of the Renaissance princes, have a terrible majesty, an aloofness, a dedication beyond the reality of common men.

So complex a society, of course, created many images that expressed its needs and hopes and aspirations, and not all mirrored egotism and the pursuit of fame. To some, Aretino or Cellini with his "Men like Benvenuto . . . stand above the Law" were tedious. Men yearn to belong, to be secure, to be accepted. At a time when the courtly graces were being practiced in London, Paris, Dijon, or Avignon, the rocky fortresses of Urbino, Rimini, or Orvieto were full of raw robber barons, uncouth, scarcely literate. Few despots could boast a long ancestry: within a mere three generations the Sforza rose from peasants to princes; even the Medici had modest origins. Rich Italy might become, but many of its prosperous men felt insecure in the luxury they could afford. Yet there existed, for them, antique patterns of behavior. The knights of the late Middle Ages had developed chivalry into a code of manners, a complex dance of love as intricate as a tarantula's; Greece and Rome offered guides to gentility and

The great classical educator Vittorino da Feltre, portrayed above in a medal by Pisanello, would not have approved of the passion for gambling and card playing that overtook Italy in the fifteenth century. In Venice it became so widespread, and ruined so many noble families, that the Council of Ten passed legislation prohibiting the sale of dice or cards. The young knight at left is one of a series of miniatures painted on a pack of Tarocchi cards. The handsome, elegantly dressed blade on the facing page was painted by the Florentine portraitist Bronzino. His subject is thought to be Guidobaldo II of Urbino.

sophistication. Above all there was Plato to teach them the efficacy of education; human nature, they hopefully believed, could be molded to what men might desire it to be.

This attitude was formulated most effectively by two men —Vittorino da Feltre, who ran an academy for boys and girls at Mantua, and Baldassare Castiglione, who became the arbiter of taste for the western world. Education, they both maintained, was more than learning: it was breeding, which might give what the heritage of blood had conferred on the nobles of the Middle Ages. Those knights had been required to learn the manners as well as the skills of the warrior's trade, to be "a verray parfit gentil knight," but the training did not confer *gentility.* That they inherited or, more rarely, won on the field of battle. The men of the Renaissance were concerned, however, to turn sow's ears into silk purses, peasants into princes.

The rough soldier of fortune and the uncouth merchant from the counting house wished to appear as men of breeding, as connoisseurs of taste, as representatives of antique virtue. Even though they spurned the fortune of birth, cared not a rap for legitimacy, they could not bear to be considered barbarous. Barbarity was shown in a man's deportment, in his attitude to women, in his pleasures, and, of course, in his possessions. Some things were easier to eradicate than others. Giovanni della Casa thought no perfect gentleman would thrust stinking fish under the noses of his friends, or closely examine the contents of his handkerchief, or sit so that the more intimate parts of his person were revealed, or pick his nose, or spit, or break wind. The fact that della Casa found it necessary to expatiate on such things in his handbook of gentlemanly behavior indicates the rudeness, the roughness, and the untutored nature of much of Renaissance society. But della Casa wanted more than behavior free from physical offense. He also stressed that no man could be a gentleman

without modesty, without being "very desirous of beautiful things, well-proportioned and comely," and squeamish of all that was not. To achieve this, Vittorino da Feltre and his imitators thought that all activities of the child should be directed to that end. Gentility, they maintained, was not an attribute of correct conversation or well-chosen clothes, on the contrary, it was the whole being of man; indeed, the highest perfection a man could achieve was to be immediately recognized as a gentleman.

The qualities of soul, the aspects of refinement and sensibility, which marked off the perfect gentleman were, of course, subject to endless debate, in which the classics were ransacked for precepts. Vittorino established a certain canon of requirements: the body as well as the soul needed to be brought to perfection. Exercise, quickness of eye, control of the muscles, and grace of movement were linked to moral qualities which the proper use of the body promoted—cour-

age, hardiness, stamina, indifference to pain and discomfort. Intellectual exercises, like physical ones, were aimed at building character, developing moral qualities, and for this purpose classical antiquities and mathematical knowledge had special merits: the former was full of the most excellent precepts, the latter revealed the harmonies of man and nature. Although many of the qualities which Vittorino sought in his pupils had been qualities of knightly perfection in earlier times, his attitude to boys and girls and to their educational needs was nearer far to Plato than to Aristotle. Above all, he believed that a gentleman should be literate and his aesthetic senses refined by teaching. Nor did he believe gentility to be conferred by birth; he educated the poor with the rich.

With the growing leisure and the growing secularization of life in the Renaissance, social pleasures became a pursuit in themselves. As ever with an emerging class, opulent but insecure, many yearned for the aristocratic distinctions of a

Baldassare Castiglione personified in his own life the high ideals of behavior set forth in The Courtier, *and when he died in 1529, Charles V sadly announced that "one of the world's noblest knights is now dead!" Raphael's portrait of the arbiter of Renaissance manners, dressed in the sophisticated court style of the time, appears on the facing page. Castiglione considered the knightly attributes—courage, horsemanship, and skill at arms, among others—requisites for the true gentleman, and no doubt the unknown knight of Carpaccio's painting (left) possessed these admirable qualities. The artist's customary attention to detail is seen in the exact rendering of the armor, animals, and flowers, and in the hovering hawk at upper left, about to strike its prey.*

previous age—long genealogies, emblazoned arms, the somewhat archaic extravagance of the joust and tourney. Some humanists, however, would have none of this hankering after the trappings of feudal nobility. "The longer the line of bold miscreants," wrote Poggio, "from which a man traces his descent, the further he is removed from true nobility." For him nobility lay in the individual heart and cultivated mind, in a man's nature and education—not in his birth. There was endless debate—snobbery, a desire for exclusiveness, drawing one way; a pride in the freshness and strength of their own world and times pulling another. In drawing rooms of courts, in the lounging places of the piazzas, in tents on the battlefield, in the country houses of bankers, men discussed over and over again the nature of men and the way of perfection. Or they argued on how they should act in love or in war, or what attributes they should cultivate, or which passions they should despise and suppress. Naturally men arose who be-

came by common consent arbiters of such matters, and the greatest of these was certainly Baldassare Castiglione, who was, as might be expected, the son of an ancient, noble, but very poor family, a man whose birth drew him toward the old, but who lacked any future except with the new and emerging world of his own time.

His long, grave, handsome face with its expression of almost careless elegance became the image of what an aristocrat and a gentleman should look like. Everyone—kings as well as commoners—immediately recognized his quality. His presence at court was eagerly sought, and he conferred immortality on Urbino by writing of the conversations about the nature of a gentleman in which he had participated under the aegis of its blue-stocking Duchess. And in his *Book of the Courtier* there is portrayed another image of Renaissance man, distinct from Aretino's man of destiny; for Castiglione's man was a social being.

Belonging though he did to the knightly class, Castiglione was open-minded about birth. It was better to be born noble, easier to become a true gentleman if one were, but it was not, he reluctantly conceded, essential. Knightly virtues were, however, a necessity, for fighting, the pursuit of arms, the cult of honor, were the life of action to which a gentleman must dedicate himself. So courage and strength were prime virtues, and the exercise of the body a necessity. Horsemanship, fencing, wrestling, swimming, tennis—all things which gave the body suppleness and grace and power were proper pursuits for a gentleman. Naturally he must excel, but should avoid seeming to do so; above all he must cultivate grace of movement, and this Castiglione thought could only be achieved by the practice of *sprezzatura*, nonchalance, "so as to conceal all art and make whatever is done and said appear to be without effort and without almost any thought about it." Polish was as necessary as prowess, in exercises of the mind as well as the

body. The gentleman was, of course, literate, knowledgeable about the classics, and eloquent. Learning must be lightly, negligently worn. Of course he should be quick in conversation but never thrusting, amusing but never mocking, humorous but never coarse, learned but never pedantic. And he must avoid being precious: eschew archaisms, never fear to use accepted colloquial speech, nor even bits of French and Spanish if they were in use in the society he frequented.

After the mind and the body came sensibility, connoisseurship. According to Castiglione, a gentleman might even be taught to paint—as, indeed, the Greek and Roman aristocrats had been. Music and its appreciation were necessities: music composed the mind, directed thought to gentle pleasures, inculcated a love of harmony. Music was essentially *right*. The lighter expressions of art as well as the weightier were proper pastimes—dances, masques, the parade of rhetoric, and, naturally, the pursuit of love (love, however, not

lust). The conquest of the heart, the possession of the mind, were a courtier's targets: the consolations of lesser delights were not altogether to be despised, even though they were improper subjects for conversation. A certain hypocrisy made for social ease.

About all activities, from the discussion of philosophy to the tilt of a hat, there must be ease, grace, and nonchalance; nobility must shine through. The princes of Italy might be murderers, adulterers, traitors, violators of boys and girls, but Castiglione depicted them as they desired themselves to be, just as Titian painted them as they wished to look—distinguished, set apart by their *virtù* and destiny from other men, yet full of ease, grace, nobility, and charm. The image created by Castiglione and his imitators, for his book enjoyed a vast success, increased the civility of Italians, made their courts a byword for sophisticated living. The cleanliness of their homes, the decorum at their tables, the beauty of their clothes and furnishings, the elegance of their manners, became models for the rude provincial gentry of the northern countries. Indeed for many generations Italy became an obsession for the less sophisticated nations of Europe, for it provided Europe not only with images of men, but also with a mirage of aristocratic and courtly life. Of course between image and reality there was frequently enough of a chasm. Most men could not live like Castiglione. Crude manners, vulgar habits, coarse pleasures, the instinctive life of which Aretino sang, lurked even in the Courtier. The importance of Castiglione lies in the fact that men thought they *ought* to be like his Courtier, and valued men who seemed to achieve it.

In the High Renaissance, aristocratic attitudes triumphed over the rough bourgeois spirit of its earlier days. Certainly in so doing the idea of what an aristocrat should be suffered a profound change. The armed knight, chivalry itself, became, as in *Don Quixote,* a pathetic joke. Much of the world

in which the new aristocracy moved with such elegance grew, after all, out of the activity of merchants, bankers, and seafarers, not out of feudalism. But the code of manners which evolved was not a merchant's code; it had little to do with the traditional attitudes of the middle class. By 1530 much that Alberti had written about the family in the fifteenth century wore an old-fashioned air, and lives devoted to the pursuit of gain were regarded as vulgar. Castiglione and others like him had helped to define the terms by which men were included in or excluded from gentility. It was essentially a private world with its own scale of values, but one that twinkled with recognition symbols. Style in the turn of a phrase or the cut of a cloak; fields of knowledge, of taste, even of sport, that a gentleman might know or practice; attitudes to love, to religion, to the prince—all these things marked off the gentleman from the man. The rich could achieve this exclusive world only by leaving the countinghouse behind and getting

away from the rattle of the loom.

This, as we shall see, had profound consequences, and still has, for Western society. But the importance of the dominating image of man created by the Renaissance lies in this: it arose after the heroic age of Italy's commercial and industrial expansion was past. It belonged to the gilded twilight world of a luxurious but defeated society—defeated not only by the discoveries of the outer world which had given Western Europe the future, but also by the exceptional resilience of its traditional class structure which triumphed over the pragmatism, the disorder, the violent economic and political changes, of Renaissance Italy.

It was against this world of Castiglione—a society at once charming, elegant, inbred, and effete—that Aretino and his followers had to rebel, and so present the image of a genius for which conventions are but naught. Castiglione taught men how to belong, Aretino how to live.

The humanist Duke of Urbino, a famous painting by Piero della Francesca.

Federigo da Montefeltro

by DENIS MACK SMITH

For a brief fifty years, a little hill town in the northern Marches was one of the great cultural centers of Europe. Urbino was the birthplace of Raphael and Bramante. Sculptors were drawn there from Milan and Florence, architects from Siena and Dalmatia, painters from Spain and tapestry workers from Flanders. Paolo Uccello worked inside its hospitable walls; so did Piero della Francesca and Melozzo da Forlì. Baldassare Castiglione emigrated from Mantua in order to live there, and was sent as the special envoy of Urbino to England, taking with him a painting commissioned from Raphael as a present for the English King. And as a result of Castiglione's much-translated *Book of the Courtier*, people all over the Western world heard of this remote mountain town, and learned from the standard of Urbino a code of manners, a way of courtesy and refinement, which became the norm of polite behavior.

The duchy of Urbino and its standards of taste in art and manners were created by Federigo da Montefeltro, whose unforgettable broken-nosed profile portrait by Piero della Francesca has helped to make him one of the best known of Renaissance personalities. Earlier Montefeltro princes had won no special reputation either in politics or culture. For three centuries they had governed no more than a few dozen square miles in the Apennines, sometimes as feudatories of the Holy Roman Emperor, but usually owing nominal allegiance to the Pope. The soil and climate were indifferent, but the precipitous hill villages were easily defensible, and their hardy mountaineers fought well, with the result that the rulers of Urbino remained independent, even though they never owned a port on the Adriatic and never penetrated far down the alluvial valleys into the fertile coastal plain of Ancona. Federigo, who ruled from 1444 to 1482, was the greatest of the Montefeltro dynasty. He consolidated several scattered mountain fiefs and extended them into a state three times larger than his original inheritance. His duchy, which reached from the environs of San Marino in the north to beyond Gubbio in the south, was about sixty miles each way at its longest and broadest, and included perhaps four hundred villages and 150,000 inhabitants. Its independence was maintained by playing off one potential enemy against another—Rome against Venice or Florence against Rome—and luckily two of the

strongest Italian states, Naples and Milan, were sufficiently remote from Urbino and sufficiently threatened by Rome or Venice to be generally friendly.

Like many prominent contemporaries, Federigo was born illegitimate. As a boy he spent a year as a hostage in Venice and then went to Mantua, where he was taught by Vittorino da Feltre, the greatest edutor of Renaissance Italy. Vittorino ran a boarding school where princes mixed with poor scholars and were given a severe classical education based on Latin and mathematics. The aim was to form character as well as mind and body. Federigo was taught frugal living, self-discipline, and a high sense of social obligation. He was made a connoisseur of literature and the arts, and also had to practice the manly sports, riding, dancing, and swordsmanship—all the accomplishments, in fact, which Castiglione later prescribed for the perfect courtier. Religion and scholarship were equally cultivated, but with a practical application: philosophy was made a guide to the art of living, and gracefulness and self-possession were inculcated as training for public life. As Federigo himself said later, Vittorino had instructed him "in all human excellence."

Few details are known about Federigo's early life. In 1432, at the age of ten, he was knighted by the Emperor, and five years later, after returning from Mantua to Urbino, he was married, after an engagement which dated from his early childhood. A few months later he set out for Lombardy with a company of eight hundred men to learn the art of war under a professional condottiere who was fighting against Gattamelata. Fighting was the occupation to which most contemporary princes were dedicated, and especially so in Urbino, where the Montefeltro family compensated for the poverty of the land and their remoteness from any significant trade routes by selling their services and their army to one side or other in most Italian wars. This was to be Federigo's chosen career. While his half brother Oddantonio succeeded their father as ruler of Urbino in 1443, Federigo himself seemed doomed to the traditionally subordinate life of the poor, illegitimate relation. But in 1444 the young Oddantonio, because of violent indignation against his debaucheries, was assassinated and his body torn to bits by the town mob. At first Federigo seems to have been refused entry to

Urbino, but eventually he was chosen to succeed "by the voice of the people" after promising not to revenge the murder.

Probably the chronicler who called this an election by popular acclaim was not romancing, for contemporaries unanimously praised the young Federigo, and later generations looked back to his reign as a golden age. Any patron as generous as he could no doubt buy adulation from that narrow but important group of writers which handed down what was likely to become the verdict of history, but with Federigo there were no dissentient voices even among commentators who did not benefit from his generosity. Unlike many Renaissance rulers, he avoided the accusation of cruelty and extravagant self-indulgence. He was magnanimous to his foes, and was rewarded handsomely when they preferred to surrender to him rather than run the risk of sack. He was also exceptional for his time in never deserting his allies for gain, and never was he known to break his word, not even when urged to do so by a papal legate. This honesty and trustworthiness were unusual in such a treacherous and brutal age. Federigo's great enemy, Sigismondo Malatesta, was in this respect more typical. Sigismondo was no less picturesque, no less refined and tasteful a patron, and equally fierce a fighter, but his atrocious cruelties were legendary; his dishonorable treatment of allies and his brutality toward subjects were common knowledge, and so was his failure to withstand such a prince as Federigo, who possessed the trust of ordinary people.

The biographers of Federigo (Raphael's father was the first of them) were concerned mainly with military exploits, and consequently there is little information about other aspects of his reign. We know, however, that he had to grant a charter of liberties at his accession. Taxes were to be reduced, some kind of public educational and medical service was promised, and the populace was to have some say in electing magistrates. Probably we should have heard further about this charter if he had governed harshly. According to one chronicler, "revisers" were sent round the country to investigate grievances and relieve poverty, and grain from Apulia was stored away so that prices could be kept steady when the harvest failed. Certainly Federigo was more gen-

erally accessible than most Renaissance rulers. Vespasiano da Bisticci described how at mealtimes the doors would be opened so that anyone might address him between courses. Furthermore, "When he rode out he met none who did not salute him and ask how he did. He went about with few attendants; none of them armed . . . He would often go afoot through his lands, entering now one shop and now another, and asking the workmen what their calling was, and whether they were in need of aught. So kind was he, that they all loved him as children love their parents. The country he ruled was a wondrous sight." This affability and accessibility were remarkable at a time when assassination was a common form of political behavior. The benevolence of Federigo's despotism was famous throughout Italy. Where his brother was said to have burnt a page alive for some minor lapse, Federigo was merciful to all offenses save blasphemy. The few recorded instances indicate a man who was just and humane, who prudently considered the welfare of his subjects. A ruler who was so often away on campaign could not afford serious discontent at home.

An important reason for this unusual domestic tranquillity was the profits of successful war, which kept taxes low. Federigo's salary, together with the wages of his army, and perhaps not least the booty they captured, were the means by which a poor country for a while became rich, civilized, and content. His employers included two kings of Naples, two dukes of Milan, and three popes, and even in winter, when not fighting, he insisted on a substantial retainer fee from them. He commanded a good price particularly because of his tried loyalty, for Federigo never kept up relations with both sides simultaneously and never surrendered an allegiance until the end of his stipulated *condotta*. His income also reflected the fact that for many years no other general possessed quite his prestige. Less brilliant than many previous condottieri, he was nevertheless more successful than any in avoiding defeat, and both Castiglione and Vespasiano proudly, if not quite accurately, boasted that he lost not a single battle even when heavily outnumbered.

Federigo was known for keeping exceptionally good discipline among troops. When he met the enemy, his usual technique was to be prudent in the early stages of a battle and impetuous and daring the moment he observed some weakness in his foe's deployment. As a young man he had lost an eye in a tournament, but otherwise he was fit and tough. People admired his swift unexpectedness, the mastery and modernity of his complicated siege works, his skill in carrying heavy guns through difficult mountain country, and his tested ability to endure fatigue, hunger, and wounds. Others admired his charity and the pains he took "to mitigate the horrors and miseries of war." Machiavelli derided the safety-first tactics of professional condottieri, and incorrectly asserted that not a single man was killed when Federigo fought the great Colleoni at Molinella in 1467. The two captains certainly met after this battle to exchange civilities, for chivalry was not extinct, but Machiavelli wrongly assumed that wars were necessarily going to be more decisive and more justifiable in the sixteenth century, when they became less humane and more destructive. Federigo had to satisfy his employers, or he would have been without a job. Wars of independence and imperialism were as real in the fifteenth century as later, even if they were smaller and less lethal.

Federigo's first regular patron was the powerful Sforza family, for whom in 1445 he helped to win Pesaro at the same time that Fossombrone was acquired for Urbino. This earned him an excommunication because it was at odds with papal ambitions, and it also increased the enmity of the Malatesta. Sigismondo Malatesta controlled a large stretch of coast above Ancona. His state and Federigo's were too close to avoid friction, and they shared an insecurity and lack of natural frontiers which led to quarrelsomeness and aggression. In between his struggles with Sigismondo, Federigo in 1448 raised an army for the Florentines. Several years later he contracted to serve the Aragonese dynasty in Naples, and this arrangement lasted almost all his life. The throne of Naples was at this point contested by the French Angevins, who found considerable support among the Neapolitan baronage, but Federigo in 1460 helped the Aragonese to resist the invaders, and in the following year he captured the important town of Aquila.

While Federigo was preoccupied in southern Italy, a Malatesta army invaded Urbino and papal

territory. The ferocious Sigismondo was therefore "canonized to hell" by the Pope and burnt in effigy before St. Peter's, while his excommunication for heresy, uxoricide, incest, and other crimes was pronounced by Cardinal Nicholas of Cusa. Federigo, as captain general of the Church's forces, seized this opportunity to destroy his rival's power for good. Sigismondo's heir was taken prisoner when Fano fell after a difficult and damaging siege, but Federigo released him without ransom despite the fact that contemporary practice made such hostages a legitimate and profitable asset. In addition to Fano, Senigallia was captured, and all that remained to the Malatesta was Rimini. Sigismondo, on his knees, publicly recanted his atheistical beliefs. Most of the Malatesta empire was claimed by the Pope and the papal nephews. Federigo, however, was allowed some fifty townships, which made him more powerful than any other ruler throughout the Marches and the Romagna. Although still a pigmy among the giant states of Milan, Venice, and Naples, he sometimes held the balance of power in Italy.

At this time the Papacy was trying to enforce its suzerainty and taxation rights over the seignorial families who ruled in central Italy. Pius II had exploited the rivalry between Montefeltro and Malatesta, employing one to subdue the other, and in 1465 his successor, Paul II, appointed Federigo gonfaloniere, or captain, of the Church's forces, in order to extend papal power still further. The condottiere from Urbino was now a famous man in Italy. In 1467 he was made commander of a league of states alarmed at the aggressive imperialism of Venice. The Venetians, retreating before the Turks on the far shore of the Adriatic, were attempting to compensate for these losses by pushing their empire westward and southward in Italy, to the consternation of their neighbors and the Pope. Federigo's own state was among those upon which both Rome and Venice might have ambitions, and this dual threat increased in direct proportion to his general political success.

In 1468 Sigismondo Malatesta died, and the Pope tried to annex Rimini. At this point Federigo, who had hitherto been more frightened of Venice, recognized the danger of further papal aggrandizement. He was a devout and loyal son of the Church, but not without qualification, for he could see that Venice and Rome between them were gradually swallowing up the Romagna. Even more alarming, the popes were trying to conquer principalities for their sons and nephews before another family succeeded them in their sacred office. Against this danger Montefeltro and Malatesta made common cause out of self-preservation, and instead of renewing his lapsed *condotta* with the Pope, Federigo supported the claims of Roberto Malatesta to Rimini. The ruler of Urbino, as captain of a league which included Naples and Milan, as well as other Romagnol *signori*, routed the papal army at Mulazzano.

Federigo's first wife, Gentile Brancaleoni, had died in 1457 leaving no children. He then married Battista, daughter of Alessandro Sforza of Pesaro. Battista's face is almost as well known to us from Piero's portrait as her husband's. Married at thirteen, she died at twenty-five, leaving one son, many daughters, and the reputation of being a formidable bluestocking who had governed the state in her husband's absence and could extemporize publicly in Latin. Federigo's half sisters had married into the neighboring dynasties of Sforza, Gonzaga, and Malatesta; two of his daughters were bestowed upon papal families, the Colonna and della Rovere, and a third upon Roberto Malatesta, the illegitimate son of his old enemy. The circle of appropriate families being limited, there was an inevitable tendency to inbreed.

In 1472, the year Battista died, Federigo was asked by Lorenzo de' Medici to raise an army against Volterra in Tuscany. (Lorenzo was defending the mining interests of Florentine citizens against nationalization in Volterra.) The military task was easy, but after the town had surrendered, Federigo could not restrain his soldiers from a terrible sack. Discipline in mercenary armies was always a problem, especially since the prospect of loot was an inducement for enlisting recruits, but this was a solitary lapse on Federigo's part. For himself he seized only a polyglot Bible of great rarity and beauty, and he was then escorted in triumph to a civic banquet in Florence and given a helmet adorned by Pollaiuolo. Another distinction received soon afterward was the Order of the Garter from England, and this emblem became a common motif in the decoration

of his palace. Such was his reputation outside Italy that special embassies arrived not only from England and Hungary but from Persia and Trebizond. A further triumph came in 1474, when Sixtus IV, solemnly receiving him in St. Peter's, changed his traditional title of Count to Duke. This acknowledged that Urbino had now reached a special position of independence and strength that distinguished it from other small city-states. It also acknowledged the Pope's need for military support for his nephews, and the formal concession of the title was designed to seal the alliance.

Federigo served Sixtus well. He tamed the insubordinate ruler of Città di Castello in Umbria, and in 1479 he campaigned against Florence after the Pope had tried and failed to assassinate Lorenzo de' Medici. Papal ambitions, however, soon became dangerous again when Sixtus began planning a conquest of Ferrara for yet another nephew. Federigo wrote to the Pope, urging him to turn against the Moslems who had just won a foothold in southern Italy; but the head of Christendom was more anxious to establish his family than to oppose the Turkish advance. As a result, war broke out over Ferrara, and Federigo aligned himself against papal aggression with Naples, Florence, Milan, Mantua, and Bologna, while his son-in-law, Roberto Malatesta, led the opposing papal forces. In the malarial swamps of Ferrara the rival commanders were stricken with the fever which was the greatest scourge of Renaissance Italy, and Federigo and Roberto died on the same day, September 10, 1482.

For a time Federigo's son and successor, Guidobaldo, was able to maintain the model state of Urbino, continuing his father's lavish patronage of the arts until his lack of success as a general lessened the profits of warfare upon which the economy depended. Then, in 1502, Pope Alexander VI persuaded Guidobaldo to loan the papal army his artillery, and at this crucial moment the Pope's son, Cesare Borgia, swept down on Urbino, forced its ruler to flee, and appropriated the priceless art collection, much of which he sold to pay his troops.

Perhaps Federigo himself would have fared no better. He had been the last of the great condottieri, and lived at a time when defense was much easier than attack. Shortly after his death that day had

passed; heavy artillery became more common and more efficient, and when it did the fortified hill towns and castles were suddenly vulnerable. The superiority of new weapons spelled ruin for the small Renaissance princedoms. A decade after his death, the perennial conflicts between Italian cities and families led to an invasion of the peninsula by France and Spain, and it was these new, large nation-states which were to dominate the next period of European history. For three centuries Italy was a convenient location where foreign armies could fight each other; and whereas Federigo had taken care to conduct his wars abroad, Urbino itself now became a battleground. By 1530 a series of invasions and counterinvasions had sacked Rome and Florence and desolated that world of small city-states which had engendered the Renaissance. Much of the surplus wealth which enlightened princes had once used for endowing culture and the arts was dissipated, and in this strange new world Urbino was too small and too awkwardly situated between rival empires to survive.

Federigo da Montefeltro is not remembered for his battles; he made no notable contribution to the art of war; his dynasty and dukedom disappeared. The one thing which survived intact was the memory of Federigo and his court of humanists and artists. In retrospect he and his son were spoken of alongside the magnificent Lorenzo. They were children of their time in a love of lavish display, in their burning drive for self-expression and a competitive urge for prestige. These instincts without doubt contributed in part to their devotion to art and learning, though both of them showed well enough that they also possessed a disinterested love of all things beautiful. Certainly they were far above all other contemporary rulers in character and intellectual refinement. Through them Urbino became a celebrated center of culture which attracted men of talent and renown from all of Europe; it was the place to which the Doria, Orsini, and Farnese families, as well as wealthy parents in other countries, sent their children to be educated. Castiglione, nostalgically recollecting that Federigo, in his day, was "the light of Italy," described life at Urbino in his delightful book *The Courtier,* in which he recorded a portrait of the model gentleman. As Vittoria Colonna wrote to him, "I do not wonder that you have depicted the

perfect courtier, for you had only to hold a mirror before you, and set down what you saw there." The conversations recorded in *The Courtier* took place in the palace which Federigo had built at Urbino.

Books of all kinds were Federigo's greatest joy, and Vespasiano described his efforts to build the great library in Urbino: "We come now to consider in what high esteem the Duke held all Greek and Latin writers, sacred as well as secular. He alone had a mind to do what no one had done for a thousand years or more; that is, to create the finest library since ancient times. He spared neither cost nor labor, and when he knew of a fine book, whether in Italy or not, he would send for it. It is now fourteen or more years since he began the library, and he always employed, in Urbino, in Florence, and in other places, thirty or forty scribes in his service . . . There are numerous Greek books by various authors, which when he was not able to get them otherwise, he sent for them, desiring that nothing should be wanting in any tongue which it was possible to acquire. There were to be seen Hebrew books, all that could be found in that language, beginning with the Bible, and all those who have commented upon it, Rabbi Moses and other commentators. Not only are those Hebrew books the Holy Scriptures, but also on medicine, on philosophy, and in all branches, all that could be acquired in that tongue.

"His lordship having completed this worthy task at the great expense of more than thirty thousand ducats, among the other excellent and praiseworthy arrangements which he made was this, that he undertook to give to each writer a title, and this he desired should be covered with crimson embellished with silver. He began, as has been noted above, with the Bible, as the foremost of all, and had it covered, as was said, with gold brocade. Then beginning with all the Doctors of the Church, he had each one covered with crimson and embellished with silver; and so with the Greek Doctors as with the Latins. As well philosophy, history, and books on medicine, and all the modern Doctors; in such a manner that there are innumerable volumes of this kind, a thing gorgeous to behold.

"In this library all the books are beautiful in the highest degree, all written with the pen, not one printed, that it might not be disgraced thereby; all elegantly illuminated, and there is not one that is not written on kidskin. There is a singular thing about this library, which is not true of any other; and this is, that of all the writers, sacred as well as profane, original works as well as translations, not a single page is wanting from their works in so far as they are in themselves complete; which can not be said of any other library, all of which have portions of the works of a writer, but not all; and it is a great distinction to possess such perfection."

Vespasiano had helped to collect this library. "Some time before," he wrote, "I went to Ferrara, being at Urbino at his lordship's court, and having catalogues of all the libraries of Italy, commencing with that of the Pope, of St. Mark's at Florence, of Pavia—and I had even sent to England to obtain a catalogue of the library of the university of Oxford —I compared these with that of the Duke, and I saw that all were faulty in one particular; that they had numerous copies of the same work, but they had not all the works of one writer complete as this had; nor were there writers of every branch as in this." Virtually the whole corpus of known classics was in the library, as well as Avicenna, Averroes, and medieval texts. Federigo was also a patron of contemporary literature. Ficino, Landino, Poggio, and Piero della Francesca dedicated writings to this man whom the humanist Piatti eulogized as *oraculum totius Italiae.*

The Duke was a competent Latinist in an age when close attention to the example of olden times was recommended for statesmen and generals. He was also an early enthusiast for Greek and hired instructors to teach it. He was able to discuss the Trojan war with Pius II and dared to contradict that learned scholar about the geography of Asia Minor. He liked to have Livy's histories read aloud at mealtimes, and was especially fond of Tacitus and the *Commentaries* of Caesar. "To return to letters," Vespasiano wrote, "the Duke of Urbino was well versed therein, not only in history and in the Holy Scriptures, but also in philosophy, which he studied many years under a distinguished teacher, Maestro Lazzaro, afterwards for his merits made Bishop of Urbino. He was instructed by Maestro Lazzaro in the *Ethics* of Aristotle, with and without comments, and he would also dispute over the difficult passages. He began to study logic with the keenest understanding,

and he argued with the most nimble wit that was ever seen. After he had heard the *Ethics* many times, comprehending them so thoroughly that his teachers found him hard to cope with in disputation, he studied the *Politics* assiduously . . . Indeed, it may be said of him that he was the first of the *Signori* who took up philosophy and had knowledge of the same. He was ever careful to keep intellect and virtue to the front, and to learn some new thing every day."

With all this, the Duke was devoutly religious. He heard Mass daily, and delighted in discussing religion with the abbot or mother superior of the monastic houses which he had endowed. He not only knew the Scriptures well, but was familiar with the great Doctors of the early Church and possessed an extensive theological library. He developed "a strong predilection" for the works of Saint Thomas Aquinas. He was no puritan, yet despite his four illegitimate children he was a moral man and, as befitted a pupil of Vittorino, recognized no dichotomy between humanist and Christian ideals.

Federigo's taste and qualities of mind were embodied most obviously in his famous palace at Urbino, for to him architecture was not only queen of the arts but the very summit of intellectual as well as aesthetic activity. Beginning around 1450 and building slowly, Federigo gradually amplified his ideas, and in 1468, after searching and failing to find an architect in the Tuscany which he so admired, he chose Luciano Laurana as chief architect. After Laurana there arrived Francesco di Giorgio, the foremost engineer in Italy, who dedicated to the Duke a celebrated treatise on architecture and gratefully acknowledged an indebtedness to his employer for many technical hints about fortification. Five architects and engineers are mentioned in a surviving list of palace officers.

The same list reveals the royal scale of life in the great palace. There were five hundred people in the court: in addition to knights and men-at-arms, these included two hundred servants, four teachers, an astrologer, five "readers aloud at meals," four men who transcribed manuscripts, two organists, the keeper of the bloodhounds, and a man who tended the camel-leopard.

But it was the buildings which struck people most.

Lorenzo de' Medici admired them, and they were to astonish Montaigne and a long succession of travelers. Federigo had furnished his palace, Castiglione wrote, "so well with every suitable thing that it seemed not a palace but a city in the form of a palace; and furnished it not only with what is customary such as silver vases, wall hangings of the richest cloth of gold, silk, and other like things, but for ornament he added countless ancient statues of marble and bronze, rare paintings, and musical instruments of every sort; nor did he wish to have anything there that was not most rare and excellent." Vespasiano da Bisticci was even more enthusiastic. (As a Florentine, Vespasiano judged by the highest standards.) "As to architecture it may be said that no one of his age, high or low, knew it so thoroughly. We may see, in the buildings he constructed, the grand style and the due measurement and proportion, especially in his palace, which has no superior amongst the buildings of the time, none so well considered, or so full of fine things. Though he had his architects about him, he always first realized the design and then explained the proportions and all else; indeed, to hear him discourse thereanent, it would seem that his chief talent lay in this art; so well he knew how to expound and carry out its principles."

Vasari was another Florentine who commented admiringly on the commodious apartments of Urbino's palace, and its stairways which were "more convenient and agreeable than any that had existed previously." Windows and doorways in admirable proportion, a graceful court with slender columns, a hanging garden, the great library, and room after room with splendid decorations in stucco and marble relief—all testifying to the sensibility as well as the munificence of the Duke. Intarsia, marquetry, polychrome marble, and *trompe-l'oeil* work on the walls represented what was best in current fashion all over Italy. Ambrogio da Milano and Domenico Rosselli of Pistoia were employed to design ornamental motifs on jambs, pediments, and chimney pieces, upon which the garter of England and the eagle of Montefeltro were frequently found. Typical of Federigo was that alongside his religious chapel, and with the same proportions, was another chapel dedicated to the Muses; and in his study were twenty-eight portraits of famous men in world his-

tory, among whom Homer was alongside Aquinas, Ptolemy with Saint Ambrose, and Seneca with Solomon. Typical also of this Renaissance prince was an inscription round the interior court which told how the great Federigo had raised this palace for his own glory and for his posterity.

In all respects, Federigo had represented the best in his age, and his example endured long after he had passed away. Through his practice the teachings of Vittorino inspired a small but noble society which, even when conquered politically, made a conquest of all Europe. At Urbino could be found an intellectual elite which believed that an integrated and disciplined education would result in proper behavior and a proper sense of duty toward God and man. Federigo's classical upbringing and intellectual curiosity in no way undermined, but rather reinforced, the teachings of orthodox religion. Nor did he tend to that all too common form of humanism which despised science; on the contrary, Vespasiano praised the Duke's skill in geometry and arithmetic. As for the arts, Federigo was enthusiastic about more than architecture. His musical tastes perhaps show the influence of contemporary Flanders, the same influence which brought Justus of Ghent and Flemish savants and textile artisans to his court. "He delighted greatly in music," Vespasiano noted, "understanding vocal and instrumental alike, and maintained a fine choir with skilled musicians and many singing boys. He had every sort of instrument in his palace and delighted in their sound, also the most skillful players. He preferred delicate to loud instruments,

caring little for trombones and the like."

Anything loud and harsh was anathema at the court of Urbino. Dress had to be sober, demeanor quiet, conversation lively but gentle. Women were given an active and respected place in this world, setting new standards for polite society. Vittorino's educational goal had been to create the complete all-round person who was courteous, upright, sensitive, but at the same time active. Federigo himself was such a man. He possessed a robust physique which resisted wounds and great hardship, yet the rough practice of war left his finer feelings unimpaired. Everyone knew him to be a man of honor as well as courage. His official portraits show him not so much as a warrior but as an intellectual, either reading, contemplating, listening to a lecture, or at prayer. Unlike many Renaissance princes, he lived without excess, "eating plain food and no sweetmeats," and the five hundred people who composed his court followed as orderly an existence as in a monastery: "Here was no romping or wrangling, but everyone spoke with becoming modesty."

What little we know about this court of Urbino gives us a precious insight into the civilization of the Renaissance in Italy at its most admirable. Piero della Francesca's work has partially perished, the superb ducal library was swallowed up by the Vatican, and Federigo's portraits were scattered to Florence, Milan, and Windsor. But time cannot easily erase his memory and example. Had he been more representative of his class, the course of the Renaissance might have followed a still more brilliant path.

Rules for Gentlemen

Intense self-consciousness marked the Renaissance man. Increasingly aware of his new importance as expounded by Pico della Mirandola and other humanists, he strove continually to prove himself worthy in the eyes of his fellows. In the open society in which he lived, where genius and character, rather than birth, were the measures of excellence, the highest goal of the educated man was to be considered a gentleman at first sight. Every detail of behavior and deportment was analyzed and discussed, and countless treatises were written on education, conduct, politeness, and good usage, as those who had risen to wealth and power through commercial or military means searched for gentility and acceptance. An example of their quest for perfection was the *Fior di Virtù,* a compilation of maxims and mores from ancient and Biblical sources, which went through sixty-six editions in less than thirty years. The most important book on the subject, however, was Castiglione's *The Courtier,* written about the court of Urbino and published in 1528. It set the pattern for gentlemanly conduct not only for its own time, but for later generations of European society and for modern times as well. With a few exceptions, its standards of propriety concur with those in general usage today. The excerpts on the following pages are taken from various Renaissance writings on behavior, and the woodcuts used in illustration are all from contemporary sources. The picture above appeared originally in a 1493 Florentine treatise on the game of chess.

The Dignity of Man, *excerpted below, was written by Giovanni Pico della Miran-dola in 1486 and reflects man's new importance. At left is the frontispiece to a 1490 edition of* Fior di Virtù, *and below, a 1523 illustration for a play by Terence.*

Now the Highest Father, God the Architect, according to the laws of His secret wisdom, built this house of the world, this world which we see, the most sacred temple of His divinity. He adorned the region beyond the heavens with Intelligences, He animated the celestial spheres with eternal souls, and He filled the excrementary and filthy parts of the lower world with a multitude of animals of all kinds. But when His work was finished, the Artisan longed for someone to reflect on the plan of so great a creation, to love its beauty, and to admire its magnitude. When, therefore, everything was completed . . . He began at last to consider the creation of man. But among his archetypes there was none from which He could form a new offspring, nor in His treasure houses was there any inheritance which He might bestow upon His new son, nor in the tribunal seats of the whole world was there a place where this contemplator of the universe might sit. . . . Finally the Great Artisan ordained that man, to whom He could give nothing belonging only to himself, should share in common whatever properties had been peculiar to each of the other creatures. He received man, therefore, as a creature of undetermined nature, and placing him in the middle of the universe, said this to him: "Neither an established place, nor a form belonging to you alone, nor any special function have We given you, O Adam, and for this reason, that you may have and possess, according to your desire and judgment, whatever place, whatever form, and whatever functions you shall desire. . . . I have set you at the center of the world, so that from there you may more easily survey whatever is in the world. We have made you neither heavenly nor earthly, neither mortal nor immortal, so that, more freely and more honorably the molder and maker of yourself, you may fashion yourself in whatever form you shall prefer. . . . O supreme generosity of God the Father! O highest and marvelous felicity of man! To him it is granted to have whatever he chooses, to be whatever he wills.

This selection, from a biography written shortly after 1460 by Leon Battista Alberti, indicates many of the attributes considered worthy in men of his time. Apparently modesty was not one of them, however; the subject of the biography was Alberti himself. At the upper right is a woodcut from a 1485 Neapolitan edition of Aesop's Fables; *the one below comes from a 1499 book on Roman perspectives.*

In everything suitable to one born free and educated liberally, he was so trained from boyhood that among the leading young men of his age he was considered by no means the last. For, assiduous in the science and skill of dealing with arms and horses and musical instruments, as well as in the pursuit of letters and the fine arts, he was devoted to the knowledge of the most strange and difficult things. And finally he embraced with zeal and forethought everything which pertained to fame. . . . he strove so hard to attain a name in modeling and painting that he wished to neglect nothing by which he might gain the approbation of good men. His genius was so versatile that you might almost judge all the fine arts to be his. Neither ease nor sloth held him back, nor was he ever seized by satiety in carrying out what was to be done. . . . to him letters, in which he delighted so greatly, seemed sometimes like flowering and richly fragrant buds, so that hunger or sleep could scarcely distract him from his books. . . . when letters began to be displeasing to him, he turned to music and painting and exercise. He played ball, hurled the javelin, ran, leaped, wrestled, and above all delighted in the steep ascent of mountains; he applied himself to all these things for the sake of health rather than sport or pleasure. As a youth he excelled in warlike games. With his feet together, he could leap over the shoulders of men standing by; he had almost no equal among those hurling the lance. An arrow shot by his hand from his chest could pierce the strongest iron breastplate. . . . he could throw an apple into the air so high that it would go far beyond the top of the highest roofs. . . . He delighted in the organ and was considered an expert among the leading musicians. . . . at the age of twenty-four he turned to physics and the mathematical arts. He did not despair of being able to cultivate them sufficiently, because he perceived that in them talent rather than memory must be employed. . . . When he heard that a learned man of any kind had arrived, he would at once work his way into a position of familiarity with him and thus from any source whatsoever he began to learn what he was ignorant of. . . . He wholly despised the pursuit of material gain [and] he always served genius rather than fame. His mind was never free from meditation and deliberation. He rarely stayed at home out of the public eye without deliberating upon something, and also pondered at dinner between courses. . . . even when he was discussing serious matters, he always showed himself agreeable, and though maintaining his dignity, even gay. . . . He could endure pain and cold and heat . . . showing by example that men can do anything with themselves if they will. . . . He took extraordinary and peculiar pleasure in looking at things in which there was any mark of beauty or adornment. . . . When his favorite dog died he wrote a funeral oration for him. Whatever was done by man with genius and with a certain grace, he held to be almost divine; and he so respected anything achieved that he insisted even poor writers were worthy of praise. The sight of gems, flowers, and especially pleasant places more than once restored him from illness to good health.

In 1489 Pope Innocent VIII, seeking an alliance between the papal see and the republic of Florence, made Giovanni de' Medici a cardinal. Since Giovanni (who later became Pope Leo X) was only thirteen, it was only natural that his father, Lorenzo, should write him a letter of advice, portions of which are printed here. The illustration is from a book of Lorenzo's canzoni, *published in Florence in 1533.*

You, and all of us who are interested in your welfare, ought to esteem ourselves highly favored by Providence, not only for the many honors and benefits bestowed on our house, but more particularly for having conferred upon us, in your person, the greatest dignity we have ever enjoyed. . . . The first that I would therefore suggest to you is that you ought to be grateful to God, and continually recollect that it is not through your merits, your prudence, or your solicitude, that this event has taken place, but through His favor, which you can only repay by a pious, chaste, and exemplary life. . . . Endeavor therefore to alleviate the burden of your early dignity by the regularity of your life and by your perseverance in those studies which are suitable to your profession. . . . I well know, that as you are now to reside at Rome, that sink of all iniquity, the difficulty of conducting yourself by these admonitions will be increased. The influence of example is itself prevalent; but you will probably meet with those who will particularly endeavor to corrupt and incite you to vice . . . To these difficulties you ought to oppose yourself with the greater firmness, as there is at present less virtue amongst your brethren of the college. . . . To give you particular directions as to your behavior and conversation would be a matter of no small difficulty. I shall therefore only recommend that in your intercourse with the cardinals and other men of rank, your language be unassuming and respectful, guiding yourself, however, by your own reason, and not submitting to be impelled by the passions of others, who, actuated by improper motives, may pervert the use of their reasons. . . . You are not only the youngest cardinal in the college, but the youngest person that ever was raised to that rank; and you ought therefore to be the most vigilant and unassuming . . . With those of less respectable character converse not with too much intimacy; not merely on account of the circumstance in itself, but for the sake of public opinion. . . . Silk and jewels are not suitable for persons in your station. Your taste will be better shown in the acquisition of a few elegant remains of antiquity, or in the collection of handsome books, and by your attendants being learned and well-bred rather than numerous. . . . Let your own food be plain, and take sufficient exercise, for those who wear your habit are soon liable, without great caution, to contract infirmities. . . . Be attentive therefore to your conduct, and confide in others too little rather than too much. There is one rule which I would recommend to your attention in preference to all others. Rise early in the morning. This will not only contribute to your health, but will enable you to arrange and expedite the business of the day . . . You will probably be desired to intercede for the favors of the Pope on particular occasions. Be cautious, however, that you trouble him not too often; for his temper leads him to be most liberal to those who weary him least with their solicitations. This you must observe, lest you should give him offense, remembering also at times to converse with him on more agreeable topics; and if you should be obliged to request some kindness from him, let it be done with that modesty and humility which are so pleasing to his disposition. Farewell.

The excerpts below, by Aeneas Silvius Piccolomini, later Pope Pius II, were addressed to the young king of Hungary and Bohemia, who had sought his advice on education. At the upper right is a woodcut from the Rime *of Bernardo Bellincioni, published in Milan in 1493. Below is an illustration from a spelling primer.*

As regards a boy's physical training, we must bear in mind that we aim at implanting habits which will prove beneficial during life. So let him cultivate a certain hardness which rejects excess of sleep and idleness in all its forms. . . . Too much importance can hardly be attached to right bearing and gesture. . . . A boy should be taught to hold his head erect, to look straight and fearlessly before him, and to bear himself with dignity, whether walking, standing, or sitting.

Every youth destined to exalted position should further be trained in military exercises. It will be your destiny to defend Christendom against the Turk. It will thus be an essential part of your education that you be early taught the use of the bow, of the sling, and of the spear; that you drive, ride, leap, and swim. These are honorable accomplishments in everyone, and therefore not unworthy of the educator's care.

As regards the use of wine, remember that we drink to quench thirst, and that the limit of moderation is reached when the edge of intellect is dulled. A boy should be brought up to avoid wine, for he possesses a store of natural moisture in the blood and so rarely experiences thirst.

Birth, wealth, fame, health, vigor, and beauty are, indeed, highly prized by mankind, but they are one and all of the nature of accidents; they come and they go. But the riches of the mind are a stable possession, unassailable by fortune, calumny, or time. . . . Literature is our guide to the true meaning of the past, to a right estimate of the present, to a sound forecast of the future. Where letters cease, darkness covers the land; and a prince who cannot read the lessons of history is a helpless prey of flattery and intrigue.

In conversation kindness and courtesy are always attractive; pertinacity or pretentiousness are odious; a turgid, affected style arouses contempt. Insincerity or malice are, of course, not mere defects in form but positive sins. So let your address be frank, outspoken, self-respecting, manly.

We must . . . insist upon the overwhelming importance of memory, which is in truth the first condition of capacity for letters. A boy should learn without effort, retain with accuracy, and reproduce easily. Rightly is memory called "the nursing mother of learning." It needs cultivation, however, whether a boy be gifted with retentiveness or not. Therefore, let some passage from poet or moralist be committed to memory every day.

I would wish the Courtier . . . endowed by nature not only with talent and with beauty of countenance and person, but with that certain grace which we call an "air," which shall make him at first sight pleasing and lovable to all who see him.

I would have him more than passably learned in letters, at least in those studies which we call the humanities. Let him be conversant not only with the Latin language, but with Greek as well, because of the abundance and variety of things that are so divinely written therein. Let him be versed in the poets, as well as in the orators and historians, and let him be practiced also in writing verse and prose, especially in our own vernacular; for, besides the personal satisfaction he will take in this, in this way he will never want for pleasant entertainment with the ladies, who are usually fond of such things.

He should also know how to swim, jump, run, throw stones; for, besides their useful-ness in war, it is frequently necessary to show one's prowess in such things, whereby a good name is to be won, especially with the crowd (with whom one must reckon after all). Another noble exercise and most suitable for a man at court is the game of tennis which shows off the disposition of the body, the quickness and litheness of every member, and all the qualities that are brought out by almost every other exercise.

When dancing in the presence of many and in a place full of people, I think he should maintain a certain dignity, though tempered with a fine and airy grace of movement; and even though he may feel himself to be most agile and a master of time and measure, let him not attempt those quick movements of foot and those double steps which . . . little befit a gentleman.

A man ought always be a little more humble than his rank would require; not ac-cepting too readily the favors and honors that are offered him, but modestly refus-ing them while showing that he esteems them highly, yet in such a way as to give the donor cause to press them upon him the more urgently. For the greater the resistance shown in accepting them in this way, the more will the prince who is granting them think himself to be esteemed, and his benefaction will appear the greater the more the recipient of it shows his appreciation and how great he con-siders the honor done him by it.

The method that the Courtier ought to follow in making his love known to the Lady would be to reveal it to her by actions rather than words, for it is certainly true that more of love's affection is sometimes revealed by a sigh, by a reverence, by timidity, than by a thousand words; next, by making his eyes be faithful mes-sengers in bearing the embassies of his heart, since they often reveal the passion within more effectively than the tongue itself, or letters, or messengers; and they not only reveal thoughts but they often kindle love in the beloved's heart.

Castiglione's The Courtier, *from which the idealistic and often snobbish excerpts on these pages are taken, became the handbook of proper behavior for generations of European gentlemen. The woodcuts at left are from a 1491 Florentine edition of the* Fior di Virtù. *On the facing page are a scene from* The Story of Two Lovers *(right), and an illustration from a 1523 edition of Boccaccio's* Decameron *(bottom).*

Our Courtier will not indulge in foolish presumption; he will not be the bearer of unpleasant news; he will not be careless in speaking words which can offend, instead of trying to please; he will not be obstinate and contentious, as are some who seem to delight only in being troublesome and obnoxious like flies, and who make a profession of contradicting everybody, spitefully and indiscriminately. He will not be an idle or lying babbler nor a boaster or inept flatterer, but will be modest and reserved, observing always (and especially in public) the reverence and respect that befit a servant in relation to his master . . .

I am not satisfied with our Courtier unless he be also a musician, and unless, besides understanding and being able to read music, he can play various instruments. For, if we rightly consider, no rest from toil and no medicine for ailing spirits can be found more decorous or praiseworthy in time of leisure than this; and especially in courts where, besides the release from vexations which music gives to all, many things are done to please the ladies, whose tender and delicate spirits are readily penetrated with harmony and filled with sweetness.

[Chess] is certainly a pleasing and ingenious amusement . . . but it seems to me to have one defect, which is that it is possible to have too much knowledge of it, so that whoever would excel in the game must give a great deal of time to it, as I believe, and as much study as if he would learn some noble science or perform well anything of importance; and yet in the end, for all his pains, he only knows how to play a game. Thus, I think a very unusual thing happens in this, namely, that mediocrity is more to be praised than excellence.

Giovanni della Casa, a papal nuncio and great friend of Cardinal Bembo, wrote the
Galateo *between 1551 and 1555, probably for a young nephew, Annibale Rucellai.*

To help you understand how to behave I must first teach you that your conduct should not be governed by your own fancy, but in consideration of the feelings of those whose company you keep. . . . For this reason it is a repulsive habit to touch certain parts of the body in public, as some people do. . . . Again, when you have blown your nose, you should not open your handkerchief and inspect it, as though pearls or rubies had dropped out of your skull. Such behavior is nauseating and is more likely to lose us the affection of those who love us than to win us the favor of others. . . . It is not polite to scratch yourself when you are seated at table. You should also take care, as far as you can, not to spit at mealtimes, but if you must spit, then do so in a decent manner. . . . We should also be careful not to gobble our food so greedily as to cause ourselves to get hiccups or commit some other unpleasantness . . . It is also bad manners to clean your teeth with your napkin, and still worse to do it with your finger, for such conduct is unsightly. It is wrong to rinse your mouth and spit out wine in public, and it is not a polite habit, when you rise from the table, to carry your toothpick either in your mouth, like a bird making its nest, or behind your ear. . . . It is also unmannerly to sprawl over the table or to fill both sides of your mouth so full with food that your cheeks are bloated. And you must do nothing to show that you have found great relish in the food or the wine, for these are the customs of the tavern and the alehouse. . . . I do not think it right to offer food from one's own plate to anyone else, unless the person who offers it is of much more exalted rank, in which case it would be a mark of honor for the other. If both are of the same rank, it is rather a presumption of superiority for one of them to offer his food to the other, and sometimes the tidbit might not be to his taste. . . . No one must take off his clothes, especially his lower garments, in public, that is, in the presence of decent people, because this is not the right place for undressing. . . . You should neither comb your hair nor wash your hands in the presence of others, because—except for washing the hands before going in to a meal—such things are done in the bedroom and not in public. . . . Again, you must not appear in public with your nightcap on your head or fasten your hose when other people are present. . . . Anyone who makes a nasty noise with his lips as a sign of astonishment or disapproval is obviously imitating something indecent, and imitations are not too far from the truth.

RENAISSANCE MEN

The individual and his aspirations became the new focus of thought during the Renaissance. And the liberal arts, pictured above in a fifteenth-century manuscript, symbolized this new goal of universality. Educators such as Vittorino taught men to be well-rounded individuals; Castiglione set forth the many skills necessary for the ideal gentleman; and Leonardo's catholicity was an example which many sought to imitate. In every field of endeavor and in all classes of society, individuals, inspired by wider freedoms and wider learning, realized new goals: doctors were polished humanists; artists excelled in the sciences; monks created artistic masterpieces; and aristocrats became accomplished musicians. The following pages suggest a few of the areas in which individuals achieved new heights of creativity.

Franchino Gafori (1451–1522) was a member of Lodovico Il Moro's brilliant circle of scholars and artists, a teacher at Il Moro's famous music school in Milan, and the most eminent Italian theorist of his time. Woodcut frontispieces from two of his many books show him (left) teaching a class in principles of harmony and (below) demonstrating the hexachord system on the organ.

THE MUSICIAN

The growing enthusiasm for popular music during the Renaissance typified man's new desire for freedom and pleasure. Music played an essential part in the great pageants and festivals of the Medici and other princes; street singers serenaded the Florentines on summer nights; crowds flocked to hear the famous cathedral organists of Milan and Florence; and the Sistine and Julian choirs in Rome attracted the best singers in Europe. The spirit of humanism which inspired poets also affected such musicians as the blind Francesco Landino, whose graceful and emotional *ars nova* compositions fill the pages of one of the loveliest of all musical manuscripts, the *Squarcialupi Codex.*

Despite its new popularity, however, music was the only art in which the Italians lagged behind in technical achievement. There were, of course, a few outstanding individual contributors: Franchino Gafori, the choirmaster of Milan, wrote several books on theory which revolutionized the rules of composition and harmony; and the works of Ottaviano de' Petrucci, the first musical printer, have rarely been matched for beauty or accuracy. But by and large most new developments up to the mid-sixteenth century were fostered by the French. Italy's principal contribution was to free music from the bonds of religious supervision. Princely salons became the centers of music during the Renaissance and vied with each other for the services of leading musicians. Humanist poems were now set to music, new and beautiful instruments were designed, and Castiglione made musical ability a requisite for his ideal courtier. In the gay and worldly atmosphere of the courts, music was able to free itself from the fetters of ancient form and began to develop along new and melodious lines.

Fra Luca Pacioli and a student, thought to be Guidobaldo, the young Duke of Urbino.

THE MATHEMATICIAN

The classical ideals of proportion and perspective espoused by Alberti and Piero della Francesca made a lasting impression on one of their young students, Fra Luca Pacioli. Instilled with a desire to see their theories put to use in everyday life, Pacioli wrote numerous mathematical books, the most important of which was a huge volume, published in 1494, which laid the foundation for most modern study of the subject. Fra Luca was the head of his monastery in his later years, as well as an inspiring teacher and author. He spent most of his time, however, in the intellectual circles of Urbino and Milan, where he was a friend of Leonardo's and tried to persuade the artist to publish his scientific drawings. But Pacioli's greatest fame came from his publication of the double-entry bookkeeping system, which was of vast importance to Italy's merchants and affected the entire business world. It was that masterwork which earned him the title, "Father of Bookkeeping."

Jupiter with two signs of the zodiac

THE ASTROLOGER

Whatever the advances in scientific thinking, there remained a widespread belief that every human action and natural occurrence was ultimately directed by the stars. Astrologers abounded, they were employed by nearly every court, and throughout Italy they busily prepared horoscopes, advising rich and poor upon the most propitious timing for everything from declaring war to planting trees. Nearly all learned men conceded the power of the planets. Even though he relegated stargazers to hell, Dante admitted the influence of cosmic forces on the soul; Pico della Mirandola wrote a treatise against astrologers, but when he died on the day they had predicted for him, his arguments lost their cogency; and even in the Church, which frowned upon the occult as bordering on heresy, Pope Julius II set the time of his coronation according to astrological calculations. In the universities, too, astrology was accorded high importance, and was regarded both as a major science itself and as the basis for all the natural sciences.

A detail from the astrological tables of G. Bianchini (left) shows the author presenting a copy to his patron, the Emperor Frederick III.

Madonna and Child *by Fra Filippo Lippi*

THE MONK

Within the monasteries of Italy were some of the brightest talents of an exceptional age—men of the caliber of Fra Angelico, Fra Filippo Lippi, Fra Luca Pacioli, and Fra Bartolommeo. And beyond the works of art produced by members of their orders, priors commissioned some of the masterpieces of the Renaissance. The monasteries continued their traditional sponsorship of schools, hospitals, and charitable institutions, but in this worldly era their secularism and immorality—tales of which fill the pages of Boccaccio's *Decameron* and other contemporary writings—were often more apparent than their virtues. Scandals and concubinage were common, and Filippo Lippi, a Carmelite, shocked even that lusty age when he ran off with a young nun. (When offered freedom from his vows to marry her, he refused, since matrimony was more binding than the monastic life.) Savonarola and other reformers fought to stem the moral laxity, but it continued to engulf all but a few of the strictest orders.

The model for Lippi's Virgin (above) was the young nun with whom he eloped. The artist's portrait, in a detail from his tomb, is at right.

THE DOCTOR

The superstitions, nostrums, and miracle cures of medieval medicine began to give way during the Renaissance to many new advances. Artists spurred on the study of anatomy, effective quarantine had controlled leprosy, hospitals multiplied, and laws restricted quack doctors. The greatest challenge to Renaissance medicine was an epidemic which broke out in Naples in 1495. The "love pestilence," as it was called, necessitated new treatments—among them city hygiene laws prohibiting mixed public baths, and a mercury cure which improved on traditional herbal remedies. A wealthy and brilliant physician, Girolamo Fracastoro, wrote a long Latin poem on the causes, symptoms, and care of the disease. Fracastoro was extremely acute in most of his observations and later won great fame for his advanced studies of other contagious infections (he was the first to recognize typhus), but in his poem he bowed to the universal belief in astrology, naming the disease syphilis after a mythical shepherd, Syphilus, who was supposedly stricken with it for offending the god Apollo.

Above is a portrait of Girolamo Fracastoro. A Fifteenth-century manuscript (below) shows doctors caring for hospitalized patients.

Cellini's portrait (by Giorgio Vasari) appears at far right. The ornate gold cup above, with its sphinx handle and brilliantly enameled dragon and tortoise base, reflects his elaborate work as well as the sumptuous taste of the time. At the right is a study for his famous statue of Perseus which still stands in the Loggia dei Lanzi in Florence. Cellini spent nine years completing it and the remainder of his life trying in vain to collect his payment.

THE CRAFTSMAN

"Men like Benvenuto, unique in their profession, stand above the law," said Paul III of Cellini, and the craftsman took him at his word. His brawls, love affairs, violent tempers, and escapades resulted in numerous enmities, eight children (one of whom was legitimate), and a bevy of dead men. But as an artist he was hard-working, tremendously talented, and his services were in demand by pope and princes alike. Michelangelo called him the "greatest goldsmith of whom the world has ever heard," and although few of his innumerable ornate works survive, the still-extant saltcellar made for Francis I and the portrait medal of Bembo amply justify the egotism which fills his *Autobiography*. That account gives a vivid picture not only of its famous author, whose seventy-one years saw countless adventures and endless wrangles over his many commissions, but also of the life of a Renaissance craftsman par excellence.

343

WOMEN
OF THE RENAISSANCE

François Villon, the vagabond poet of France, wondered, as he drifted through the gutters and attics of fifteenth-century Paris, where were the famous women of the days long past? Where Héloïse, for whom Abelard had endured such degradation? Where Thaïs, Alis, Haremburgis, where the Queen Blanche with her siren's voice, where were these fabled, love-haunted, noble women, of more than human beauty? Gone, he thought, gone forever. Even the rough Viking bards sang of their heroic women, of Aud the Deep-minded who "hurt most whom she loved best." The lives of these fateful, tragic women, medieval heroines of love and sorrow, became themes of epic and romance which were told in the courts of princes; yet even as Villon bewailed their loss, men were growing tired of them.

The age of heroes was dying. The unrequited love of Dante for Beatrice, the lyrical attachment of Petrarch for Laura, and, in a different mood, the agreeable pleasantries of Boccaccio, had domesticated love, making it more intimate. The dawn of a carefree, less fate-ridden attitude to woman was gentle, undramatic, and slow, beginning way back with the wandering troubadours and scholars who moved from castle to farm, from monastery to university, singing their light-hearted lyrics to earn their keep.

> *Down the broad way do I go,*
> *Young and unregretting,*
> *Wrap me in my vices up,*
> *Virtue all forgetting,*
> *Greedier for all delight*
> *Than heaven to enter in:*
> *Since the soul in me is dead,*
> *Better save the skin.*

Sit you down amid the fire,
Will the fire not burn you?
Come to Pavia, will you
Just as chaste return you?
Pavia, where Beauty draws
Youth with finger-tips,
Youth entangled in her eyes,
Ravished with her lips.

So sang the nameless Archpoet, young, consumptive, in love, as he wandered down to Salerno to read medicine. The time was the twelfth century—three hundred years before the haunting love poems of Lorenzo de' Medici were written. Yet the sentiments of both men were a part of the same process, part of the lifting tide of Southern Europe's prosperity, of its growing population, of the sophistication that wealth and leisure brought: for in leisure lies dalliance. The wandering scholars were few; their mistresses, chatelaines or girls of the

town: yet they were the naïve harbingers of a world that was to reach its fullness in Italy in the fifteenth century.

It was the new prosperity that influenced the lives of women most profoundly. It brought them fresh opportunities for adornment; it increased their dowries and their value. It emancipated many from the drudgery of the household and from the relentless, time-consuming demands of children. Women entered more fully into the daily lives and pursuits of men. And, of course, the new delights of the Renaissance world—painting, music, literature—had their feminine expression. Much of the artistic world was concerned with the pursuit of love in all its guises. Women were a part of art.

Except for the very lowest ranks of society, women were inextricably entangled in the concept of prosperity, and their virtue was a marketable commodity. They were secluded from birth to marriage, taught by women and priests, kept constantly under the closest supervision in the home or in the con-

In a square outside the Baptistery of Florence, richly dressed couples parade under a striped canopy in celebration of the Adimari wedding, which took place in the middle of the fifteenth century. At far left, pages carry serving vessels of gold, while musicians play a fanfare on trumpets decorated with the lily of Florence. Both visitors and servants wear bright colors, but those in the wedding party are dressed mainly in black and gold. Paintings such as this often decorated the bride's cassone, *a wedding chest designed to contain her trousseau.*

vent. Marriage came early: twelve was not an uncommon age, thirteen usual, fifteen was getting late, and an unmarried girl of sixteen or seventeen was a catastrophe. Women conveyed property and could often secure a lift in the social scale for their families. Even more important was the use of women to seal alliances between families, whether princely, noble, or mercantile. The great Venetian merchants interlocked their adventures overseas with judicious marriages at home. The redoubtable Vittoria Colonna was betrothed at the age of four to the Marquis of Pescara to satisfy her family's political ambition. Lucrezia Borgia's early life was a grim enough reminder of the dynastic value of women. Her fiancés were sent packing, her husbands murdered or declared impotent, so that Alexander VI could use her again and again in the furtherance of his policies. In less exalted ranks of society women were still traded. It took Michelangelo years of horse-trading to buy a young Ridolfi wife for his nephew and so push

his family up a rank in Florentine society. Marriages so arranged were symbolic of power and social status as well as of wealth, and their celebration, in consequence, demanded the utmost pomp and splendor that the contracting parties could afford. Important Venetian marriages were famed for an extravagance that not even the Council of Ten could curb. The festivities began with an official proclamation in the Doge's Palace. The contracting parties and their supporters paraded the canals *en fête.* Gondoliers and servants were dressed in sumptuous livery; the façades of the palaces were adorned with rare Oriental carpets and tapestries; there were bonfires, fireworks, balls, masques, banquets, and everywhere and at all times—even the most intimate—serenades by gorgeously dressed musicians. Of course, such profusion acted like a magnet for poets, dramatists, rhetoricians, painters, and artists of every variety. For a few ducats a wandering humanist would pour out a few thousand words, full of recon-

dite references to gods and heroes; poets churned out epithalamiums before they could be asked; and painters immortalized the bride, her groom, or even, as Botticelli did, the wedding breakfast. And they were eager for more mundane tasks, not for one moment despising an offer to decorate the elaborate *cassoni* in which the bride took her clothes and linen to her new household. Indeed, the competitive spirit of both brides and painters in *cassoni* became so fierce that they ceased to be objects of utility and were transformed into extravagant works of art, becoming the heirlooms of future generations.

The artistic accompaniment of marriage became the height of fashion. When the Duke and Duchess of Urbino returned to their capital after their wedding, they were met on a hilltop outside their city by all the women and children of rank, exquisitely and expensively dressed, bearing olive branches in their hands. As the Duke and Duchess reached them, mounted choristers accompanied by nymphs *à la Grecque* burst

into song—a special cantata which had been composed for the newlyweds. The Goddess of Mirth appeared in person with her court, and to make everyone realize that jollity and horseplay were never out of place at a wedding, hares were loosed in the crowd. This drove the dogs insane with excitement, to everyone's delight. No matter how solemn the occasion, marriage always involved coarse farce, usually at the climax of the wedding festivities, when the bride and groom were publicly bedded. Although there was no romantic nonsense about Italian weddings, certainly few marriages for love, everyone knew that the right true end of the contract was the bed. The dowager Duchess of Urbino, something of a bluestocking and a Platonist, and a woman of acknowledged refinement, burst into her niece's bedroom on the morning after her marriage and shouted, "Isn't it a fine thing to sleep with the men?"

Marriage for the women of the Renaissance gave many

their first taste of opulence, leisure, and freedom. They were very young, the atmosphere of their world was as reckless as it was ostentatious, and furthermore, they had not chosen their husbands, who frequently were a generation older than themselves. Their men, who were frequently soldiers or courtiers who lived close to the razor edge of life, fully enjoyed intrigue, so the young wife became a quarry to be hunted. As she was often neglected, the chase could be brief. Even Castiglione, who was very fond of his wife, treated her somewhat casually. He saw her rarely, and made up for his absence with affectionate, bantering letters. Of course, she was a generation younger than himself and therefore hardly a companion. Such a situation was not unusual: a girl of thirteen might excite her mature husband, but she was unlikely to entertain him for long. She fulfilled her tasks by bearing a few children and running a trouble-free household, and neither matter was too onerous for the rich. Nurses took

over the children as soon as they were born; a regiment of servants relieved wives of their traditional housewifely duties. So the leisure which had previously been the lot of only a few women of very high birth became a commonplace of existence for a multitude of women.

The presence of these leisured women in society helped to transform it. It created the opportunity for personality to flourish, for women to indulge the whims of their temperaments—free from the constraining circumstances of childbirth, nursery, and kitchen. There were men enough to adorn their vacant hours. Italy was alive with priests, many of them urbane, cultured, and idle, whose habit acted as a passport, hinting a security for husbands which their actions all too frequently belied. Nevertheless, they were the natural courtiers of lonely wives, and they swarmed in the literary salons of such distinguished women as Elisabetta Gonzaga at Urbino, the Queen of Cyprus at Asolo, or Vittoria Colonna at Rome.

Poets and their allegories were high on the list of feminine interests. On the facing page is a strange, mystical allegory, The Maiden's Dream, painted by Lorenzo Lotto, whom Titian called "as good as goodness, and as virtuous as virtue." Above, a maid crowns a poet with a laurel wreath.

Soldiers as well as priests needed the sweetness of feminine compassion to soften their tough and dangerous lives. Fortunately, military campaigns in Renaissance Italy were short and usually confined to the summer months, and so the horseplay, the practical jokes, and the feats of arms which were as essential to the courtly life as literary conversations or dramatic performances were provided by the knights. In addition to soldiers and priests, there were the husbands' pages, all in need of the finer points of amorous education. For a princess, further adornment of the salon was provided by an ambassador—often, true enough, a mere Italian, but at times French or Spanish, which gave an exotic touch that a woman of fashion could exploit to her rivals' disadvantage. Naturally, these courts became highly competitive: to have Pietro Bembo sitting at one's feet, reading his mellifluous but tedious essays on the beauties of Platonic love, was sure to enrage the hearts of other women. In fact, the popularity of

Bembo illustrates admirably the style of sophisticated love that the extravagant and princely women of Italy demanded.

Pietro Bembo was a Venetian nobleman, the cultivated son of a rich and sophisticated father who had educated him in the height of humanist fashion at the University of Ferrara, where he acquired extreme agility in bandying about the high-flown concepts of that strange mixture of Platonism and Christianity which was the hallmark of the exquisite. Petrarch, of course, was Bembo's mentor, and like Petrarch he lived his life, as far as the pressures of nature would allow him, in literary terms. He fell verbosely and unhappily in love with a Venetian girl; his ardent longings and intolerable frustrations were committed elegantly to paper and circulated to his admiring friends. This experience provided him with enough material for a long epistolary exchange with Ercole Strozzi, who was as addicted as Bembo to girls in literary dress. Enraptured by the elegance of his sentiments, Strozzi invited

Bembo to his villa near Ferrara, doubtless to flaunt his latest capture, Lucrezia Borgia, as well as to indulge his insatiable literary appetite. However, the biter was quickly bitten, for Bembo was just Lucrezia's cup of tea. A mature woman of twenty-two, thoroughly versed in the language as well as the experience of love, she was already bored with her husband, Alfonso d'Este, and tired of Strozzi. Soon she and Bembo were exchanging charming Spanish love lyrics and far larger homilies on aesthetics. After a visit by Lucrezia to Bembo, sick with fever, the pace quickened. Enormous letters followed thick and fast. Bembo ransacked literature to do homage to Lucrezia; they were Aeneas and Dido, Tristan and Iseult, Lancelot and Guinevere—not, however, lover and mistress. For a time they lived near each other in the country, while Ferrara was plague-ridden. Proximity and the furor of literary passion began to kindle fires in Bembo that were not entirely Platonic, and, after all, Lucrezia was a Borgia. Her

tolerant but watchful husband, however, had no intention of being cuckolded by an aesthete, and he rattled his sword. Bembo did not relish reliving the tragedy of Abelard; he might love Lucrezia to distraction, but he cherished himself as only an artist can, so he thought it discreet to return to Venice (he had excuse enough, as his brother was desperately sick). There he consoled himself by polishing his dialogue, *Gli Asolani,* which already enjoyed a high reputation among those to whom it had been circulated in manuscript. Resolving to give his love for Lucrezia its final, immortal form, he decided to publish it with a long dedication to her. To present her with his divine thoughts on love was a greater gift by far, of course, than his person. Doubtless both Lucrezia and her husband agreed; whether they read further than the dedication is more doubtful.

Bembo had written these highfalutin letters—informal, mannered, obscure, and so loaded with spiritual effusions on

*In long blonde curls, a young Sienese maiden,
the grandniece of Pius II, posed for her portrait.*

before meant that the jealous competition between them was intensified.

Yet it would be wrong to think that the gilded lives of Renaissance princesses were merely elegant, sophisticated, and luxurious, or that flirtation took place only in the most refined language. Few could concentrate their thoughts year in, year out, on the nobility of love like Vittoria Colonna. She, who inspired some of Michelangelo's most passionate poetry even as old age was ravaging her features, could and did live in an intense world of spiritual passion, in which the lusts of the flesh were exorcised by an ecstatic contemplation of the beauties of religion. The miracle was that she retained her charm, avoided the pitfalls of hypocrisy, and secured without effort the devotion of Castiglione and Bembo as well as Michelangelo. Even the old rogue Aretino attempted to secure her patronage, but naturally she remained aloof. In her the Platonic ideals of love and beauty mingled with the

Christian virtues to the exclusion of all else. Amazingly, no one found her a bore. However, few women could live like Vittoria: they sighed as they read Bembo, became enrapt as they listened to Castiglione, but from time to time they enjoyed a quiet reading of Boccaccio and, better still, Bandello.

Matteo Bandello had been received as a Dominican and spent many years of his life at the Convento delle Grazie at Milan, which seems to have been a more exciting place for a short-story teller than might be imagined. He acted for a time as ambassador for the Bentivoglio and so came in contact with that remarkable woman Isabella d'Este Gonzaga, whose court at Mantua was as outstanding for its wit, elegance, and genius as any in Italy. There Bandello picked up a mistress, which put him in no mind to hurry back to his brother monks. At Mantua, too, he laid the foundations of his reputation for being one of the best raconteurs of scandal in all Italy, Aretino not excepted. How true Bandello's stories are is still a

d bores were
more likely
for her insa-
r eloquence;
after night
ut the spir-
stupid as to
abetta could
interlarded
vith a warm
etic aspects.
ly modestly
to declaim
excessively
papal secre-
e the word
ible arms of

The delicate features and blonde hair in the Florentine bust at right represent an ideal of beauty ardently pursued by Renaissance women. Ignoring sumptuary laws, ladies of fashion paid fanatical attention to their appearance. Like the girl drawn by Pisanello (opposite), their elaborate gowns reflected the beauty of Renaissance art. Pisanello himself designed textiles, and the hand of a skilled artist is apparent in the decorated comb above, carved with Biblical scenes. Fancy clogs, such as the one shown below, protected women from mud; eventually they became so high that ladies had to be supported by maids when they walked.

matter for fierce warfare among scholars, but this they agree on: they did not seem incredible to those who read them. That being so, they give a hair-raising picture of what was going on at courts, in monasteries, in nunneries, in merchant houses, in the palaces and parsonages of Italy. The prime pursuit, in the vast majority of Bandello's stories, is the conquest of women, and to achieve success any trick, any falsehood, any force, is justifiable. His heroes' attitude to success in sex was like Machiavelli's to politics—the end justifies any means. The aim of all men is to ravish other men's wives and daughters and preserve their own women or revenge them if they fail to do so. Vendettas involving the most bloodcurdling punishments are a corollary to his major theme. In consequence, Bandello's stories, cast in a moral guise, nevertheless read like the chronicles of a pornographer. Here are the themes of a few that were thought to be proper entertainment for the lighter moments of court life or for quiet reading by a bored wife—the marriage of a man to a woman who was already his sister, and to his daughter; the adultery of two ladies at a court and the death of their paramours, which is a vivid record of sexual pleasure and horrifying punishment; the servant who was decapitated for sleeping with his mistress; the death through excessive sexual indulgence of Charles of Navarre; Gian Maria Visconti's burial of a live priest; the autocastration of Fra Filippo—and so one might go on and on, for Bandello wrote hundreds of short stories and they were largely variations on a single theme. The women of the Renaissance loved them, and few storytellers were as popular as Bandello (such abilities did not go unmarked, and he finished his career as Bishop of Agen). Nor was Bandello exceptional: there were scores of writers like him. Malicious, distorted, exaggerated as these tales were, they were based on the realities of Italian life. Undoubtedly the increased leisure of men and women released their ener-

Beauty substituted for comfort in the wooden chair shown on the facing page, which was made in the fifteenth century for the Strozzi, a Florentine family rivaling the Medici in culture and wealth. More often, Renaissance craftsmen succeeded in combining beauty with convenience, as evidenced by the beautifully wrought silver service below, made by a Roman artisan (the substitution of forks for fingers was a recent innovation). The rigors of housekeeping were eased for many rich ladies by slaves, two of whom are illustrated here in charming silhouettes. Pope Innocent VIII once received a gift of one hundred Moorish slaves, whom he distributed as a gratuity to cardinals and friends.

gies for a more riotous indulgence of their sexual appetites.

However daring the Italian males of the Renaissance were, the prudence of wives and the vigilance of husbands prevailed more often than not. The Emilia Pias, Elisabetta Gonzagas, Isabella d'Estes, Lucrezia Borgias, Costanza Amarettas, and Vittoria Colonnas were all too rare—particularly for cardinals and bishops ravenous for Platonic love. So in Rome, in Florence, in Venice, and in Milan there developed a class of grand courtesans, more akin to geisha girls than to prostitutes, to the extent that the *cortesane famose* of Venice despised the *cortesane de la minor sorte* and complained of their number, habits and prices to the Senate (they felt they brought disrepute on an honorable profession). Grand as these Venetian girls were, they could not compete with the great courtesans of Rome, who not only lived in small palaces with retinues of maids and liveried servants, but also practiced the literary graces and argued as learnedly as a Duchess

of Urbino about the ideals of Platonic love. Imperia of Rome, for example, held a salon for priestly humanists and gratified their spiritual as well as their carnal lusts with a delicacy and grace that made her name legendary. Her virgin daughter had been brought up so immaculately that she even threatened suicide to escape the amorous advances of a randy cardinal. Such a quean did honor to Rome, and her death was celebrated as a day of public mourning.

Even Imperia, however, could scarcely hold a candle to Tullia d'Aragona, the authoress of *On the Infinity of Perfect Love,* a subject for which her profession, perhaps, gave her special insight. Certainly she drove the aesthetes crazy. She was rhapsodized on her arrival at Ferrara in June, 1537, in these terms: "There has just arrived here a very pretty lady, so staid in deportment, so fascinating in manner, that we cannot help finding in her something truly divine. She sings all sorts of airs and motets at sight; her conversation has

Leisured Florentine women might devote their time to studying Latin, but Venetian ladies, like the one shown at right, were apt to spend hours on a rooftop with their hair spread out in the sun to bleach. Wide brims protected their skin, since a white complexion was prized as highly as blonde hair. Washing in a liquid distilled when a dove was cooked in its feathers was guaranteed to make skin beautiful; to keep it that way, Venetian ladies usually wore veils in the streets. This custom gave them an appearance of modesty not usually associated with the Renaissance, but the effect was diminished by the décolletage then in fashion, which reduced the illusion of decorum to a bare minimum.

matchless charm; she knows everything and there is nothing that you cannot talk to her about. There is no one here to hold a candle to her, not even the Marchioness of Pescara" (*i.e.*, Vittoria Colonna!). Tullia actually preferred her clients to be philosophers or historians. After Leo X had chased her and her sisters from Rome, she settled in Florence, where the reigning Duke insisted that all whores should wear yellow as a mark of their infamy. Her admirers, however, protested so vehemently on Tullia's behalf that she was publicly excused by the government on the grounds of "literary talents that are found in her to the great joy of noble minds."

Italy during the Renaissance was a country at war, plagued for decades with armies. A well-versed condottiere might battle with skill even in the wordy encounters of Platonic passion, but the majority wanted a quicker and cheaper victory. For months on end the captains of war had nothing to do and money to spend; they needed a metropolis of pleasure

and vice. Venice, with its quick eye for a profit, provided it and plucked them clean. There girls were to be had for as little as one *scudo*, well within the means even of a musketeer. And it was natural that after Leo X's purge, the majority of the fallen from Rome should flow to Venice. That city, with its regattas, *feste*, and carnivals, with its gondolas built for seclusion and sin, became a harlot's paradise. The trade in women became more profitable and extensive than it had been since the days of Imperial Rome. The Renaissance recaptured the past in more exotic fields than literature or the arts.

Life, however, for the noble women of the Renaissance was not always cakes and ale; it could be harsh and furious: the male world of war, assassination, and the pursuit of power frequently broke in upon their gentle world of love and dalliance. Indeed, Caterina Sforza, the woman whom all Italy saluted as its *prima donna*, won her fame through her dour courage and savage temper. Castiglione tells the story

of the time she invited a boorish condottiere to dinner, and asked him first to dance and then to hear some music—both of which he declined on the grounds that they were not his business. "What is your business, then?" his hostess asked. "Fighting," the warrior replied. "Then," said the virago of Forlì, "since you are not at war and not needed to fight, it would be wise for you to have yourself well greased and put away in a cupboard with all your arms until you are wanted, so that you will not get more rusty than you are." Violent, sensual, inexhaustible, contemptuous, and credulous, she is more a figure of a saga than a woman of the Renaissance. Three of her husbands were assassinated. At one time she defied the French, at another Cesare Borgia, who caught her and sent her like a captive lioness to the dungeons of Sant' Angelo. She told her frantic sons that she was habituated to grief and had no fear of it, and as they ought to have expected, she escaped. Yet tough and resourceful as she was,

Caterina could be a fool in love—much more of a fool than the Duchess of Urbino or Vittoria Colonna. Time and time again her political troubles were due to her inability to check her strong sensual appetite, which fixed itself too readily on the more monstrous of Renaissance adventurers. So eventful a life induced credulity, and like the rest of her family, Caterina believed in the magical side of nature, dabbled in alchemy and mysteries, and was constantly experimenting with magnets that would produce family harmony, or universal salves, or celestial water, or any other improbable elixir that the wandering hucksters wished on her. At any age, at any time, Caterina would have been a remarkable woman, but the Renaissance allowed her wild temperament to riot.

Certainly the women of the Renaissance were portents. Elisabetta Gonzaga and Isabella d'Este are the founding sisters of the great literary salons that were to dominate the fashionable society of Western Europe for centuries. But the courts

Gardens were a proper setting for dalliance. When Lorenzo de' Medici planted a myrtle, sacred to Venus, in his botanical garden, he made the spot an appropriate setting for scenes such as the one on the facing page—a Florentine engraving depicting the Garden of Love. Milan had no great botanical garden, but Leonardo da Vinci made one room of the Sforza palace into a verdant bower by painting branches on its ceiling. The interlaced pattern on the sleeve of a girl thought to be Lodovico Sforza's daughter (right) was probably designed by Leonardo, too, but the lovely portrait is now attributed to Ambrogio de Predis.

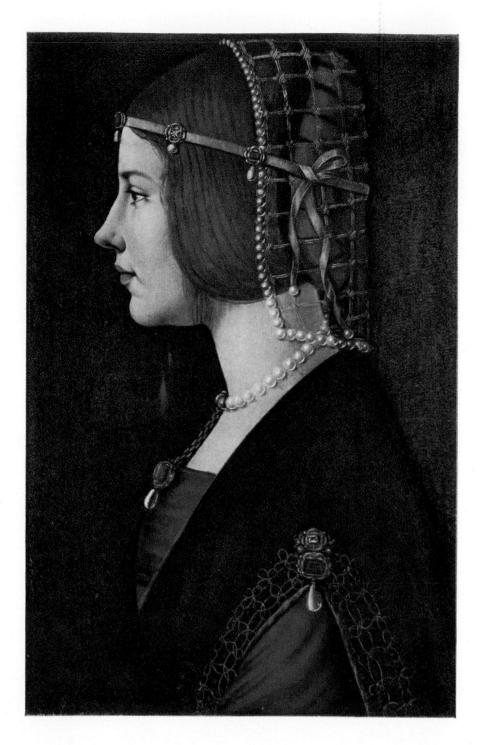

of Italy were few, the families that were rich enough to indulge the tastes and pleasures of sophisticated women never numerous. The lot of most women was harsh; they toiled in the home at their looms or in the fields alongside their men. They bred early and died young, untouched by the growing civility about them, save in their piety. In the churches where they sought ease for their sorrows, the Mother of God shone with a new radiance, a deeper compassion, and seemed in her person to immortalize their lost beauty. Even the majority of middle-class women knew little of luxury or literary elegance. Their lives were dedicated to their husbands and their children; their ambitions were limited to the provision of a proper social and domestic background for their husbands; and they were encouraged to exercise prudence, to indulge in piety, and to eschew vanities. Yet their lives possessed a civility, a modest elegance, that made a strong contrast to the harsher experiences and more laborious days of medieval women. Their new wealth permitted a greater, even if still modest, personal luxury. They could dress themselves more finely, acquire more jewels, provide a richer variety of food for their guests, entertain more lavishly, give more generously to charity. Although circumscribed, their lives were freer, their opportunities greater. It might still be unusual for a woman to be learned or to practice the arts, but it was neither rare nor exotic. And because they had more time, they were able to create a more active social life and to spread civility. After the Renaissance, the drawing room becomes an integral part of civilized living; indeed, the Renaissance education of a gentleman assumed that much of his life would be spent amusing women and moving them with words. As in so many aspects of life in Renaissance Italy, aristocratic attitudes of the High Middle Ages were adopted by the middle classes. Courtesy and civility spread downward, and the arts of chivalry became genteel.

The bust of Beatrice is by Gian Cristoforo Romano, Isabella's portrait by Leonardo.

Beatrice and Isabella d'Este

by MARIA BELLONCI

The stories of the two sisters, Beatrice and Isabella d'Este, are not easily interwoven in a single brief account, nor would either of them have relished such a thing, for they were lively, even peremptory individualists. Then, too, the span of their lives was very different. Of Beatrice, who died when she was twenty-two, we know only the transports, the vehemences, the proud and ambitious passions of adolescence. On the other hand, we know, step by step, Isabella's magistral development from youthful potential to the maturity that unfolds and reveals the meaning of a human life. They were born in Ferrara one year apart, Isabella in 1474 and Beatrice in 1475, thus preceding their four brothers—Alfonso, Ferrante, Ippolito, and Sigismondo.

The Este, one of the most ancient dynasties in Italy, had dominated Ferrara—a strategic area between Lombardy, Venice, and Emilia—and the broad luxuriant valley of the Po since the thirteenth century. They belonged to the Guelph party and for centuries had fought the Ghibellines in defense of the Church—and even fought the Church on those occasions when the popes had sought to meddle unduly in their affairs. These struggles, added to embroilments with neighboring powers or within the Este family, had forged a race of men who, no matter what their individual temperaments, were bold statesmen. In proof of this, the Ferrarese, a people proud to the point of arrogance and brave to the point of temerity (a Ferrarese proverb states that no man is too poor to own a dagger), never, not even when sorely provoked, rebelled against their masters.

It was Niccolò III, coming to power in 1402, who with the unsparing energy of his forebears consolidated the domain on a grand scale. Niccolò III was a resolute soldier, an astute manipulator of circumstance, and a man of constructive intelligence, who founded a university and was so solicitous of the people's welfare as to stipulate in his will that the monies allocated for his own funeral should be donated instead to public charity. Variously magnanimous and cruel (he ordered his son Ugo and his second wife, Parisina, beheaded when he discovered that they were lovers), Niccolò had exceptional sons who reigned in succession after him, the first two illegitimate, the third legitimate. Leonello, a level-headed, shrewd politician, sowed the seeds of the flowering of humanism in Ferrara; Borso, also a statesman of peace, was equally devoted to the arts. The first legitimate son to rule was Ercole, a man

whose temperament was so icy that it won him the nicknames "North Wind" and "The Diamond."

In 1473, two years after he ascended the throne at the age of forty, Ercole made the most political of marriages, wedding Leonora of Aragon, the daughter of King Ferrante of Naples, who was at the time a very powerful sovereign. The bride was beautiful —indeed, more than beautiful. Naturally regal, endowed with sound bourgeois sense and queenly courage, she was a sensitive, warm woman in whose company even the chilly nature of her husband was somewhat thawed.

Into this noble house and into a court traditionally cultivated and schooled in all the humanistic sciences, Isabella and Beatrice d'Este were born. From birth their destinies seem both divergent and parallel, patterned in counterpoint. Isabella, the first child, was born in May, 1474. She was welcomed with enthusiasm by parents, court, and populace, who saw in the blonde, softly rounded, comely infant girl the herald of the male, the heir to come. Beatrice was born a year later, in June, 1475, and the arrival of this second girl aroused no joy whatever. For her there were no celebrations, royal or popular, and no sign of love except perhaps the slightly humiliated tenderness of a mother who was beginning to feel marked by the most mortifying attribute of a princess —that of being "the mother of females." Both infants were given the names of queens, Isabella being called after her grandmother, the Queen of Naples, and Beatrice named for her aunt, who was wife to Matthias Corvinus, King of Hungary. One year passed and, fortunately, a son was born; Alfonso was received with noisy jubilation and festivities by all Ferrara. The next year another son, Ferrante, arrived. The girl infants had been redeemed.

Ferrante was born in September, 1477, in the Neapolitan palace of the grandfather whose name he took. That year the King, who was even less old in feeling than in fact, had married for the second time, taking as wife the delicate, elegant Giovanna of Aragon. Leonora was bid to pay her respects to her father and stepmother, and she went to Naples carrying with her not Alfonso—the heir had to remain in Ferrara—but the two girls and the still unborn child. The King of Naples, a dissipated man, richly endowed with ambiguous charms and a taste for the grandiose, took an immediate fancy to Beatrice. He recognized in her the long face and heavy cheeks, the jet-black hair and eyes, and the sulky, heavy-lidded

glance of the true Aragon. His marriage was duly celebrated, and Leonora's second son was born shortly thereafter, whereupon she was recalled in haste to Ferrara by Duke Ercole, who sniffed the scent of war in the air. She took only Isabella with her, leaving Beatrice and Ferrante in Naples, where they stayed for eight years. The little Este children played with their cousins, among whom was Isabella of Aragon, betrothed to Gian Galeazzo Sforza, who would one day clash with Beatrice in a mortal match.

In her grandfather's court in Naples, Beatrice learned that pride is vital and splendid, that every gesture of King and nobles was governed by an etiquette compounded equally of pomp and fantasy, and she realized, too, that power must be deserved. Accordingly, she began then to develop the intrepid patience that would stand her in such good stead when she returned to Ferrara to find herself in a position secondary in every respect. There was no doubt about it; the child who reigned in the Este palace was the elder sister, the gay and witty and wise Isabella. Everyone adored Isabella. No one had ever seen such an intense and vivacious feminine intelligence, such a felicitously inventive art in arranging things to her own liking while capturing the consent of others. Even the judicious Leonora was beguiled into calling her "my dearest and sweetest of daughters." Perhaps Isabella was not as beautiful as they say: she was not very tall and her features were not perfect, but she had a clear, rosy-cheeked complexion and a bearing of incomparable elegance. And her intelligence was prodigious. Her teachers were stunned when she translated smoothly and rapidly a selection from Virgil's *Bucolics* or a letter of Cicero; she mastered Greek and Latin grammar, committed Terence and Virgil to memory, learned to perform songs and madrigals on the lute, was first in perfecting the steps of a new dance, embroidered faultlessly, conversed —and held her own—with ambassadors.

The year 1480 was a year of engagements in the Este house, and it brought Isabella the worst bit of sheer bad luck that she was to suffer in her whole life. In April a marriage contract was signed between her and Francesco Gonzaga, heir of the neighboring Marquis of Mantua. Scarcely a month later, an ambassador arrived from Milan to ask for Isabella's hand on behalf of Lodovico Sforza. Il Moro, as he was called, was the guardian of his young nephew, the Duke of Milan, but in actuality Lodovico was master of both his nephew and half of Italy. Since

Duke Ercole would never offend the Marquis of Mantua, who was his friend and ally, by reneging on agreements already signed, he took advantage of Il Moro's suit to marry off both of the pawns he held in the game of alliances. Let the first daughter go to the Marquis of Mantua, and let the second, who was the equal of her sister—legitimate, healthy, intelligent, and cultivated—go to Il Moro. (Alfonso d'Este, his eldest son, was already affianced to Anna Sforza, the Duke of Milan's sister.) Lodovico was not enthusiastic, and he accepted this engagement of expediency with perceptible disappointment.

Happily, a fresh and quite unusual relationship developed between Isabella and Francesco; the innocent and touching charm of the girl surprised and beguiled her fiancé, a vigorous and already experienced fifteen-year-old youth, even before it made him fall in love with her. But between Beatrice and Lodovico there was nothing of this sort. He who was judged the first man in all Italy, and who was certainly one of the richest, scarcely remembered the dark-haired girl, twenty-five years younger than he, who awaited him in Ferrara. On the contrary. Surrounded by the elaborate pomp of his court, he was flaunting his passion for the beautiful, exquisitely mannered Cecilia Gallerani (*see* page 122), the unofficial queen of Milan. It is not certain whether Beatrice knew of her rival or not, for contemporary accounts record only the silences of the young Este girl in this period.

In February of 1490, ten years after her engagement, Isabella went as a bride to the castle in Mantua, her resolute, slim sixteen years transported there in the triumphal carriage designed by Ercole de' Roberti; his, too, was the hand that painted the thirteen chests that followed her, in which her elegant trousseau was packed. She was followed also by her father, mother, sister, her three brothers, the whole band of her Este relatives, and the acclamations of seventeen thousand spectators. Isabella was going to a youthful court, since her delightful parents-in-law, Federigo and Margherita, who so warmly wanted her in their family, had died while still young. Her husband was twenty-five, his two brothers twenty-one and sixteen. Her new eighteen-year-old sister-in-law was Elisabetta Gonzaga, a woman of pale and heraldic beauty, who was the wife of Guidobaldo, Duke of Urbino. (For a time no one suspected the burning secret of the unconsummated marriage which Elisabetta endured with love and shame and a pas-

sional exhaustion which bordered on despair.)

That February, the most gloomy, foggy month in the year for lacustrine Mantua, was for Isabella a period of acquisition, confirmed by a whole series of new possessions beginning with her husband. She served no novitiate as daughter-in-law, but came at once into both title and power, rising to the demands of her role with the sparkling glance and lightness of step that lent wings to her sixteen years. Isabella realized that her marriage had the rigorous political significance of an alliance between reigning families, for on this score she had learned her father's lesson well, and she responded to her husband's passion like a woman who appreciates the quality of being warmly involved in marriage without being swept away or losing her own identity thereby. As for her young husband, one of the most ugly and fascinating men in Italy, he was the brave soldier, the complete gentleman, a graceful and entertaining conversationalist in the Lombard style, a lover of gentle sensuality—and so delightfully ingenuous as to have his humanists compose poems that he sent to his literary-minded wife as his own. He, too, was overcome with admiration for Isabella, but this admiration, which perforce grew greater day by day, was destined to alter in kind. Francesco Gonzaga scarcely realized it, but presently he began to lose confidence in this wife who was like no one else, and who, while obedient to his smallest wish, seemed always to protect a growing independence of her own. Yet she was so loyal, so adroit in sensing whatever could benefit the little Mantuan state and the Gonzaga family, that it was difficult to find cause for reproach. The new Marchioness of Mantua was clearly the pride of the city; her praises were sung, indeed, throughout Italy.

In Ferrara, Beatrice was awaiting her husband. She should have married immediately after her sister, but Lodovico Il Moro was bound to his Cecilia Gallerani and showed not the least concern about joining his betrothed. However, Ercole d'Este was not a man to accept even a small affront, and at a certain point he allowed a hiss of irritation to reach Lodovico's ear. Il Moro, knowing that he needed Ferrara to protect Lombardy against the threat of its centuries-old enemy, the republic of Venice, and further pressured by the marriage pact between his niece Anna and the Este heir apparent, finally brought himself to a decision. And once he had decided, he threw the gates of the Lombard palaces wide, opened the coffers of his treasury, and set in

motion the mighty machinery of the Milanese court, which teemed with artists, poets, mathematicians, scholars, and a spirited nobility well disposed toward any courtly enterprise. The wedding date was set for January, 1491, and the place chosen was the castle in Pavia. Whereupon not a day passed without messengers arriving in Ferrara from Milan; they brought gifts, like the famous necklace of pearls strung with flowerets of gold and embellished with splendid drops of rubies, pearls, and emeralds; the masters of ceremonies came to arrange for the bride's journey —and to recommend that Beatrice bring many embroidered and bejeweled gowns; artists came, like Gian Cristoforo Romano, sculptor and engraver, accomplished lute player, and a man of wide literary attainments, who did the bust of Beatrice that is now preserved in the Louvre (*see* page 360).

With an intent, childish frown, Beatrice set about preparing herself for her unknown future, and she scarcely noticed the fearsome and memorable trip, as the ice-encrusted bucentaurs passed between the snowy banks of the canals. They arrived, finally, in a Pavia blanketed in snow, but inside the castle everything exuded warmth, wealth, and ease. Lodovico led his bride and her entourage through the princely dwelling, judged the most sumptuous in the world. At the last, he showed them its greatest treasure, the library begun by Gian Galeazzo Visconti and now rich in illuminated volumes and Greek and Latin manuscripts that Sforza had had copied in the most remote sanctuaries where they were preserved. In the face of all this splendor Beatrice appeared reserved, which everyone took to mean that she was timid. She had, in any case, no time to recover her self-possession after the wedding (which took place on January 17, the day chosen by the astrologers as propitious), for the next morning Il Moro left for Milan, to arrange, he said, for the celebrations, on which a legion of artists captained by Leonardo da Vinci and Bramante from Urbino were assigned to work. Yet how could one forget that Cecilia Gallerani was living there in the castle?

Eventually, the whole company moved on to Milan, and the spectacle in the great Lombard city surpassed belief: imaginatively staged tournaments, elegant dances, theatricals, masquerades, concerts of rare music, and fantasies of every kind. Energy, grandeur, verve, intelligence, and beauty joined to compose around the bride—who until yesterday had been quite obscure—a magnificent show of which she was the sole heroine. She could, it seemed, be sure even of her husband, from the moment she realized that her youth attracted him. She led him on to fondle her, used every charm to beguile him into kissing her before everyone; she offered him an olive-toned, girlish face that was flushed and alight with happiness; everything she did expressed her joy in having been called to so full a life. Before the eyes of her startled mother and sister, Beatrice let go; this was her moment, and it was as if she cut herself off from all else in a frenetic drive to seize it.

Once back in Mantua, Isabella saw to it that she was kept informed daily of what was going on in Milan. The accounts that reached her told of a whirl of amusements; of a morning, Beatrice, Galeazzo di Sanseverino, and Diodato the jester would set out in a carriage, singing three-part songs. They fished, they lunched, they played ball and fished again, and returned home in the evening deliciously exhausted. Beatrice won quick ascendancy over her husband, and if she did not succeed in dislodging Cecilia Gallerani from the castle, she did manage to break off, officially at least, that lady's relationship with Il Moro. In 1491 Cecilia married Count Bergamini, shortly after she gave birth to a son by Lodovico.

Beatrice never wearied of thinking up masquerades, jokes, or expeditions, with herself and her ladies dressed like commoners and spoiling for a squabble with some plebeians. His wife's exploits were irresistibly amusing to Il Moro, who laughed and applauded the girl. In Milan, Beatrice had found her cousin again—that Isabella of Aragon with whom she had played at the court in Naples some years before. From the day Beatrice arrived, she had had to concede first place in the city to Isabella, acknowledging the unchallengeable primacy of her position as wife of the actual Duke, Gian Galeazzo Sforza. However, Isabella of Aragon's greatness of spirit, her courage, and the exquisite refinement of her nature (later, her court was considered an incomparable school for pages and courtiers) did not suffice in her efforts to support her husband, given his weaknesses. The young Duke of Milan appeared to combine the vices of his Visconti and Sforza forebears, although in him they were enfeebled by a congenital frailty that enervated both his physical and intellectual capacities to the point of decay. The courageous daughter of King Alfonso took an unblinking view of her present and her future. The desire for power that she had recognized in Gian

Galeazzo's uncle and guardian was now increased by Beatrice's appetite, which had all the fierceness of youthful passion. And the moment was propitious for the ambitious couple. The French King, Charles VIII, was girding himself for the conquest of the kingdom of Naples; the Borgia Pope, Alexander VI, was unable to dissuade him; and Il Moro favored the foreigners' coming, calculating that in this way he could be quit once and forever of all difficulties with the Aragons, who were the natural protectors of Isabella and her children. Without a thought for her grandfather, King Ferrante, who had so doted on her, Beatrice abetted her husband ardently. When in January, 1493, Beatrice's first son was born—Ercole, later called Massimiliano—and royal celebrations were held in his honor, the unfortunate Duchess Isabella of Aragon wept her eyes out.

But her protests accomplished nothing. Late in 1494, Charles VIII was in Italy, received with a whirlwind of festivities by Lodovico and by Beatrice, who dazzled the King, even if she could not prevent some of his French followers from maliciously evaluating her and her displays of costume and charm with the observation that "the husk is worth more than the kernel." At Pavia the tragic colloquy between Isabella of Aragon and the French King took place, in which Isabella fell to her knees before him, in tears. With a vague promise of protection for the Sforza children, Charles VIII left. While the French King was on his way to the easy conquest of Naples, the ailing Gian Galeazzo succumbed to tuberculosis; the young Duke's last request was to see his horses and his greyhounds.

Lodovico quickly set in motion the plan he had long since prepared, and had himself proclaimed master of Milan by his fellow citizens. Shortly thereafter Emperor Maximilian granted the title to the dukedom to him and to his direct heirs, disregarding Gian Galeazzo's son. The fame and fortune of Beatrice, now crowned Duchess of Milan and applauded and sung and glorified by all, glowed brilliantly above the downfall of Isabella of Aragon.

But the Italian states quickly realized that the French King was not a guest to be taken into the house so casually, and they hastened to repair the damage already done. Even Milan joined the league established among Venice, Mantua, the Pope, and other principalities, for Il Moro had come to see that if foreign invasions were dangerous for all, they were most dangerous for him, since Charles made no

secret of his wish to annex the duchy of Milan, which, he said, was his by right of inheritance. The armies gathered, and to avoid being captured in the kingdom he had just conquered, Charles VIII withdrew rapidly up the peninsula, and at Fornovo di Taro met the allied armies of the league in a battle from which he managed, as a result of the Italians' incompetence, to escape and to return to France. Italy rejoiced in her recovered liberty, and in Mantua, Isabella rejoiced to see her husband, Marquis Francesco Gonzaga, captain general of the league, the hero of Italy's liberation.

As the characters of the Este sisters became more differentiated, a disquieting rivalry gradually unfolded; it was in no sense petty, for both were women of noble spirit and bound by family loyalties, but it was perceptible, nevertheless. Beatrice's accent on luxury was too loud, verging on the satanic. Everyone found her eighty-four new dresses, heavily embroidered with gold thread, jewels, and pearls, excessive; they hung in a great room that, as her mother, Leonora, observed with graceful irony, resembled a "sacristy hung with all the canonicals." Too many rooms were too full of silver, ivories, precious glass, paintings, perfumes, lutes, clavichords, in quantities sufficient to "fill all the shops." Her unchecked imperiousness, her inconsiderate way of treating people about her, her cruel little games (she used to terrify ladies in waiting by pretending to set her horses upon them at an unbridled gallop), were in the same measure her way of vindicating her humiliated adolescence. When Isabella realized that the festivities and gifts that always awaited her in Milan were contrived to oppress her with honors, she found excuses to accept no further invitations. The immense wealth and the traditional magnificence of the Sforza court allowed Beatrice to have about her men like Bramante and Leonardo; she made her presence felt even in politics, and could engage in well-informed arguments with heads of state.

Another source of bitterness for Isabella was their relative maternal status. In the Sforza household there were two sons, Ercole and Francesco; in the Gonzaga household there were two daughters, Eleonora and Margherita. When Beatrice sent her congratulations on the birth of Eleonora, there was a hint of self-satisfaction in her including the greetings of her little son to the newborn girl. Isabella was so infuriated that when she bore her second daughter, she insisted that the infant be removed

from the sumptuous cradle which had been prepared for a boy. But the fabulous life story of Beatrice hung suspended by the thread of fortune that had created it. Something had already gone wrong when, around 1495, Il Moro had fallen in love with an exquisite lady of the court, Lucrezia Crivelli, and had refused to give her up. Wounded in her feelings and in her pride, Beatrice had pretended to see nothing in order to preserve her own happiness intact, and she had mastered her pain with great strength of spirit. She was pregnant for the third time, and by dint of will power she managed to save appearances, laughing, singing, arranging, commanding. On January 2, 1497, she held a ball in her apartments, with the whole court present. Toward evening she was taken ill; she was carried to her bedchamber; at two o'clock that morning she gave birth to a stillborn son, and within an hour and a half she died.

The chronicles of all Italy were filled with accounts of Lodovico's immoderate, theatrical, and romantic grief, of his repentant self-reproaches, his passionate lamentings, of the funeral at Santa Maria delle Grazie in the midst of a thousand flaming torches and thousands upon thousands of wax tapers, and of the final appearance of Beatrice robed in gold upon her bier. The blinding suddenness of the misfortune had moved everyone; and those twenty-two years consumed with such intensity and fervor had, it seemed, upheld not only the fortunes of the Sforza family but also the destiny of the duchy. From the moment of Beatrice's death, the future of Milan began to cloud; soon after followed the French invasions, the fall of the Sforza, and the imprisonment of Lodovico, who was fated to die in exile, in the castle of Loches.

Isabella's sorrow, like her character, was genuine but controlled. Having shed her tears, she kept assiduously in touch with her brother-in-law, feeling for Il Moro—powerful and superstitious, fanciful and realistic, indecisive and stubborn as he was—the attraction that strong, clear-headed women feel for men who are full of self-contradictions and, when all is said, are weak. She recovered quickly from her grief, for she had to ward off the perils represented by the French flanking her to the north, Cesare Borgia threatening from the south, papal interventions, and the bitter hostility of the Venetians. With disdainful patience she endured a family tie with the Borgia when, in 1501, with the Borgia star in full ascendancy, Lucrezia married her brother Alfonso d'Este, the widower of Anna Sforza, and came to reign in Ferrara as its Duchess.

To Cesare Borgia she sent masks, perfumes, and compliments to hold him at bay; at the same time she exulted when the troops of Faenza successfully withstood the Borgia forces, which led her to formulate her clear concept of domestic policy: the prince must deserve to have the people make his cause their own by making their cause his. This was the traditional Este idea of good government and, joined with a feminine nature, it was now translated into a series of sustained, sensitive political moves. All Mantua acknowledged the efficacy of Isabella's policies during her regency in 1509, a period when the League of Cambrai united Europe in an alliance against the excessive power of Venice. It so happened that Francesco Gonzaga, commander for the league, was taken prisoner while he was sleeping, to the anger and disgust of his allies. The little Mantuan state faced a grave danger then, but Isabella demonstrated her courage and the growth of her personality by calling the people together, offering her young son for the public's acclamation, and enjoining the strictest orders upon the army—forbidding the garrisons of the fortresses bordering Venice to open their gates even were the Venetians to lead Marquis Francesco to the foot of the glacis and murder him before their eyes.

And so Francesco Gonzaga, languishing and ill in Venetian prisons, waited to be liberated, while, in Mantua, Isabella played a most artful hand. Caught in a fearsome vise between venomous foes and suspicious friends, she succeeded in keeping the Mantuan frontier free not only of enemy assaults but also of allied garrisons. But because she had governed too well and ably, she found in 1512, the war ended, that she had lost the love of her husband. Shortly after his return from prison, Francesco Gonzaga wrote her in these words: "*We are ashamed* that it is our fate to have as wife a woman who is always ruled by her head." Not at all intimidated, Isabella replied with icy pride: "Your Excellency is indebted to me as never husband was to wife; nor must Your Excellency think that, even did you love and honor me more than any person in the world, you could repay my good faith." Day after day she watched as her husband became increasingly alienated. When she sensed that she had fallen from power, she protested in a way all her own—not in words but in action. She traveled, and one of her destinations was Rome.

Isabella arrived in Rome like a reigning sovereign who was securely established in her own kingdom.

No one suspected her real situation. In the splendid company of the papal court of Leo X, surrounded by a continuous thunder of acclamation, amid all the banquets and theatricals and the penetrating, brilliant talk, she permitted no one to guess the contrast between such homage and her true vagrant isolation. She was buoyed up by her taste for experimentation, and the thought of her children helped her—the sons, that is, who must be guided toward great futures. (Her daughters she cared very little about—at least at this time. When two of them, Ippolita and Paola, entered a convent, she did not weep, but with a license verging on blasphemy, declared herself content, since this son-in-law would cause her no trouble.) Her sons, Federigo, Ercole, and Ferrante, were educated and watched over with daily, unremitting attention. The first was destined to the throne, the second to the Church, the third to the army. But Federigo was clearly her favorite; her affection for him was the supreme expression of her maternal love, her pride, and even a kind of hope in the future. This explains how she should separate from the husband who had stripped her of all authority, for she knew that in Federigo she had a future, and she planned her own vindication in that future. When Francesco Gongaza died in 1519, worn down by illness, Isabella's tears paid tribute only to the memories of her youth. Since her son was far away in France, the one urgent and essential thing for her to do was to rule.

It was 1519, Isabella was forty-four, and to reign was the natural expression of her nature. "She trusts no one and will know the motive of everyone," observed the Mantuans, who were never displeased to have power exercised by a woman of her sort of matriarchal nobility.

Federigo, the nineteen-year-old Marquis, was at first overwhelmed by his mother and lived in a state of admiring subjugation, with little more than the occasional restiveness of an unruly colt. She governed well; she maintained a difficult equilibrium among the great powers that divided Italy, and she was the first to foresee that Charles V would prevail over the French King, Francis I. But Federigo presently discovered that his life was partitioned into two roles: one, that of the submissive son, and the other his own, that of an independent, effective man. It was only natural that the second seemed to him the good and true self, all the more so since he had the support of a young and extremely beautiful woman in proving it. The young Marquis was so in love with

Isabella Boschetti, called La Boschetta, that he refused to marry to ensure the continuity of the dynasty. The young woman fueled Federigo's idea of his total independence, and he responded by surrounding her with every royal honor, costly and magnificent gifts, courtiers, artists, and literary figures, while by sly, imperceptible moves he eliminated his mother little by little from direct participation in the government. He asked her advice, but privately —and gradually Isabella was relegated to the role of an elderly woman.

No moment in her life had been so serious as this, and once again she bided her time, waiting for her son's mistress to fall from favor. Isabella was coming to recognize bitterly that her beloved Federigo was a weak man, and worse. "The Marquis of Mantua is not good for much," Guicciardini wrote with terse accuracy in 1527, when Federigo and the Duke of Urbino opened the way by their betrayal for the German mercenaries to march south to sack the city of Rome.

Isabella d'Este had returned to Rome in 1525, and so shared in the final days of that tempered, cultivated, Christian paganism that was to be shattered by the brutal impact of the Lutheran gangs from Frundsberg. Rome had received her gloriously in the time of Leo X, and now, under another Medici, Clement VII, it welcomed her again. And again Isabella stood firm in her loyalty to Mantua and to the Gonzaga who had so often betrayed her. Thanks to her subtly modulated tactics, she succeeded in securing the red hat for her second son, Ercole, only a few days before the dreadful pillage of the city began. Federigo was writing her from Mantua meanwhile. He had seen the imperial hordes at first hand, and found them crude, fanatical, blasphemous, and innately hostile to the soil and civilization of Italy. Again and again he begged his mother to return to Mantua, but these entreaties had the opposite effect: they suggested a strengthening of her position that might restore her to an ascendancy over her son far above the poor physical expedients of La Boschetta. And then the terrible day, May 6, 1527, arrived. From within Palazzo Colonna, where she was securely housed, she heard the mercenaries howling through the streets, bent on robbing, killing, and torturing. Isabella remained steadfast; she took in gentlewomen, princes, ambassadors, priests, and friars who were seeking shelter; she encouraged them, shared her meager food with them, and with them

trembled and hoped. Only when they were out of danger did she leave the ravaged city and make her way northward to Mantua without undue haste. Fired by the evidences of her courage, the populace was all for her and against La Boschetta. And gradually La Boschetta had to give in, retreat, and remove herself, allowing Federigo to marry Princes Margherita Paleologa—the wife chosen for him by Isabella.

Margherita was gentle, sensible, and in love; she had just the right degree of native shrewdness; and as her dowry she brought with her nothing less than a whole region—Monferrato. She bore her husband numerous sons, gave him constant, discreet support, and got along extremely well with her great mother-in-law, who gladly placed full confidence in her. Federigo's political future was a limited one, subject as it was to the will of Charles V, but within the sphere of his large and splendid court he was active, buying painting and sculpture, building extensively with his Giulio Romano, quarreling with his Aretino. Toward the mother to whom he owed so much, including his title of Duke, which Charles V granted to the rulers of Mantua, he continued to behave courteously and even affectionately, but he persisted in keeping her isolated. Her greatness of spirit was truly tried, yet her response was a gesture generous to the point of scorn; in effect, she offered to be his accomplice against her own interests, helping him to conceal her humiliation so that no one could suspect him of an unworthy action.

The futures of the other sons had been secured. Ferrante, the future Viceroy of Milan, would be a good general. Ercole would be a great cardinal, a major figure at the Council of Trent, and would come very near to wearing the triple crown; and when his elder brother died at barely forty years of age, leaving an infant heir, he would assume the regency of the duchy of Mantua and perform his duties with the prudence, the severity, and the awareness of his mother.

Although no one needed Isabella now, as she moved into her sixtieth year, she was stronger and more animated and gay than ever, always ready and eager to go to the heart of a problem. Respect and consideration were paid her in abundance; her court was, as always, exemplary and, as always, crowded with literary figures, courtiers, and beautiful and witty young women whom she formed and trained in her own school according to her own bold and modern moral concept—allowing them freedom but insisting that they be virtuous. In her new apartments on the ground floor of the ducal palace, she collected about her the noblest and finest creations that her age was producing. The famous rooms, the *Studiolo* and the *Grotta* with the celebrated door by Tullio Lombardo, were the talk of all the courts of Italy. Poems, songs, travel memoirs, writings of every description, flowed into Mantua from all over to satisfy her ever livelier curiosity. Nor did the heavy traffic in elegant luxuries diminish—the gowns, jewels, perfumes, cosmetics, adornments, and extraordinary objects like the doll "dressed inside and out exactly like her [Isabella]," which Francis I requested and received to send to his wife in France. But above all this, Isabella's inner life was fortified by a secret. This secret was called Solarolo.

Solarolo was a tiny possession in Romagna that belonged to her. This was all Isabella needed. She received secretaries as if they were ministers; she directed and adjudicated and enforced her own methods of management with almost affectionate ease, since here she was legitimately fulfilling her true nature and was finally giving expression to the passion for ruling that could have made her a magnificent queen. As she listened to her secretaries' reports, with the maps of Solarolo spread before her, and around her her collections of paintings, marbles, bronzes both ancient and modern, her crystal and her alabaster and her ornate clocks, she was expressing her personality fully and harmoniously.

Most rare Phoenix, the humanists called her, reviving the worn image to honor her—but more than that, a most rare woman. Yet why does posterity remember her? In both her marriage and her maternity she was sorely disappointed; emotionally hers was a wintry life. She has survived thanks to her individuality, to the awareness of self that she sustained with all the force and conviction of a style. It was a style fashioned by the mind; it was the effective alliance of idea and action; and it characterized Isabella's life until her death on February 13, 1539. It is impossible to say whether Beatrice would have been able to develop in the same way, had she lived to the same age. But both these princesses, these creatures of lucid and resolute intelligence, had understood one thing—the necessity of living according to an inner order that vibrates in continual response to the external world, and by which we surmount the error of facts, the harshness of circumstance, and the inertia of our surroundings.

Translated by Adrienne Foulke

THE NEW WOMAN

In a world which idolized beauty, princesses, courtesans, and housewives spent hours enhancing their charms. "Neither Giotto nor any other painter uses color better than the Florentine women," one critic complained, but the monk Angelo Firenzuola gallantly announced that "The beautiful woman is the loveliest object of contemplation, and beauty is the best of God's gifts to the human being." His enthusiasm exemplified the age's new liberalism, which gave woman the time and the freedom to display her beauty as well as the opportunity to write sonnets and rule duchies. Venus was the symbol of beauty and womanhood, and it was under her sign that astrologers located the Garden of Delight, which is illustrated in the charming miniature above, depicting men and women bathing in a fountain of love, while musicians, singers, and a pair of ardent lovers echo their harmony.

THE BRILLIANT
ESTE COURT

An unfinished Este family tree shows Isabella as a baby, dressed in a white gown and a tightly fitted cap. Her mother, the Duchess Leonora, is shown next to her, beside a frame left empty for a picture of Beatrice, whose name and birth date are written under it. Duke Ercole appears in the top row, under a list of his accomplishments; on either side are his two illegitimate children, Lucrezia (at right) and Lorenzo, whose early death in 1471 is recorded beneath his portrait.

When Borso d'Este (below) died of malaria, his brother Ercole became Duke of Ferrara. He wed a Neapolitan princess, the beautiful Leonora (left), and their daughters married well, too. Above are Isabella's and Beatrice's husbands, the bearded Francesco Gonzaga and Lodovico Sforza.

The aunt of the Este sisters, Bianca, "The Virgin of Este," was famous for her writings; they displayed a Latin style rivaled in purity only by her virtue. The girls' mother, the Duchess Leonora, was an accomplished harpist, and the future Duke Alfonso, their brother, performed on the violin in public, with talent inherited from an Este uncle, the late Duke Leonello, who had been a virtuoso at the guitar. Duke Ercole, the father of the girls, translated Latin plays and staged them in the palace courtyard, while their cousin wrote pastoral dramas and composed musical settings of sonnets for Isabella to sing.

The sisters' talents equaled those of their relatives, and they were notable as well for their generous patronage of artists. The masque, which mixed comedy with dancing and music, developed at Ferrara, and the first permanent theater in modern Europe was constructed there. Piero della Francesca and Francesco Cossa frescoed rooms in Este palaces, and Cosimo Tura earned four golden florins when he painted a portrait of ten-year-old Beatrice to be sent to her fiancé as a Christmas present. The Duchess Leonora brought to Ferrara embroiderers from Spain and tapestry makers from Florence and Milan, and her collection of jewelry was considered the most artistic in all Italy (although it was often pawned to raise money for her husband's wars). With these female paragons of culture and virtue, the court of Ferrara provided a congenial shelter for the poets Boiardo and Ariosto, whose romances of chivalry, based on an idealization of women, established a new tradition of courtly poetry.

CHILDHOOD

Curious but shy, the little girl at right (a detail of the Crivelli Annunciation *on page 383) peeks from behind a wall to inspect an angel. Above, a boy of the same age looks trustingly at his grandfather, a Florentine merchant painted by Ghirlandaio.*

Despite the antics of his schoolfellows and a dwarf, Beatrice d'Este's son Massimiliano (right) briefly heeds his tutor's lesson. With fewer distractions, the boy below studies Cicero, whose initials M. T. C. are inscribed on the bench behind him.

Man's happiness, wrote Agnolo Pandolfini, lay not in public office or fame, but in his wife and children, his financial success, his reputation, and his friends. To ensure a happy marriage, he ought to wed a woman sufficiently young to be malleable, since he would have to teach her the obligations of motherhood and the art of managing the home. Paternal authority was supreme in the Renaissance household, but in all normal circumstances the mother was expected to supervise the day-to-day routine.

High on the list was the children's education, which began early, under the aegis of a tutor. Prodigies of ten or eleven wrote Latin letters, memorized pages of poetry, and entertained state visitors with eloquent and prolonged recitations from the classics. When it came to learning, there was little distinction between the sexes. "A little girl ought to learn Latin," Cardinal Bembo wrote. "It puts a finishing touch to her charms." They were also taught to embroider and to dance, and to supervise servants, but most of their domestic training was postponed until after marriage, when the real molding process began.

In a detail of Botticelli's The Birth of Venus *(left), the goddess, riding the waves on a gleaming shell, is wafted toward shore by zephyrs amid a shower of roses. The painting illustrates part of a long poem which Poliziano wrote in commemoration of Simonetta's tourney. Years after Simonetta's death, Piero di Cosimo, in a memorial portrait (right), symbolized her fatal illness by painting an enamel serpent coiled around her neck.*

GODDESS OF LOVE

Born at Porto Venere, the legendary site of Venus' rising from the sea, the lovely Simonetta Vespucci came to Florence and dazzled the city with her beauty. Giuliano de' Medici, falling in love with her, ordered a lavish tourney held in her honor, and commissioned Botticelli to paint her portrait on the banner which he carried into the lists. With that exception, all of the supposed portraits of Simonetta were done after she had died from consumption at the age of twenty-three. Sandro Botticelli recalled her loveliness years later when he used her likeness in the *Primavera*. "It seemed impossible," Lorenzo de' Medici said, "that she was loved by so many men without any jealousy and praised by so many women without envy," yet it seems to have been true. Faithful to her husband (a cousin of the navigator Amerigo Vespucci), Simonetta became a symbol of beauty for artists and poets, an embodiment of the Renaissance belief that perfection was possible.

OVERLEAF: *With her hand raised in blessing, Venus welcomes the advent of spring in Botticelli's allegory,* La Primavera. *The artist is thought to have painted Simonetta Vespucci as Venus, as the three Graces, and as the flower-decked nymph standing at the right.*

In a series of water-color miniatures, an anonymous Venetian artist recorded scenes of a courtesan's life. Above, a harlot leans provocatively out of her window to dicker with two prospective customers dressed in carnival costume; below, another entertains a bearded guest within her sumptuous chamber, while a pet dog looks on.

THE COURTESAN

Standing nude at their windows to entice customers inside, the harlots of Venice enjoyed the busiest professional practice in all Italy. Rome had a more distinguished collection of learned courtesans, whose intellectual attainments rivaled their other skills, but when the popes periodically expelled all harlots from the city they gravitated to Venice. Even there, however, they found professional hazards. They could be punished with a flogging for trafficking with Turks or Jews, and the prevalence of the dreaded French disease daily jeopardized their careers, if not their lives. Harlots had to take a holiday to celebrate religious festivals, even though the republic lost tax revenues when the profits of their trade decreased. Still, almost 12,000 registered prostitutes managed to eke out a living at a time when Venice's total population was only 300,000. One catalogue, listing the city's most notorious harlots, names 215 who were especially accomplished, but warns the enterprising tourist, who might be interested in striking up friendship with all of them, that his curiosity would cost a total of 1,200 scudi.

Prices were high, but the more cultivated courtesans provided their customers with intellectual refreshment, too. Despite clients' complaints that conversation was as expensive as love, salons held by famous courtesans often rivaled those of the great princesses like Isabella d'Este. Open to the public for a fee, the salons attracted the greatest men of the age to listen to music, to dance, and to engage in philosophical conversations. Courtesans were trained to be intelligent company; and in studying for their profession they took lessons in singing, dancing, Latin, letter-writing, painting, and deportment, and one earned immortality by memorizing everything that Petrarch and Boccaccio ever wrote. In tribute to their unsurpassed command of the courtly graces, humanists coined the euphemism *cortigiana* to distinguish these talented ladies from their less fortunate sisters toiling in ordinary brothels.

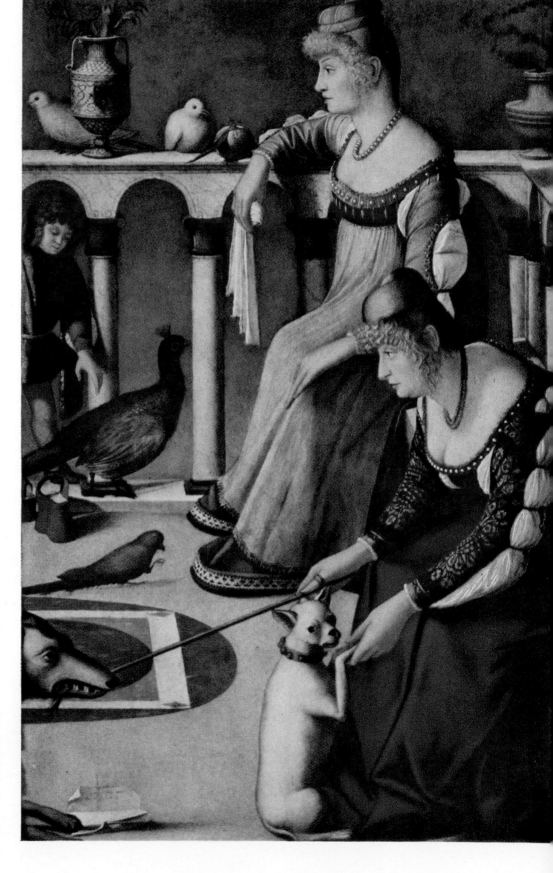

In décolleté finery, a pair of Venetian courtesans (right), in a painting by Carpaccio which Ruskin called "the best picture in the world," take the air on a balcony, surrounded by their pet birds and dogs, a peacock, and a page. The Senate tried to limit the splendor of harlots' costumes, but its efforts were in vain; to keep pace with honest women, prostitutes flaunted costly dresses, bleached their frizzed hair, and tottered about on high clogs like the red ones in Carpaccio's picture (beneath the peacock's tail). Dressed as elegantly, if more sparsely, another Venetian courtesan appears above, wearing richly jeweled headdress, earrings, necklace, and opulent red cloak.

"Melancholy shows in his work," reported Vasari in his biography of Correggio, the painter who drew the shrieking woman at left, posed in a classical attitude symbolizing suffering. Her features, contorted by grief, resemble a mask of the Greek theater.

THE FACE OF REALITY

Painters, poets, and courtiers chattered endlessly about beauty, but beauty faded quickly in fifteenth-century Italy. Brutal wars racked the countryside, plague raged in the cities, and the image of love, like Dante's Beatrice, Petrarch's Laura, and the adored Simonetta Vespucci, perished quickly. Brides were often widowed while still young, for Renaissance men preferred to marry late in life; and remarriage was frowned upon, for it was considered a disgrace to the memory of a dead husband. In Perugia second marriages had to take place after dark, and they were often disrupted by rioters, hooting derisively outside the wedding chamber. Maidens without dowries were even less fortunate than widows; with no prospects of marriage, they were sent off to finish their days virtually imprisoned in a convent. Theorizing about ideal proportions and the spiritual value of beauty, artists painted idyllic scenes of life as they wished it to be, but there were some who preferred to portray it as they saw it. Mary Magdalen, weeping over her sins in the desert, only made Titian see another plump Venetian nude with long ringlets and a fresh complexion, but Donatello, treating the same austere theme, had chosen instead to carve a haggard, repentant Magdalen (opposite), whose gaunt face and deep-set eyes reflect her suffering.

Pointing to herself as an example, a worn and aged woman (right), painted by Giorgione, displays the motto COL TEM-PO, *to warn that "with Time" everything meets destruction. The ravages of both sin and time show in the deeply moving face of Mary Magdalen (opposite), Donatello's last statue.*

THE IMAGE
OF MARY

In contrast with the calm beauty of Antonello da Messina's Virgin Annunciate *(above), Crivelli's* Annunciation *(opposite) shows Mary in a scene of splendor. Curiously, neither artist was in the main stream of the Italian Renaissance. Antonello was a follower of the Van Eycks; Crivelli worked in Padua, only lightly touched by the surge of culture.*

When workmen digging on the Appian Way in 1485 unearthed the perfectly preserved corpse of a Roman maiden, thousands of pilgrims filed by to marvel at her unequaled beauty. It seemed to prove what humanists had claimed—that the ancient world was superior to the Christian era. But most Italians of the time never lost sight of another, far more compelling ideal of incorruptible beauty—the Virgin, whose image protected every house, church, and wayside shrine. Despite the inroads of paganism, the Church kept a firm hold on Renaissance Italy. Whatever the signs of corruption in the Church, the great mass of the people retained their genuine devotion. Even the warring factions of Siena, once they had placed the keys of the town before the image of Mary and vowed to maintain civil peace, faithfully kept their promise for years. And for every woman acclaimed for her beauty or her wit, the Renaissance produced its saints. Many of them were simple women, like the Genoese matron, Caterinetta Fieschi, who established shelters for incurables who had been expelled from hospitals to die on the streets. Housewives gave their time and money to orphanages, nursed the sick, and distributed alms, and when they died, asked to be buried in the habit of a nun. Even Martin Luther, who deplored most Italian practices, found himself admiring the good works of Italian women.

OPVS CARO
LI·CRIVELLI
VENETI

·1486·

THE SPREAD OF THE
RENAISSANCE

In the autumn of 1511, Erasmus, the most distinguished scholar of Northern Europe, took up his lodgings again in Queens' College, Cambridge—a cold, bleak room that overlooked the marshes of the fens. He was poor, he was frightened of the plague that raged about the University, he was very lonely. He had been swept to England by the tide of the Italian Renaissance, not for the first but for the third time. For five wearisome years Erasmus moldered in Cambridge until he could stand the poverty and the ignorance no longer, and off he went on his journeys again, to the Netherlands, to Switzerland, to Germany, always carrying with him the memory of those years in Italy when he had discovered himself. The new learning had filled him with such hope that not even the sorrows and hardships of his personal life could eradicate it. In 1517 he could still write, "Immortal God, what a world I see dawning! Why can I not grow young again?" Nor was Erasmus unique. In London one of the most

gifted, yet wayward, of Florentine sculptors, Torrigiano, was modeling, under the soaring Gothic arches of Westminster Abbey, the first Renaissance tombs of Northern Europe, built to immortalize Henry VII and his wife, Elizabeth of York. For decades the currents created not only by cataclysmic events such as the invasion of Italy by the French kings, but also by the excitement of the new learning, had been drawing such men as Erasmus and Torrigiano into or out of Italy. And that sense of wonder, of a new world and a new dawn of the spirit, touched less sensitive men than Erasmus. Edward IV conferred the Garter, the highest order of English chivalry, on the Duke of Urbino, and the court of Windsor witnessed the embassy of Castiglione who came to receive it for his master. So profound was Henry VII's respect for the Italian scholarship that he asked Polydore Vergil to write what became the first serious and dispassionate study of England's history. Indeed, the presence of Erasmus in England

The bronze figures of King Henry VII of England and his Queen, Elizabeth of York, rest atop their elaborate Renaissance tomb in Westminster Abbey. Made by an Italian sculptor, Pietro Torrigiano, who had the dubious distinction of having broken Michelangelo's nose in a youthful brawl, the tomb is one of the earliest monuments of the Tudor style. Francis Bacon later commented that the penny-pinching King Henry "dwelleth more richly dead than he did alive in any of his palaces."

was due entirely to a devoted band of humanists—Linacre, Grocyn, and Colet—who had studied in Padua, Florence, and Rome, seeking to acquire facility in Greek and a knowledge of the old as well as the new philosophies. Their attitude was deeply Christian, and their aim was to perfect their theology through a more exact knowledge of the early Fathers. The employment of Pietro Torrigiano was also due to the same band of humanists, which included Lord Mountjoy as its patron and John Fisher as its chaplain, both of whom were intimately connected with the English royal family. What was true of England was also true of the Netherlands, of Germany, and of Spain.

As the Renaissance spread beyond the Alps, it was checked in Italy. In 1495 Charles VIII invaded Naples and in so doing unleashed thirty years of carnage. In the Lombard plain battle followed battle, draining away wealth, disrupting trade, heaping up taxes, destroying conditions favorable to art and learning. Furthermore, the riches of the New World, so recently discovered, poured into Spain, the Netherlands, France, and England, but not into Italy; wealth went west, and with it art. And then came Luther, who in 1517 hammered his Protestant theses to the church door of Wittenberg. To hold off the Reformation, the Papacy needed a sterner spirit; the luxurious and wanton times of the Borgia and Medici were brought to an end, and a militant asceticism replaced the self-indulgence of Renaissance Rome. No wonder Vasari regarded the venerable Michelangelo as a relic of the age of heroes. This lonely, solitary artist had become the symbol of a time that had passed.

By 1500 Italy exerted a hypnotic influence, and just as the princes of the Western world wished to acquire the services of Italy's great painters and sculptors, so, too, did the artists of this outer world feel themselves drawn to Italy. The great Flemish school of painters might be secure within its own

Notoriously vain, Dürer portrayed himself many times. Above he is seen as a youthful apprentice (left), holding an aphrodisiac herb (center), and at right piously posing in imitation of Christ, in a painting influenced by the newborn Reformation. Dürer's religious mentors, Luther and Melanchthon, are shown at left, in a double portrait by Lucas Cranach the Younger. Melanchthon had been a promising humanist scholar, but he soon came to devote most of his energies to the Protestant cause.

great tradition and therefore possess little or no sense of inferiority when confronted with the brilliance of the Italian achievement; and in fact it contributed as much in technique and originality as it derived from Italy. The same was not true, however, of the French or the German artists. They had been ravished by the books of engravings of Italian pictures that had begun to circulate after 1470. Crude as these were, they sufficiently hinted the beauties of the masters they copied to excite an overwhelming curiosity. Albrecht Dürer, as a young apprentice at Nuremberg, somehow acquired engravings of Pollaiuolo and Mantegna. Already in a tentative, schoolboyish, and rather shocked manner he had begun to draw from the nude, but these engravings helped to release his spirit from the harsh, moral, and cruelly realistic treatment of naked women that had become traditional in Gothic Germany. Engravings were not enough, however, and try as he might the secret of the Italian painters seemed to

elude him. He believed that the formula for successful painting of the human figure, like some ancient mystery, was kept hidden by Italian artists. He sought the magic formula in Italy itself, deepened his imagination, improved his technique, but never found what he sought, and to his death the Gothic tradition into which he had been born held him in thrall. Yet without his Italian experiences and without his preoccupation with Italian art, his own achievement would have been less noble. As with Dürer, so with scores of artists great or small over the next four hundred years. They came to Italy as on a pilgrimage, for here was the source of their art. The painting of El Greco is as idiosyncratic as any artist's of Western Europe, yet his art is indelibly stamped with the years that he spent in Venice. The way he draws, the glittering light that runs along the edge of his figures, derives from Tintoretto, as his color does from Titian. The two greatest French artists of the seventeenth century—Nicolas Poussin

Giorgione's dreamlike Venus *(upper left) was one of the first classical reclining nudes in Venetian art, and was the model for many great paintings in the succeeding four centuries.* Titian's Venus of Urbino *(see page 301) is almost a direct copy. Although a great admirer of Titian, Diego Velázquez took a different and unusual pose for his* Rokeby Venus *(lower left), portraying her with her back discreetly turned. As paintings of the female nude were all but forbidden in inquisitorial Spain of the seventeeth century, it was perhaps the artist's way of appeasing the puritans.*

and Claude Lorraine—spent most of their working lives in Rome. Titian—his color, his atmosphere, even his figures—entranced Poussin. Again and again, artists of the highest genius—Velázquez, Rubens, Rembrandt, Goya, Renoir—paint the same themes, sometimes even copy the same pictures, that the artists of the Renaissance had first conceived and executed. Giorgione's reclining Venus haunts European painting like a dream. All who aspired to greatness in painting needed to make the long journey to Italy. Some, like Sir Joshua Reynolds, went in great comfort under the patronage of the rich; others, like Richard Wilson, went on foot and in poverty, painting for their bread. Until the twentieth century, the traditions created by the Italian Renaissance were those in which all Western European artists worked.

The French kings and their courtiers during their invasions of Italy were delighted by much that they saw in Milan and Venice: the Certosa of Pavia especially caught their imagina-tion. On the other hand, the austere and more truly classical buildings of Florence left them unmoved. So at first Italian influences on the new luxurious hunting lodges that the French nobility were building along the Loire combined, as at Chambord, the basic plan of a traditional medieval castle with the sophisticated elevation and greater comfort of an Italian palace. For a time this marriage of the old and the new satisfied Western Europe, but in the end, no matter how much inspiration might twist and turn within its national traditions, or frolic in the riotous decoration of the Baroque, it was drawn back, time and time again, to the purity of classical achievement, to Brunelleschi, to Bramante, to Palladio, and, finally—just before the Gothic revival destroyed architectural taste throughout Western Europe—to the Greek. In the visual arts, in its themes as well as its techniques, the achievements of the Italian Renaissance permeated Europe like an indelible stain. They expressed the world in which

men wished to live—their dreams, their aspirations, as well as their actualities.

The arts of the Renaissance were not the only achievements that seeded themselves throughout the countries of the Western world. Changes that had taken place in Italy generations earlier were happening in Western Europe in the sixteenth century, with the result that a similar sort of society grew up with similar needs. Its basis, like Italy's, was mercantile and urban; and it was ambivalent toward the old feudal nobilities—longing for their grace, their courtliness, and their sense of privileged destiny, yet hating their special rights, their selfish and jealous independence that could cut so savagely across the needs of society as a whole, to the detriment of trade and profit. The new men longed for professional government, for a powerful person who could secure order and inculcate into a barbarous and anarchic society the *civilitas* of the ancients. For them the fountain of this politi-

cal knowledge was Italy: there the wisdom of the classical world, of Plato, of Aristotle, of Cicero, had been sifted and refined and adjusted to modern necessities. Even more importantly, the University of Padua could teach them the secrets of Roman government through the study of its laws. Again, the Italians had made a profession of diplomacy in Europe of the fifteenth century which had come to be regarded as essential to good government as statistical analysis is in the twentieth. Men of affairs in London, in Paris, in Brussels, in Madrid, in the towns and states of Germany, thought that they could only manage their new and baffling societies if they or their subordinates had studied in Italy. Most of Henry VIII's ministers of state—Wolsey, More, and Thomas Cromwell—were fascinated by the new learning, and they encouraged scholarship whenever they could. Wolsey endowed Christ Church, Oxford, in order to establish the study of the new humanities in England. Thomas More became the

life-long friend of Erasmus. Cromwell lent his rare and precious Italian books to his friends and encouraged young men such as Thomas Starkey, who had spent years studying civil law at Padua in the household of Reginald Pole. (Pole, who was a Plantagenet and a kinsman of Henry VIII, maintained a small court of English scholars at the University of Padua.) This interest in Italian learning certainly had its practical aspects, but it captivated them all—even Cromwell, that hammer of the monasteries—at a deeper level than practical usefulness.

This new learning seemed to hold the secrets of life itself for most of them and, for the more sensitive, some of the secrets of eternity. More and his friends—Colet, Linacre, Grocyn—were deeply religious men. So were Lefèvre d'Étaples and his colleagues in Paris; so were Ulrich von Hutten and Reuchlin in Germany. They reverenced Italian scholarship, for it took them, via a knowledge of Greek, to the

purest texts of the New Testament. Here, they felt, they would find a faith cleansed from the impurities and evasions created by centuries of comment and explanation. By applying the new skills of philology and textual criticism which the Italian humanists had perfected, they would, they hoped, lay bare Christianity in its purest and most historical form and thereby strengthen the Church. This attitude toward religion fused with another, equally serious, but Flemish rather than Italian in origin. Before Renaissance influence had touched Northwestern Europe there had been a strong revival of religious mysticism, led by the Brethren of the Common Life, which had been given literary and devotional form by Thomas à Kempis in his *Imitation of Christ*. This mysticism stressed the importance of the individual's direct relation with God, and, by implication, lessened the importance of the priesthood and the Church. The search for historical truth, through scholarship, became linked with

As the alma mater of Pico della Mirandola and Bembo, the University of Padua (opposite) was one of the chief
centers of Italian humanism, and
throughout the sixteenth century its
famous teachers (Galileo was one) attracted students from all over Europe.
Among them were youths who were to
become kings of Sweden and Poland,
scholars who were to spread the Renaissance throughout Northern Europe.
Erasmus, shown at right in a portrait by
Hans Holbein the Younger, never studied at Padua, but did work at the library
of the University of Bologna. During
his lifetime, his satirical masterpiece
The Praise of Folly was printed forty
times; at left is the title page of an English edition published posthumously.

this search for truth in the exercise of the individual's religious conscience; and both became the seeding ground of
Protestantism.

No one is more typical of the linkage between Italian humanism and reformed Christianity than Erasmus, who prepared the ground for Luther. A bastard son of a priest, half-
tricked into monastic life, sensitive, excluded both by his habit
and temperament from an active life of the instincts, he concentrated his heart and mind on friendship with scholars of
like tastes. A man of formidable intellectual ability and exquisite literary gifts, his vast reputation was built up not only
by personal contact and familiar letters, but also by the new
invention of the printing press. His sharp satire—*The Praise
of Folly*—exploited the sensationalism which only the press
can give, and his Latin translation of the Greek Testament
established his reputation as a scholar with a rapidity that no
one could have achieved in earlier centuries. For Erasmus, the

institutions of the Church and its learning were encrusted
with silliness, stupidity, and barbarity. Christian faith could
never regain its pristine clarity until this dross of centuries
was cleared away. Yet he was no Protestant, no revolutionary,
and he retreated rapidly from the position toward which
Luther with his furious denunciations and precipitate actions
seemed to be dragging him. Naturally he refused to listen to
Albrecht Dürer's ardent plea: "O Erasmus of Rotterdam,
where wilt thou tarry? . . . Hear, Christian knight, ride
forth with the Lord Jesus . . . defend the right, obtain the
martyr's crown!" He preferred to die in his bed: scared of the
new age whose coming in 1517 he had welcomed with such
joy. But for Dürer the reformation of religion was an inspiration greater and deeper than any experience of his life, greater
even than his artistic experience in Italy.

Undoubtedly the scholars and critics had undermined, by
their sharp attack on contemporary religious practices, the

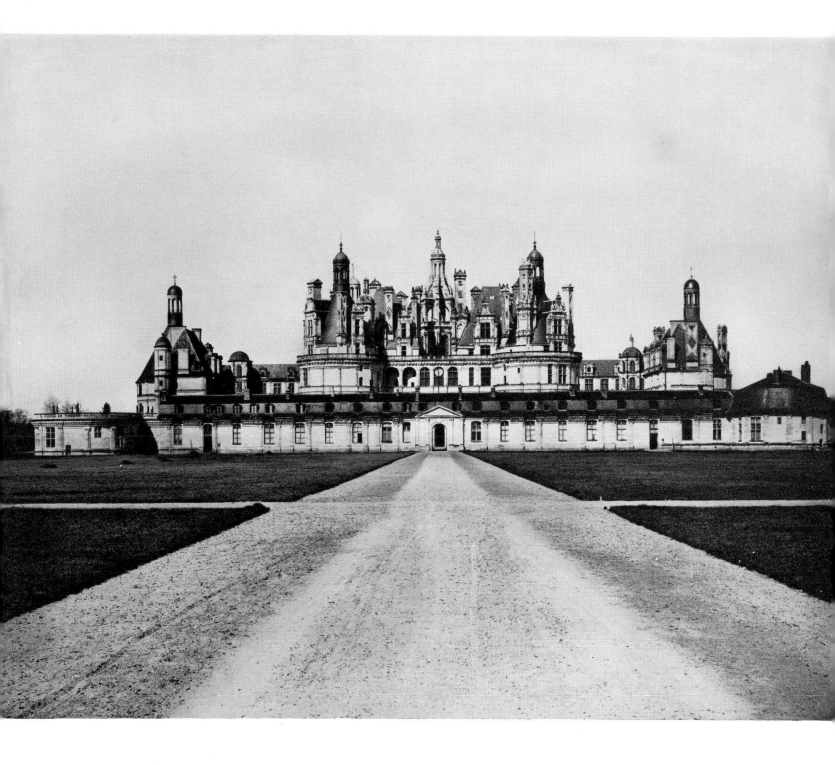

institutions of the Church; they mocked priests, bred resentment against papal taxation, and held the popes themselves up to the ridicule many deserved. Although some like Erasmus drew back, others such as Melanchthon and Peter Martyr, the Italian humanist, were prepared to go forward with Luther, feeling that he was leading them to the true dawn of a new age, to the rebirth of Christianity as Christ preached it. So the spirit of the Italian Renaissance, once it crossed the Alps, was diverted into new channels, plunging from the broad, sunlit meadows of secular delights into the dark ravines of religion.

Yet this political and religious twist to Italian influence was, for the early part of the sixteenth century, largely, if not entirely, confined to England, the Netherlands, and Germany. In France there were men like Erasmus, friends of his, deeply concerned with theology, deeply distrustful of scholasticism, as ardent as he was for pure religion. Yet they were not typical of French society as More and Colet or even Thomas Cromwell were typical of England. French society was more sophisticated, more secure, readier far to pursue that language of personal expression which lies at the heart of the Italian Renaissance. Much of Italian civilization—the gardens, the clothes, the furnishings and decoration of houses and palaces, the general civility of life, had entranced Philippe de Comines and many another noble Frenchman with the invading armies of Charles VIII and Louis XII. But it was Francis I who really fell in love with Italy and things Italian in spite of the fact that the greatest humiliation of his career —his defeat by the Emperor Charles V—took place at Pavia. He was the first prince outside Italy to begin a collection of paintings and sculpture by the great Italian masters. He persuaded Leonardo da Vinci to spend his last years at Amboise, close to his great hunting lodges at Blois and Chambord. He did everything he could to entice Michelangelo to live in

France and nearly succeeded. (He had to be content with a *Hercules* his agent bought.) With Benvenuto Cellini he was more successful. This fabulous rogue, a boastful, swashbuckling liar yet a craftsman of genius, entranced Francis, who tolerated his extravagance and forgave his bad temper for the sake of the embellishments (among them Cellini's superb gold saltcellar which is so justly famous) with which he was adorning his châteaux.

Francis I was not merely a collector; he wanted his court to outshine in literature and in manners, as well as in art, the most famous courts of Italy, and he flung his cloak of patronage on all who might bring distinction to his country. In this he was aided by his remarkable sister, Marguerite of Navarre, who can claim, perhaps, to be one of the most outstanding women of the Renaissance. She wrote the *Heptameron*, a bawdy collection of stories, after the style of Boccaccio; a mystical tract called *The Mirror of the Sinful Soul*, and a number of outstanding spiritual hymns. She corresponded with Erasmus, befriended Protestants, was accused herself as a heretic by the Sorbonne, and patronized Rabelais. Her court contained the whole world of letters, as complex and as strange as her own temperament. Indeed, many of the contradictions in her own self-expression reflected the contradictions of French artistic and intellectual society as it struggled to assimilate the achievements of Italy not only with its own Gothic traditions but also with those new horizons—intellectual as well as geographical—which the great discoveries had disclosed to the Western world. For Italian humanists, discovery lay in the past, in the art and history of their ancestors or their country's ancestors, the Greeks. With Frenchmen and with Englishmen, discovery also meant new worlds that knew neither Christianity nor Christian government nor Christian morality. To men such as Rabelais, Montaigne, Marlowe, Shakespeare, or Bacon, in-

security, anxiety, and elation mingled haphazardly and fused into art. Reverence for the past, a yearning for the safety of tradition, alternated with the intoxicating sense of the capacity of man, the uniqueness of his experience, and the splendor and freshness of the world about him.

In Rabelais, the greatest writer of the French Renaissance, this conflict was apparent both in his restless, troubled life and in his writings. Like Erasmus, he was a rebel monk who hated the ignorance and immorality of monastic life. He sought truth in the world. "Abandon yourself," he wrote, "to Nature's truths, and let nothing in this world be unknown to you." Rabelais followed his own dictum and it led him to strange places—to alchemy, to astrology, to the mysterious exoticism which seemed to offer new truth in the intellectual chaos of sixteenth-century Europe. And his great work *Gargantua and Pantagruel* is as odd and as moving as Rabelais' own quest for self-knowledge. Gargantua, Panta-

gruel, and Grangousier, the chief characters of this extraordinary fantasia, have the twisted extravagance of Gothic gargoyles. They are gross representatives of the instinctive life, yet full of satire and wisdom, capable of nobility and understanding. Above all they are in search of life and truth. And in the midst of their fantastic adventures comes the description of the Abbey of Thelema, a Utopian world that might have been dreamed by Castiglione. The turmoil and confusion of real life is stilled by the contemplation of realized ideals; men and women achieve the noble life. The whole book is written in a fabulous style, by a man utterly drunk with words. It is almost as if Rabelais had himself discovered language. This mixture of barbarity and civility, of satire and sincerity, entranced the French court. The Church might be scandalized, the Protestants outraged, but Pantagruelism became chic, the fashion of the aristocracy. It was original, it was in tune with the medley and confusion of contem-

A contemporary drawing (right) shows Marguerite of Navarre, beloved sister of Francis I, fondling her pet dog. Marguerite was equally protective toward artists, and Rabelais gratefully dedicated one volume of Gargantua and Pantagruel *to her. Although his chronicle of the lusty giant (left), a figure borrowed from French folklore, was condemned as obscene, Rabelais retained the royal patronage. Marguerite's own novellas were hardly less bawdy, but she composed devotional poetry as well. The miniature at far left shows her dressed in mourning for her son, giving Francis' mistress, the Duchess d'Étampes, a copy of one of her works.*

porary life, and above all, it was French.

As soon as a literary renaissance begins to flourish either in France or in England or in Spain, a strong nationalist sentiment rapidly infuses it, and the delight that writers and artists took in the Italian achievement led not only to emulation but also to envy. In 1549 Joachim du Bellay published his pamphlet *La Défense et illustration de la langue française* (cribbed almost entirely from Speroni's defense of Italian) in which he exhorted Frenchmen to challenge in their own language the triumphs of antiquity. The same court circle that patronized Rabelais took du Bellay's exhortation as a battle cry. Fortunately, du Bellay could practice what he preached. He and his friend Ronsard and their group, *La Pléiade,* produced excellent lyrics. They, too, were preoccupied with the loneliness of men and their dependence on love and affection to save them from unbearable solitude. In Marguerite of Navarre, Ronsard, Rabelais, du Bellay, and the rest,

the court of Francis I possessed a galaxy of talent that would have been a credit to any court of Italy. Owing vast debts to the Italian Renaissance, they nevertheless achieved a style, an idiom, and a theme that were distinctly French.

The same was to be true of the great efflorescence of literature that took place in England shortly afterwards. Plots, characters, in fact entire plays were lifted wholesale from Italian authors. The intentions of Edmund Spenser would have drawn from Castiglione nothing but his entire approval, and Spenser's debt to Ariosto's *Orlando Furioso* is as obvious as it is large. Yet there is no plagiarism: all is transmuted, Englished. Like Rabelais, the Elizabethans grew drunk on the discovery of their language. At the same time they were even less confined by tradition than the French, and their sense of achievement was far sharper, for the English were closer in time to barbarity and to anarchy. The great promise of the days of Chaucer, Langland, and Wycliffe had been checked

by the maelstrom of the fifteenth century. The Wars of the Roses had ripped apart the fabric of English life. The violent class turmoil of the early Tudor period which followed, which had led men of affairs to seek guidance in politics and diplomacy in Italy, had begun to settle by the reign of Elizabeth I into a new pattern of society in which gentlemen—but not noblemen—predominated. The break with the Church, combined with increasing knowledge of the worlds beyond Europe, intensified this sense of a new age, of an original time. Yet the very dissolution of the past created anxiety, insecurity, a sense of isolation, and a longing to discover standards. The dramatists held up a looking glass to this society in conflict. The violence, the rapacity, the passion of their age was more acceptable to the audience that thronged to see their plays if they were cast in Italy, in ancient Rome, or more daringly in their own historic past. For their crude audience, the crimes in the *Duchess of Malfi* or the *White*

Devil possessed a further dimension of evil and horror if set in the criminal splendor of an Italian court where incest, riot, poison, and murder were, everyone believed, commonplaces of life. As well as stimulating the poetic imagination of a Webster or a Tourneur, however, Italy and its Renaissance still possessed a serious purpose for Englishmen. Long after politicians had given up expecting to find the secrets of their craft there, and long after dramatists had exhausted the plots of its authors, Italy continued to exert the deepest influence.

Profoundly important as the influence of the Italian Renaissance might be on art and literature and learning, it was greater still in education, using that word in its widest possible sense. This possessed two aspects—one for the narrow circle of intellectually creative men, the other for the world at large. How far the intellectual skepticism of the Renaissance, with its search for truth in the evidence presented by men and events rather than in dogma and authority, stimu-

Quentin Matsys was the dean of Flemish art during the early sixteenth century, and such paintings as The Moneylender and His Wife *(facing page) illustrate the transition from religious preoccupation to an interest in the common man and his surroundings. The mirror in the foreground reflects what is probably the artist's self-portrait. In England, the influence of Italy is most clearly seen in Elizabethan drama. William Shakespeare, whose portrait (below) appeared as the frontispiece of his first folio, used numerous Italian scenes, names, and tales in his plays. His dramas were enthusiastically received in such London theaters as the Swan (right), sketched in 1596 by Johann de Witt, a visiting Dutchman.*

lated the growth of a rational attitude to the world is difficult to know. Certainly without the greater stimuli of the discovery of the world beyond Europe and the revolutionary achievements of science in the seventeenth century, it might easily have come to naught. However, to belittle the importance of those first broad cracks that were made in fifteenth-century Italy in the all-embracing dome of dogma is to falsify history. Ideologies were still to rage in the heart of man and haunt his destiny, but for Western man never again could there be two opposed worlds of Christians and heretics. Important though this impetus was to the habit of truth, to the growth of a scientific and skeptical spirit in the world of learning, it is of minor significance compared with the influence which the Italian Renaissance had on the social patterns which Western Europe adopted.

Italy, with Flanders, had been the first country in Europe to grow really rich on commerce, to throw up a middle class which could challenge the economic, political, and social power of the aristocracy. These merchants, bankers, craftsmen, found their first real security in economic life. This they knew; this they controlled. And so they organized their political and social life about their economic activity—in guilds —and ignored as far as they could the structure of the world about them. But the pressure of their wealth and the needs of their professions forced them from their exclusive habits, forced them into contact (and at times into conflict) with the aristocracy, whose sources of wealth, invigorated by the rise of commerce, remained large enough to maintain their privileged place in society. In the end a linkage was made between the aristocracy and the middle class: they remained distinct but joined by paths that men could traverse, and this mingling wrought a profound change in social customs, in manners, in education, in the images of man that seemed socially valuable. In its search for standards, Italy could look where

the Flemish could not—into its highly sophisticated past, to the days of Rome and Greece when life had also been urban, rich, and aristocratic, yet commercially minded. Although antiquity could provide some ingredients, it could not provide all, and the merchants' hunger to belong drove them to accept readily many of the concepts of feudal aristocracy.

By 1530 or so, however, Italian society had brought into being an idea of a gentleman that was neither classical nor feudal, neither noble nor bourgeois, neither rural nor urban, but a fusion of all of these. The projection of this image acquired such intensity because Western Europe had begun to undergo the same sort of violent social revolution that Italy had undergone between 1300 and 1450. In the sixteenth century commercial wealth poured into Cadiz, Lisbon, Bordeaux, Nantes, London, Antwerp, Hamburg. It raced through the veins of rural society, erupting, creating, destroying. The new men of this age—and there were thousands of them—felt great social insecurity. They had to learn to be gentlemen, to move at ease in the aristocratic world which they could not or would not eradicate. They adopted the pattern of compromise which the Italians had established. They wolfed down the courtesy books—della Casa as well as Castiglione. They adopted Italian clothes and Italian manners. They educated their children according to Italian precepts. A knowledge of a great deal of Latin and a little Greek became an absolute necessity for anyone who aspired to gentility, from the North Cape of Norway to the Strait of Gibraltar. And a gentleman was not only delineated by his education, he also required breeding—those aristocratic airs, that easy nonchalance, that assumption of privileged position lightly borne, which Castiglione had emphasized over and over again. A taste in the visual arts, or connoisseurship, was as essential a part of breeding as skill in sitting a horse. As Europe assimilated its vast wealth,

and society became more ordered, so this image of a gentleman became more tenacious. It represented, as it did in Italy, the triumph of the aristocracy at the expense of the middle class, whose own merits—prudence, reticence, professional education—came to be regarded as either boorish or comic, from which the young not only wished to escape but were encouraged to do so. This is why the possession of land achieved such sanctity in Western Europe—it was the way to salvation, the route by which a merchant's children might become gentlemen and gentlewomen. Excluded from true social power, hypnotized by the snobbery and sophistication of aristocratic life to which the Italian Renaissance had given such vivid definition, the merchant classes of Europe lost much of their dynamic and creative energy, and it took nearly two centuries of frustration before they challenged, in the age of Napoleon, the aristocratic foundations of European society.

During this period from the Reformation to the French Revolution the spirit of the Italian Renaissance pervaded Europe. It taught the rough and very raw provincial aristocracies of the West how to live, how to move at ease through a world of bourgeois delights, without being contaminated by it. Certainly it intensified snobbery, hardened the stratification of classes of men, and checked the scientific imagination by insisting on the education of character rather than of aptitudes. In return it gave much. It taught the new men of Europe that the purpose of art, the call of learning, were an essential part of the use of wealth. And it projected a theme—the uniqueness of personal experience, the idea of man caught in the jaws of Time—that has given rise to the world's greatest art and literature. The spirit of the Italian Renaissance broods over these centuries which link the age of feudalism to modern times, and makes them a part of itself.

ITALY'S RENAISSANCE
MOVES NORTHWARD

Federigo da Montefeltro called upon a painter from Flanders to decorate his new palace at Urbino. King Alfonso urged Jan van Eyck to emigrate to Naples, and when Rogier van der Weyden came to Rome for the Jubilee of 1450, Italian painters crowded around him like rustics gawking at a king. Flanders, along with the other domains of the Duke of Burgundy, was the only part of Europe which could claim to rival Italy's own Renaissance. Combining the trappings of knightly life with rich commercial activity, the Burgundian realms produced schools of painting which were to impose a lasting influence on European art. Italy was in constant commercial and artistic contact with the triple capitals of Ghent, Bruges, and Dijon, as indicated by Jan van Eyck's famous wedding portrait (opposite) of a Tuscan merchant and his bride. The painting, which reveals the passionate attention to detail for which Flemish artists were famous, is an example of the crosscurrents which flowed between the two lands.

Burgundy, which rivaled Italy's progress, was soon to foreshadow Italy's fate. With the death of Duke Charles the Bold in 1477, Burgundian territory fell prey to the battling powers of France and the Empire. Seizing most of the French-speaking hinterland, France established a national power which was to set the stage for the splendid reign of Francis I. Imperial Spain and the Flemish lowlands were less fortunate; they inherited each other, and soon were locked in mortal combat. Burgundy and Flanders, lands which Charlemagne had envisioned as part of a middle kingdom between France and Germany, became mere satellites of Paris and Madrid; yet those capitals, despite their political supremacy, looked to Italy for rules of art and diplomacy, manners and education. Italian universities lured students and visitors from all over Europe, who returned to implant Renaissance ideas in lands as distant as Sweden and Poland. But it was where political power was centered—in Spain, France, and later England—that the Renaissance flourished most brilliantly.

The pages that follow, briefly summarizing the spread of the Renaissance beyond the Alps, barely hint at the richness of the age, for merely a list of the men who reflected the Renaissance spirit would be an awesome one. In its heyday Spain boasted of Cervantes and Lope da Vega, El Greco and Velázquez. England gave birth to no great painters, but where Italy a century before had found its noblest expression in painting and sculpture, Elizabeth's kingdom had its poets —Spenser and Shakespeare, Marlowe, Jonson, and the translators of the Bible—who produced what is one of the few bodies of work in history which can stand beside the art of the Italians. Nevertheless, it was France which gained most from Italy: except for Rabelais and Montaigne, there were no great native names to equal the giants of Spanish or English literature, but France assimilated the Renaissance experience so thoroughly that in the centuries which followed she succeeded Italy as the light of Europe.

Once the King had an actor whipped for satirizing his court, but behind his back contemporaries still called Francis "Le Roi Grand Nez." Despite his long nose, the King was very vain of his good looks. Clouet's portrait shows him splendidly arrayed in a feathered bonnet and a robe of gold brocade with immense puffed sleeves.

THE RENAISSANCE
IN FRANCE

Louis XII, invading Milan in 1499, was so impressed by Leonardo's fresco of the Last Supper that he proposed cutting it down from the wall and carrying it back to France. His courtiers finally dissuaded him, and the King was forced to appease his hunger for Italian art by commissioning a group of minor Italian craftsmen to work for him in France. Louis' successor, Francis I, was more fortunate; he managed to employ the great Leonardo himself by promising him 7,000 pieces of gold and "a palace of his own choice in the most beautiful region of France." Francis also brought in other Italian painters to decorate his palace walls with frescoes celebrating royal patronage and power. This was not hollow symbolism; the King's devotion to art and letters almost equaled his notorious enthusiasm for philandering.

During Francis I's reign, Paris was the largest city of Western Europe; the population of his kingdom was five times that of England and more than twice as large as Spain's. As the King traveled with a retinue of thousands from one castle to the next, his court consumed wealth as industriously as the country produced it. Along the valley of the river Loire, Francis and his nobles built splendid châteaux, designed by Italian architects and adorned in Renaissance style. One of the earliest was Azay-le-Rideau (*see* page 384), which was erected by the royal treasurer, who devoted ten years to its construction, only to have Francis quickly requisition the château for himself.

Château life recreated the ideal courtly society envisioned by Castiglione. Catherine de' Medici, whom Francis had imported from Florence as a wife for his son, brought with her the tastes of the Medici as well as some of their cash. Under her aegis the French court achieved a splendor which foreshadowed Versailles. A circle of poets attached to the Valois dynasty reflected its Renaissance spirit. Led by Ronsard and du Bellay, they proposed a rigid set of rules to make French poetry classical (Ronsard followed them so closely that his countrymen sometimes needed a guide to understand him). When Mary Queen of Scots, the wife of Francis' grandson, persuaded Ronsard to publish his odes, he became so famous that students in Paris fought to touch his robes as he passed by. The royal women—Mary, Catherine, Marguerite of Navarre, and Henry II's mistress, the fascinating Diane de Poitiers—gave the courts of Renaissance France much of their luster, and artists looked to them for patronage almost as much as to the kings themselves.

"This is a hundred times more divine a thing than I had ever dreamed of," Francis I exclaimed when Benvenuto Cellini showed him a wax model of the golden saltcellar shown above. When the work was finished, the King was even more effusive. "He uttered a loud cry of astonishment," Cellini proudly reported, "and could not satiate his eyes with gazing at it." The female figure on the saltcellar symbolizes earth, while the male opposite her, holding a trident, represents the sea. Cellini earned the same salary which Leonardo da Vinci had received at the French court, but Francis gave Leonardo 4,000 additional crowns when he purchased the famous Mona Lisa *portrait (below).*

With the English Channel visible in the distance, Henry VIII (left) rides out of Calais on a white palfrey to meet Francis I. Their famous encounter took its name from the cloth of gold which covered the pavilion (top, center) where the kings met. The monarchs jousted and wrestled; after Francis won one of their matches, he showed his chivalrous nature by venturing into Henry's camp unarmed.

THE FIELD OF
THE CLOTH OF GOLD

The meeting between "those suns of glory, those two lights of men," Francis I and Henry VIII, on the Field of the Cloth of Gold near Calais in 1520, was the last splendid display of the age of chivalry. Shakespeare described the fortnight of celebration: "Today the French All clinquant, all in gold, like heathen gods, Shone down the English; and tomorrow they Made Britain India: every man that stood Show'd like a mine." Both Henry and Francis were heirs of kings who had suppressed nobles to unify their countries. Both were young and chivalrous. Both were patrons of the arts, and the accession of each promised his kingdom a new age of gold. "What may we not expect," rhap-

sodized Sir Thomas More, "from a King who has been nourished by philosophy and the nine Muses!" Henry gave England far more than the utopian Sir Thomas had anticipated; the King's break with Rome, which cost More his life, strengthened the doughty national spirit that kept England alive during the century's titanic battle between France and Spain. With the decline of medievalism, Europe's nation-states began to emerge. Enriched by the wealth of the New World and the expansive spirit of the Renaissance, they forged affluent new cultures which were to clash with each other far more ferociously than their small Italian counterparts had done a century before.

A panorama of the sack of Rome, probably painted by Pieter Brueghel the Elder, shows a horde of German and Spanish troops pouring into the city. The biggest contingent storms the palace of the popes at upper right (twin towers); below, its triple bastions overlooking the river, is Castel Sant' Angelo, where Clement took refuge. The invaders even massacred refugees who sought shelter in St. Peter's.

THE SACK OF ROME

All Italy agreed that the iniquities of papal Rome merited punishment, but no one imagined the extent of the catastrophe that befell the city in 1527. Emperor Charles V, warring with Francis I, had signed a treaty with Henry VIII undoing the results of the Field of the Cloth of Gold, and sent a German army into Italy. Reaching Rome, thirty thousand uncontrollable troops slaughtered hospital patients, raped nuns, stabled horses in shrines, and kindled campfires with precious manuscripts. Many were Lutherans who had joined the army to pillage Rome: convinced that the city's wealth came from milking Christian nations dry, they sought revenge by requiring every citizen to pay a ransom for his life. Pope Clement VII was impotent; imprisoned in Castel Sant' Angelo, he let his hair grow as a sign of mourning and roamed about repeating Job's lament to God: "Wherefore then hast thou brought me forth out of the womb!" When he was finally restored to power, only one-fifth of the city's houses were inhabited. Diplomats forced the Emperor to abandon his resolution to strip the popes of temporal power, and soon the Papacy, with characteristic elasticity, was as splendid as ever. Rome was lavishly rebuilt, and Michelangelo was called on to design a dome for St. Peter's, but Clement was the last of the great Renaissance popes. With the sack, his humanist scholars had fled, and in succeeding decades theologians took their place. Reacting to the forces of nationalism unleashed beyond the Alps, Rome now belonged to the Counter Reformation.

THE ENGLISH RENAISSANCE

The Renaissance in England was an age of new men. Within two decades after Henry VIII's dissolution of the monasteries, one-fifth of the country's land came up for sale, and merchants and lawyers, their purses fattened by trade and the burgeoning legal profession, acquired as much of it as they could. Many, like Shakespeare after his first success in London, commissioned heralds to design a coat of arms. "As for gentlemen," one observer complained, "they be made good cheap in England." Not as cheaply as he imagined, however; it took a fierce spirit to rise in that dangerous age. Still the list of gentry swelled with England's wealth, and as poets and population eagerly

borrowed foreign words and ideas, England's language
changed too. The verbal extravagance of Elizabethan poetry reflected an age of extremes, in which men fanatically
pursued riches or power, learning or gentility, with texts
provided by Italy. Scholars tapped the wealth of Renaissance humanism, playwrights requisitioned the plots of
Italian *novelle*, the new aristocracy found its pleasures in
fanciful country houses built in the Italian style. For the
ambitious, there was "the murderous Machiavel" to study,
and for those who were yearning to be gentlemen, there
was *The Courtier* and the dozens of imitative tracts which
it had spawned.

A SON OF THE RENAISSANCE

When a generous Venetian colleague revealed the mathematical secrets which would enable Albrecht Dürer to draw a perfectly proportioned human body, the German painter declared that his new-found knowledge was more precious than a kingdom. He had first come to Italy in 1494 on a pilgrimage to see for himself "what had been hidden for a thousand years." The Renaissance was at its height, and young Dürer soon was converted by it. He copied the classical nudes of Mantegna and studied mathematics, read Poliziano's Latin poetry and later made an engraving inspired by it. In Nuremberg after a second trip, he wrote a treatise on painting and a book on human proportions which, along with his paintings, were to revolutionize German art. Despite his wife's nagging, Dürer refused to leave his books and attend strictly to his trade as an artisan-painter. He found his cronies among humanists and scholars, not in the painters' guild. Although he assimilated Italian ideas, Dürer still retained his own intensely northern character, alien to the flowing rhythm of Italian art. In this his painting reflects the fate of the Renaissance in Germany, which soon abandoned the easy acceptance of life inherent in the humanism and art of Italy. Like Dürer himself, Germany was overwhelmed by the Reformation, and its artists, scholars, and princes were dominated by the towering figure of Martin Luther. Aroused by his cause and prey to fanatical religious life, that country had little room for the spirit of humanism.

Dürer's watercolor of the landscape at Arco (upper left) is a memento of his Italian journey. Although The Four Witches *(left) is based on Italian studies of the nude, and* The Nativity *(opposite) uses a sophisticated perspective scheme learned in Venice, both retain Gothic touches, such as the tiny foreground figures in* The Nativity.

IMPERIAL SPAIN

Charles V ruled an empire that stretched from Prussia to Peru, and the heart of its power was Spain, where the gold of the New World had built a kingdom which was to dominate Europe for a century. Charles collected paintings as he collected provinces; his successor, Philip II, inherited dozens of Titians and Tintorettos to hang in the Escorial, his new royal palace near Madrid. Yet even that great collection was dwarfed by the immense palace, so Philip called on the artists of Spain to decorate it with paintings worthy of his royal taste and their country's new role in the world. Despite his challenge, the rooms devoted to Spanish art remained half empty, and most Spanish paint-ings only imitated, but could not equal, Italian art. El Greco, who had studied with Titian and worked with Tintoretto, was unsuccessful in his efforts to attract royal notice. When he sent a canvas to the King, it failed, as one contemporary noted, "to find favor with His Majesty." "That was natural enough," the critic added, "for it finds favor with few people." El Greco left Philip to his empty rooms, settled in Toledo, and there, in the ancient capital of Spain, he continued painting, surrounded by the poets and scholars who inaugurated the Spanish Renaissance. Another generation went by before Velázquez again gave Spanish royalty the chance to patronize a painter as great.

El Greco painted The Adoration of the Shepherds *(right) to hang over his tomb in Toledo. The dramatic movement of figures recalls Tintoretto's painting, but the unique style of his remarkable pupil is evident in the immensely elongated forms of the shepherds. Velázquez deeply admired El Greco and owned some of his paintings. In* The Surrender of Breda *(opposite) he based the portraits of Spanish soldiers, visible under the line of lances, on a group of similar figures painted by El Greco. The canvas commemorates a victory over the Dutch in one of the many wars which Catholic Spain carried on against the Protestants.*

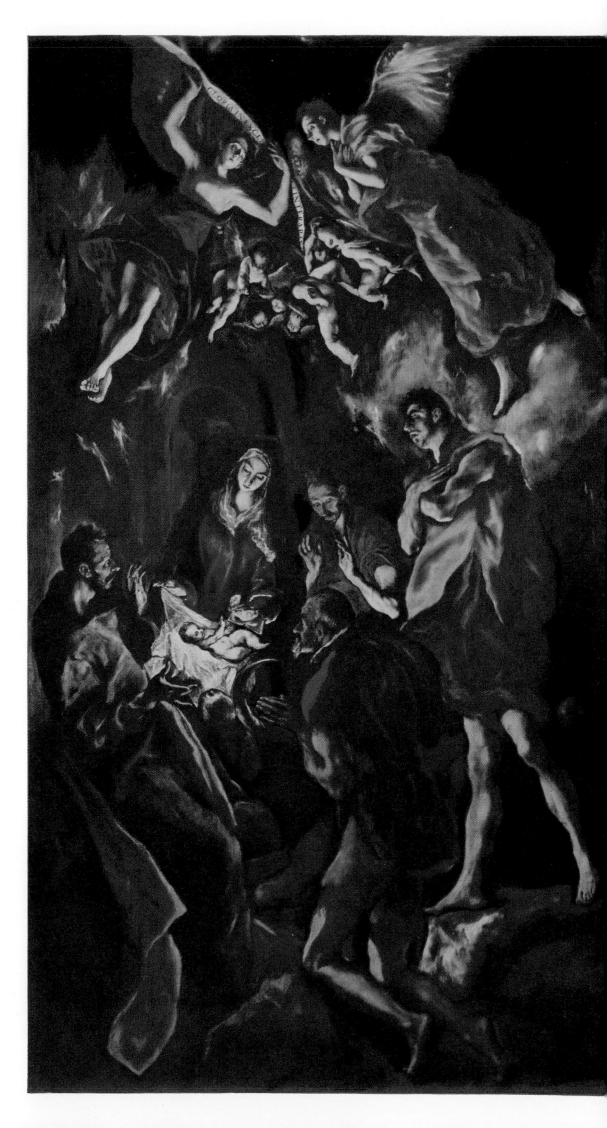

THE GRAND TOUR

"A man who has not been in Italy," Dr. Johnson proclaimed, "is always conscious of an inferiority." English gentlemen agreed. Although Trinity College in Dublin was once praised for keeping young men from being "infected with popery and other ill qualities" while studying abroad, the lure of Italy proved too strong; gentlemen were soon required to complete their education with a Grand Tour which reached its climax in a visit to Rome, the very font of popery. A thriving English guide service welcomed them to the city, ready to lead Gibbon on an eighteen-week tour of antiquities or stroll with Boswell through the Forum, conversing in Latin to sustain the classical ambience. By the nineteenth century, Lord Byron found the city "Pestilent with English—a parcel of staring boobies who go about gaping." But they did not gape alone. Even when Dürer visited Venice to plumb the secrets of Renaissance art, the *Wanderjahr* had been a tradition for German students. They made Rome the focus of their trip, and eventually they were followed there by awed visitors from Scandinavia and America. The Grand Tour was *de rigueur* for gentlemen educated on the Renaissance model, and even more necessary for painters and poets. The dedication with which they inspected Roman remains and Renaissance monuments equaled the fervor shown centuries before by Brunelleschi and Donatello, who first traveled to the city at the dawn of the Renaissance to immerse themselves in the spirit of the past.

Zoffany, an eighteenth-century favorite, painted some of the treasures of Florence's Uffizi Gallery in a souvenir picture for Britain's royal family. Titian's Venus of Urbino *dominates the foreground; at left is a Raphael Madonna surrounded by a swarm of connoisseurs.*

OVERLEAF: *Canaletto, who grew affluent painting views for nostalgic tourists, shows a group of them amid the ruined grandeur of the Forum, studiously inspecting the source from which the Renaissance sprang.*

ACKNOWLEDGMENTS AND INDEX

ACKNOWLEDGMENTS

The Editors are especially grateful to the following individuals and institutions for their generous assistance, and for their co-operation in making available pictorial material in their collections:

Archivio di Stato, Siena
 Dr. Sandro de' Colli
Archivio di Stato, Venice
 Prof. Conte Raimondo Morozzo della Rocca
Biblioteca Estense, Modena
 Prof. Pietro Puliatti
Biblioteca Marciana, Venice
 Prof. Tullia Gasparrini Leporace
Biblioteca Mediceo-Laurenziana, Florence
 Prof. Irma Merolle Tondi
Biblioteca Nazionale, Florence
 Dr. Eugenia Levi
Biblioteca Riccardiana, Florence
 Dr. Berta Maracchi Biagiarelli
Biblioteca Trivulziana, Milan
 Prof. Caterina Santoro
Bibliothèque de l'Arsenal, Paris
 Jean-Pierre Seguin
Bibliothèque Nationale, Paris
 Jean Porcher
 Jean Babelon
 Jean Vallery-Radot
Book-of-the-Month Club, New York
 Harry Dale
British Museum, London
 Manuscripts, Prints, and Drawings Departments
Donna Lelia Caetani, Rome
Casa Editrice Aldo Martello, Milan
 Aldo Martello
Centre National de la Recherche Scientifique, Paris
 Miss Jeanne Vielliard
Dr. Enrico Ceramelli-Papiani, Florence
City Art Gallery, Bristol
 H. Schubart
Civici Musei Veneziani d'Arte e di Storia, Venice
 Prof. Giovanni Mariacher
Lord Chamberlain's Office, St. James's Palace, London
 The Comptroller of Paintings
Marcel Destombes, Paris
Prof. H. J. Dow, Sweet Briar College, Virginia
P. Duchartre, Paris
Dr. Colin Eisler, New York
Ente Nazionale Industrie Turistiche, Rome
 Dr. Gian Piero Gallian
Fitzwilliam Museum, Cambridge
 Carl Winter
Frick Art Reference Library, New York
Galleria e Museo Estense, Modena
 Dr. A. Ghidiglia Quintavelle
Prof. Marvin T. Herrick, University of Illinois
Dr. Gilbert Highet, New York
Istituto Geografico de Agostini, Novara
 Dr. M. Nilo
Istituto Italiano d'Arti Grafiche, Bergamo
 Antonio Mancia
Istituto e Museo di Storia della Scienza, Florence
 Prof. Maria Luisa Bonelli
Dr. Hellmut Lehmann-Haupt, New York
Federico Arborio Mella, Milan
Sir Thomas Merton
The Metropolitan Museum of Art, New York
 Marshall B. Davidson
 Stephen Grancsay
 Miss Lillian Green
 Mrs. Edward S. McGill
Mrs. Clarice Milani-Comparetti, Florence
Monumenti, Musei e Gallerie Pontificie, Vatican City
 Prof. Filippo Maggi
 Dr. D. Redig de Campos
Musée de Cluny, Paris
 Francis Salet
Musée Condé, Chantilly
Musée Longchamp, Marseille
 Mrs. Jacques Latour
Musée du Louvre, Paris
Musée Royal des Beaux Arts, Antwerp
 W. Vanbeselaere

Museo Civico, Siena
 Dr. Aldo Cairola
Museo del Prado, Madrid
 Francisco J. Sánchez Canton
Museum of Fine Arts, Boston
 Miss Elizabeth Riegel
Museum of History of Science, Oxford
 H. Josten
 Francis Maddison
National Gallery, London
 Publications Department
National Gallery of Art, Washington
 John Walker
 Huntington Cairns
 Mrs. Elizabeth Ostertag
New York Public Library, New York
 Karl Kup
 Miss Elizabeth Roth
 Wilson G. Duprey
Opera della Metropolitana, Siena
 Conte Ugo del Vescovo Sterbini
Marchesa Iris Origo, Rome
Palazzo Ducale, Venice
 Prof. Egle Trincatanto
The Pierpont Morgan Library, New York
 Frederick B. Adams, Jr.
 John H. Plummer
 Miss Mary M. Kenway
Pinacoteca Ambrosiana, Milan
 Mons. Carlo Castiglioni
Pinacoteca di Brera, Milan
 Dr. F. Russoli
"Réalités-Connaissance des Arts," Paris
 Mrs. Lily LeRoux
Lessing J. Rosenwald, Jenkintown, Pennsylvania
Royal Academy of Arts, London
 Humphrey Brooke
Scala, Florence
 John Clark
Janos Scholz, New York
Soprintendenza alle Gallerie di Firenze, Florence
 Prof. Filippo Rossi
Soprintendenza alle Gallerie per il Lazio, Rome
 Prof. Emilio Lavagnino
Soprintendenza alle Gallerie di Mantova, Mantua
 Prof. Giovanni Paccagnini
Soprintendenza alle Gallerie, Naples
 Dr. Bruno Molajoli
Soprintendenza alle Gallerie di Torino, Turin
 Dr. Noemi Gabrielli
 Col. Vittorio Maglioli
Soprintendenza alle Gallerie, Venice
 Prof. Vittorio Moschini
Time, Inc., New York
 Miss Dorothy L. Smith
Royal Library, Windsor Castle
 Miss A. Scott-Eliott
 Miss Olwen Hedley
Yale University Library, New Haven
 Thomas Marston
Conte Ottavio Zasio, Venice

Grateful acknowledgment is made for permission to quote from the following works:

Michelangelo: A Record of His Life, translated and edited by Robert W. Carden, Constable & Co., London, 1913. *The Notebooks of Leonardo da Vinci,* translated and edited by Edward MacCurdy, Jonathan Cape Ltd., London; Harcourt, Brace & World, Inc., New York (by permission of Mrs. S. W. A. McCurdy). *The Venetian Republic* by William Hazlitt, A. & C. Black, London, 1915. *The Portable Renaissance Reader,* edited by James Bruce Ross and Mary Martin McLaughlin, The Viking Press, Inc., New York, 1958 (from "The Dignity of Man" by Giovanni Pico della Mirandola, translated by M. M. M., and "Self-Portrait of a Universal Man" by Leon Battista Alberti, translated by J. B. R.). *The Book of The Courtier,* by Baldassare Castiglione, copyright ©1959 by Charles S. Singleton and Edgar de N. Mayhew, Doubleday & Company, Inc., New York. *Galateo* by Giovanni della Casa, translated by R. S. Pine-Coffin, Penguin Books, 1958.

PICTURE CREDITS

The source of each picture is listed below. The title or description appears after the page number, which is in boldface type, followed by the artist (where appropriate) and the location of the work. Where the location of a museum or library is obvious, the city has been omitted. Photographic credits appear in parentheses. Where two or more pictures appear on one page, they are separated by dashes. Many of the woodcuts appear in such works as Italian Woodcuts *by Sanders and* Les Livres à Figures Venitiens *by Messena.*

The following abbreviations are used:

Amb.—Biblioteca or Pinacoteca Ambrosiana, Milan
BAV—Biblioteca Apostolica Vaticana
BEM—Biblioteca Estense, Modena
BLF—Biblioteca Laurenziana, Florence
BM—British Museum
BN—Bibliothèque Nationale, Paris
BNF—Biblioteca Nazionale, Florence
ENIT—Ente Nazionale Industrie Turistiche, Rome
LC—Library of Congress, Washington
MMA—Metropolitan Museum of Art, New York
MNF—Museo Nazionale, Florence
NGAW, Kress—National Gallery of Art, Washington, Kress Collection
NGAW, Mellon—National Gallery of Art, Washington, Mellon Collection
NGAW, Widener—National Gallery of Art, Washington, Widener Collection
NGL—National Gallery, London
NYPL—New York Public Library
SGF—Soprintendenza alle Gallerie di Firenze

FRONT MATTER—Jacket: "Portrait of a Youth" by Filippino Lippi. NGAW, Mellon. Back jacket: Lodovico Sforza and nephew, Velins 724, BN. **Title page:** "Triumph of Venus" by Francesco Cossa and others. Detail: Palazzo Schifanoia. Ferrara **4** Angel. Drawing by Filippino Lippi. Collection of Janos Scholz. **8-9** Map by David Greenspan.

THE DAWN OF THE RENAISSANCE

10 Cathedral, Orvieto (John Ross) **12-13** "Effects of Good Government in the City and Country" by Ambrogio Lorenzetti. Palazzo Pubblico, Siena **14-15** Guidoriccio da Fogliano by Simone Martini. Palazzo Pubblico, Siena **16** Genoese banking scene. Add. ms. 27,695, BM—Astrolabe. The Royal Scottish Museum, Edinburgh **17** *Statuti della Società dei Drappieri e Bracciaioli.* Museo Civico, Bologna (Alinari-Giraudon) **18** 14th-century Crusade miniature. Ms. Français 24209, BN **19** Frederick II. Cod. Pal. Lat. 1071, BAV—Castel del Monte (Dr. C. A. Willemsen) **20** "Temptation on the Mountain Top" by Duccio di Buoninsegna. The Frick Collection—Boccaccio Ms. II. II. 38, BNF **21** Sketch by Petrarch. Ms. Latin 6802, BN—Dante. 15th-century copy of lost Taddeo Gaddi fresco. Ms. Palatine 320, BNF **22** Venice. Ms. 264, Bodleian Library, Oxford **23** Miniature by Simone Martini. Amb. **24** Petrarch by Lombardo della Sala. Ms. Latin 6069 F, BN **33** Plaques on Campanile, Florence, by Giotto, Andrea Pisano, and others (All: Alinari) **34-5** "The Crucifix" by Cimabue. S. Domenico, Arezzo (Scala) **36-7** "St. Ambrose, St. Michael, and St. Augustine" by Simone Martini and assistants. Fitzwilliam Museum, Cambridge **38** "The Kiss of Judas" by Giotto. Detail. Scrovegni Chapel, Padua (Anderson) **39** "Pietà" by Giotto. Scrovegni Chapel. Padua (Scala).

THE PRINCE AND THE STATE

40 San Leo, designed by Francesco di Giorgio (ENIT) **42** Guelph emblem (Brogi) **42-3** Orvieto (John Ross) **44** Horrors of tyranny. *De Sphaera.* Ms. A.X. 2.14, BEM (Aldo Martello Editore) **45** "Triumph of Death" attributed to Francesco Traini. Detail. Camposanto, Pisa (Alinari) **46** Presumed portrait of Roberto Malatesta. "Passage of the Red Sea" by Piero di Cosimo. Detail. Sistine Chapel, Vatican (Anderson)—Piccinino by Pisanello. MNF (Alinari) **46-7** *Bastone di comando.* Giovanni Erole, *Erasmo Gattamelata da Narni,* 1877 **47** Gattamelata by Donatello. Piazzo del Santo, Padua (Anderson) **48** "Scene from the Life of San Bernardino" by the Master of Legend of San Bernardino. Pinacoteca Vanucci, Perugia—"Il Bravo" attributed to Titian. Kunsthistorisches Museum, Vienna (Kunst-Verlag Wolfrum) **49** *Biccherna* cover, 1468. Archivio di Stato, Siena (ENIT) **50** Building the Tempio Malatestiano. Ms. 630, Bibliothèque de l'Arsenal—Crab by Agostino di Duccio. Tempio Malatestiano. Rimini (Alinari)—Tempio Malatestiano (Ediz. RIMA) **51** "A Princess of the Este Family" by Pisanello. Louvre (Giraudon) **52-3** "The Return of Lodovico from Exile" by Mantegna. Camera degli Sposi, Castello di Corte, Mantua **53** Federigo da Montefeltro. Urb. Lat. 508, BAV **54** Deposition. Drawing by Raphael. Uffizi (Anderson) **55** Griffin. *L'Histoire et Vite di Braccio Fortebracci et di Nicolo Piccinino,* Perugia, 1623. BAV—"San Bernardino Preaching" by Sano di Pietro. Cathedral, Siena (Anderson) **56** Machiavelli by Santi di Tito. Palazzo Vecchio, Florence **65** Condottiere. Drawing by Leonardo da Vinci. BM **68-9** Battle of Fornovo. A. Vérard. *Mer des Histoires,* Paris, *ca.* 1503 **70-1** Scaling ladder, attack platform, battering ram, and cannon. Valturius, *De Re Militari.* LC, Lessing J. Rosenwald Collection—Mine. Drawing by Francesco di Giorgio Martini, *Trattato di Architettura Civile e Militare,* BLF—Fortress. Drawing by Francesco di Giorgio Martini, *Trattato di Architettura Civile e Militare,* BNF **72** Arabian engine and repeater gun. Valturius, *De Re Militari.* Library of Congress, Lessing J. Rosenwald Collection—Mortar. Drawing by Leonardo da Vinci. *Codice Atlantico,* Amb. **73** Mars. *De Sphaera.* Ms. A.X. 2.14, BEM (Aldo Martello Editore) **74** Presumed portrait of Astorre Manfredi attributed to Romagnol School. Detail of "Beato Bernardino de Feltre." Pinacoteca, Faenza (Alinari)—Letter. Archivio di Stato, Siena—Presumed portrait of Caterina Sforza by Lorenzo di Credi. Pinacoteca, Forlì—Presumed portrait of Duke of Gandia by Pinturicchio. Detail of "Dispute of St. Catherine." Appartamento Borgia, Vatican (Alinari)—Sword. Collection of Donna Lelia Caetani **75** Cesare Borgia, anonymous copy of authentic portrait. Palazzo Venezia, Rome **76** Colleoni hunting, attributed to Girolamo Romanino. Castello di Malpaga, Bergamo **77** Colleoni by Verrocchio. Detail, Campo SS. Giovanni e Paolo, Venice (Anderson) **78-9** "The Rout of San Romano" by Uccello. Uffizi (Aldo Martello Editore) **80** "Battle of the Bonacolsi and Gonzaga" by Domenico Morone. Detail. Castello di Corte, Mantua—"Madonna of Victory" by Mantegna. Louvre **81** "Return of Cardinal Francesco Gonzaga from Rome" by Mantegna. Camera degli Sposi, Castello di Corte, Mantua **82** Gibbet by Pisanello. Detail of "St. George and the Princess of Trebizond." S. Anastasia, Verona **83** Medal of Isotta da Rimini by Matteo de' Pasti. NGAW, Kress—Sigismondo Malatesta by Piero della Francesca. Detail of fresco. Tempio Malatestiano, Rimini (Scala) **84** Document. Detail. Archivio Segreto, Venice **84-5** "King Maurus Dismissing the English Ambassadors" by Carpaccio. Accademia, Venice **86-7** "Fleet of Ferrante I in the Bay of Naples," anonymous. Museo di San Martino, Naples—Four details. M. 801, The Pierpont Morgan Library.

THE ARTS

88 S. Francesco, Arezzo (Gjon Mili) **90-1** "The Tribute Money" by Masaccio. Brancacci Chapel, Sta. Maria del Carmine, Florence (Dmitri Kessel, courtesy *Life*) **92** "David" by Donatello. MNF (Alinari) **92-3** Ideal city attributed to Piero della Francesca. Palazzo Ducale, Urbino (Anderson) **93** Drawing tools. Museum of the History of Science, Oxford **94** Unloading wheat by Fra Angelico. Detail of "Scene from the Life of St. Nicholas of Bari." Pinacoteca Vaticana (Istituto Italiano d'Arti Grafiche, Bergamo) **95** "Madonna and Child" by Piero della Francesca and assistants. Brera, Milan **96** "St. George and the Dragon" by Uccello. NGL **97** Star of Bethlehem and other plants by Leonardo da Vinci. Royal Collection, Windsor Castle. Copyright reserved **98** "St. Jerome in His Study" by Antonello da Messina. NGL **99** "The Castelfranco Madonna" by Giorgione. Cathedral, Castelfranco Veneto (Conzett & Huber) **100** "Hercules and Antaeus" by A. Pollaiuolo, MNF (Alinari) **100-101** Bas-relief of craftsmen by Nanni di Banco. Orsanmichele, Florence (Alinari) **101** Plate from Cafaggiolo. Victoria and Albert Museum. Copyright reserved—Old woman. Tuscan majolica. Fitzwilliam Museum, Cambridge **102** "Apollo and Daphne" by A. and P. Pollaiuolo. NGL **103** "The Feast of the Gods" by Giovanni Bellini and Titian. NGAW, Widener **104** Michelangelo, from his atelier. Louvre **113** Drawings of Hercules by Michelangelo. Royal Collection, Windsor Castle. Copyright reserved **114** Torso of a seated man by Michelangelo. BM—Model of a river god by Michelangelo. Galleria dell' Accademia, Florence **115** Nude athlete by Michelangelo. Detail of ceiling. Sistine Chapel, Vatican (Anderson) **116** "Captive" by Michelangelo. Galleria dell' Accademia, Florence (Evelyn Hofer) **117** "Rondanini Pietà" by Michelangelo. Castello Sforzesco, Milan (Arc. Fot. dei Civici Musei, Milan) **118-19** Ceiling of the Sistine Chapel by Michelangelo. Detail. Vatican (Anderson) **120** Chalice by Uccello. Uffizi (SGF)—Face by Leonardo da Vinci. Palazzo Reale, Turin (Anderson)—Mosaic attributed to Uccello. Atrium, San Marco (Osvaldo Böhm)—Head by Piero della Francesca, *De prospettiva pingendi.* Amb. **120-21** "The Flagellation of Christ" by Piero della Francesca. Palazzo Ducale, Urbino (Scala) **122** Presumed portrait of Cecilia Gallerani. "Lady with an Ermine" by Leonardo da Vinci. Museum Czartoryskich, Cracow (Kindler Verlag, Munich)—Leonello d'Este by Pisanello. NGAW, Kress **123** Giovanni di Pierfrancesco de' Medici by Botticelli. Collection of Sir Thomas Merton **124-25** "Diana and Actaeon" by Titian. Ellesmere Collection, National Gallery, Edinburgh (Larry Burrows, courtesy *Life*) **125** Drawing by Signorelli. Louvre (Giraudon) **126** "The Adoration of the Shepherds" by Giorgione. Detail. NGAW, Kress—"Thebaid" attributed to Starnina. Detail. Uffizi—"St. Jerome" attributed to Lazzaro Bastiani. Museum of Fine Arts, Boston **126-27** "St. Francis in Ecstasy" by Giovanni Bellini. The Frick Collection (courtesy *Time*).

FLORENCE CRADLE OF HUMANISM

128 View from Boboli Gardens (Robert Descharnes) **130** Arms of Arte della Lana attributed to Luca della Robbia. Museo dell' Opera del Duomo (Alinari)—Woodcut of market. *Contrasto di Carnevale e Quaresima*—Woodcut of money changer. Jacopo de Cessolis, *Libro di Giuoccho di Scacchi,* 1493—Silk reeler. Ms. 2580,

Biblioteca Riccardiana 130-31 Facsimile of woodcut in Staatliche Museen, Berlin. Print Division, NYPL 132 Abundance. *Il Biadajolo.* Tempiano 3, BLF (ENIT) 133 Famine. *Il Biadajolo.* Tempiano 3, BLF (Scala) 134 Plaques attributed to Luca della Robbia. Campanile del Duomo (Alinari)—St. Augustine. Manuscript initial. Spencer Collection, NYPL 135 Coluccio Salutati. Cod. Strozziano 174, BLF—Primer. Ms. 2669, Biblioteca Riccardiana 136-37 "Story of Theseus and Ariadne," school of Piero di Cosimo. Musée des Beaux Arts, Marseilles 138 Cosimo de' Medici. Detail of "Procession of the Magi" by Benozzo Gozzoli. Palazzo Medici-Riccardi (Scala) 138-39 Drawing by Filarete. BNF (SGF) 139 "Triumph of Fame" attributed to Francesco di Antonio Banchi. New-York Historical Society 140 Giuliano de' Medici by Botticelli, NGAW, Kress 141 Medal by Bertoldo di Giovanni. NGAW, Kress—"Pallas and the Centaur" by Botticelli. Uffizi (Scala) 142 Astrology woodcut. *Tractato contra le Astrologi,* 1490—Savonarola preaching. *Compendio di Rivelazione,* 1496 142-43 Cloister of San Marco (Anderson) 144 Lorenzo de' Medici by Verrocchio. NGAW, Kress (William Sumits, courtesy *Life*) 153 "Allegory of the Divine Comedy" by Domenico di Michelino. Detail. Cathedral (Istituto Geografico de Agostini, Novara) 154 "Adoration of the Magi" by Fra Angelico and Fra Filippo Lippi. NGAW, Kress—Cup. Museo degli Argenti (SGF)—Medici manuscript. Plut. LXXXII, BLF 155 "Judith and Holofernes" by Donatello. Piazza della Signoria (Alinari) 156-57 "The Procession of the Magi" by Benozzo Gozzoli. Palazzo Medici-Riccardi (Fernand Bourges, courtesy *Life*) 158-59 Self-portrait (Brogi)—Doors (Anderson)—Sacrifice of Isaac (Anderson)—Squirrel (Brogi). All from second doors by Ghiberti. Baptistery 160-61 "Tournament in the Piazza Santa Croce" by the Master of the Jarves *Cassone.* Jarves Collection, Yale University Art Gallery 160 Engraving of man in a fantastic helmet. Anonymous. NGAW, Lessing J. Rosenwald Collection 161 "The Youthful David" by Andrea del Castagno. NGAW, Widener (Courtesy *Metropolitan Museum of Art Miniatures* and Book-of-the-Month Club) 162 Medal of Pico della Mirandola attributed to Niccolò Fiorentino. BN (Giraudon) 163 "St. Augustine" by Botticelli. Ognissanti 164 Poliziano and Giuliano de' Medici by Domenico Ghirlandaio. Detail of "Pope Honorius Setting Up the Franciscan Order." Sassetti Chapel, Sta. Trinità 165 Hands by Raphael. Detail of "Pope Leo X." Uffizi—Four humanists by Domenico Ghirlandaio. Detail of "Scenes in the Life of the Baptist." Sta. Maria Novella 166-67 "Burning of Savonarola." Anonymous. Museo San Marco 167 Savonarola by Fra Bartolommeo. Detail. Museo San Marco.

MILAN
CITY OF STRIFE

168 Cathedral (Foto Paoletti) 169 Milan plan. Urb. Lat. 277, BAV 171 Gian Galeazzo Visconti by Pisanello. Louvre (Giraudon)—Bernabò Visconti monument by Bonino da Campione. Detail. Castello Sforzesco (Perotti) 172 Lady with Visconti shield. Ms. Lat. 6340, BN—Visconti family tree. Ms. Lat. 5888, BN 173 Crowning G. G. Visconti. Ms. Lat. 5888, BN 174 Cloister of Certosa di Pavia (Chiolini) 175 Filelfo. BN—Lecture. Certosa di Pavia (Chiolini) 176 Medal of Filippo Maria Visconti by Pisanello. NGAW, Kress—Francesco Sforza. Detail of illumination. Velins 724, BN 177 Hunting scene. Ms. 1375, Musée Condé, Chantilly 178 Sebastian Muenster, *Cosmographia,* 1588. LC 179 Galeazzo Maria Sforza by Piero Pollaiuolo. Uffizi (Alinari)—Assassination. Lorenzo della Rota, *Lamento del Duca Galeazo,*

Florence, 1505 180-81 Details from Velins 724, BN 181 Drawing, presumed portrait of Isabella of Aragon, by Beltraffio. Amb. (Anderson) 182 Battle of Marignano. Ms. Fr. 1738 BN (Giraudon) 183 Study for Sforza monument by Leonardo da Vinci. Royal Collection, Windsor Castle. Copyright reserved 184 Self-portrait by Leonardo. Palazzo Reale, Turin (Alinari) 193-94 All from Royal Collection, Windsor Castle. Copyright reserved 195 Study for "Battle of Anghiari." Budapest Museum of Fine Arts (Roger-Viollet)—Vitruvian man. Gallerie dell' Accademia, Venice (Alinari) 196 Deluge. Royal Collection, Windsor Castle. Copyright reserved. 197 Horse's foot. Royal Collection, Windsor Castle. Copyright reserved—*Lilium candidum.* Royal Collection, Windsor Castle. Copyright reserved.—Dogs. BM—Bramble. Royal Collection, Windsor Castle. Copyright reserved—Crabs. Kölnisches Stadtmuseum, Cologne—198 Wing and leverage demonstration. Ms. B, Institut de France. Facsimile—Parachute. *Codice Atlantico,* Amb.—Perpetual motion studies. Victoria and Albert Museum. Copyright reserved 199 Weirs on river. *Codice Atlantico,* Amb.—Snorkel. Cod. Arundel, BM—Dredge. Ms. E, Institut de France (Giraudon)—Automotive wagon. *Codice Atlantico,* Amb.—Two-decker city and spiral staircase. Ms. B, Institut de France. Facsimile 200 Cats. Royal Collection, Windsor Castle. Copyright reserved 201 Certosa of Pavia. Detail of "The Carthusians Following Christ" by Borgognone. Musei Civici, Pavia 202-3 Portals by Giovanni Antonio Amadeo. Certosa di Pavia (Alinari)—Francesco Sforza with classical heroes. Manuscript leaf by Giovanni Pietro Birago. Uffizi 204-5 Massimiliano Sforza: portrait, on horseback, and riding in triumph. Cod. 2167, Biblioteca Trivulziana 205 Massimiliano Sforza with Emperor Maximilian. Cod. 2163, Biblioteca Trivulziana 206-7 Armor. MMA.

ROME
SPLENDOR AND THE PAPACY

208 Tempietto. S. Pietro in Montorio, Rome (Georgina Masson, courtesy Thames and Hudson) 210 Tomb of Antipope John XXIII by Donatello and Michelozzo. Detail. Baptistery, Florence (Brogi)—Tomb of Martin V by Simone Ghini. Detail. S. Giovanni in Laterano (Anderson)—Eugenius IV by Filarete. Detail of bronze doors. St. Peter's, Vatican (Anderson)—Paul II, Sixtus IV, Innocent VIII, Pius III, Julius II. All: BN—Leo X. NGAW, Kress 211 Nicholas V and Calixtus III. BN—Pius II by Paolo Romano. Appartamento Borgia, Vatican (Anderson)—Alexander VI, Adrian VI, Clement VII. All: BN—Cameo of Paul III. BN (Giraudon) 212 Pilgrimage churches. Gabinetto Nazionale delle Stampe 265 Mosaic of John VII. Grotte Vaticane 214 "Laocoön." Musei Vaticani (courtesy Prof. F. Maggi) 214-15 Ancient wolf; Romulus and Remus by A. Pollaiuolo. Palazzo dei Conservatori (Alinari) 215 Drawing of palace of Septimius Severus by Marten van Heemskerck. Staatliche Museen, Berlin—"Apollo Belvedere." Musei Vaticani (Anderson) 216-17 The Forum (Dmitri Kessel) 217 Castel S. Angelo. *Codex Escorialensis.* Biblioteca del Escorial 218 Sixtus IV frescoes. Florentine School, 16th century. Ospedale di Santo Spirito (courtesy Prof. Pietro De Angelis) 218-19 Drawing by Raphael. Louvre (Alinari) 219 Anonymous drawing. Egger, *Romische Veduten,* Vienna, 1931-32 220 "Moses" by Michelangelo. S. Pietro in Vincoli (Gabinetto Fotografico Nazionale) 221 Julius II by Raphael. Detail of "Mass of Bolsena." Stanze, Vatican 222 Intarsia of Baraballo. Stanze, Vatican—Majolica plate. Museo Civico, Bologna 223 Campidoglio (Dmitri Kessel) 224 Pius II. Codex 147, Biblioteca Corsini 233 Widowed Rome. Ms. Ital. 81,

BN 234 Drawing by Pinturicchio. Uffizi (Alinari) 235-37 Frescoes of life of Pius II by Pinturicchio. Libreria Piccolomini, Siena 235 Poet laureate (Fernand Bourges, courtesy *Life*) 236 Congress of Mantua (Alinari)—Crusade (Anderson)—Miter. Museo d'Arte Sacra, Pienza 237 Canonizing St. Catherine of Siena (Fernand Bourges, courtesy *Life*) 238 Votive picture of Jacopo Pesaro by Titian. Musée Royal des Beaux-Arts, Antwerp (Malvaux) 239 Djem. Ms. Lat. 6067, BN—Petition. The Pierpont Morgan Library 240 "Paul III with Alessandro and Ottavio Farnese" by Titian. Galleria Nazionale, Naples 240-41 Miniatures from Messale Borgia. Chieti (Ente Provinciale Turismo) 241 Golden Rose by Simone de Firenze. Museo dell' Opera Metropolitana, Siena (Alinari) 242 Sixtus IV and Platina by Melozzo da Forlì. Pinacoteca Vaticana (Scala) 243 Count Tommaso Inghirami by Raphael. Isabella Stewart Gardner Museum 244-45 St. Peter's. Anonymous. Staatsgalerie, Stuttgart 245 Medal by Caradosso. NGAW, Kress 247 Sistine Chapel 248 "St. Jerome" by Leonardo da Vinci. Pinacoteca Vaticana (Eric Schaal, courtesy *Time*) 249 "St. Lawrence Giving Alms" by Fra Angelico. Chapel of Nicholas V—Doors of St. Peter's by Filarete. Detail (Alinari) 250-51 "Punishment of Korah, Dathan, and Abiram" by Botticelli. Sistine Chapel 252 "Pietà" by Michelangelo. St. Peter's (Anderson) 253 Grotesque by Giovanni da Udine. Logge (Archivio Fotografico, Mus. Vat.)—Geometry and perspective by A. Pollaiuolo. Grotte Vaticane (Anderson) 254 "School of Athens" by Raphael. Stanze (Archivio Fotografico, Mus. Vat.)—Swiss guards by Raphael. Detail of "Mass of Bolsena." Stanze 255 "Disputation on the Sacrament" by Raphael. Detail. Stanze (Scala).

VENICE
THE GOLDEN YEARS

256 Piazza San Marco (G. E. Kidder Smith) 258-59 View of Venice by Jacopo de' Barbari. Facsimile NYPL, Print Division 260 Tournament by Domenico Morone. NGL—Woodcut from *Il Lamento della Femena di Padre Agustino*—Lion's mouth. Museo Correr 261 "The Return of the Ambassadors" by Carpaccio. Detail. Gallerie dell' Accademia 262 Mercantile arithmetic book. Collection of Thomas Marston, New Haven 263 Velvet. MNF (Giraudon)—Negress. MMA—Embroidery. Musée des Arts Decoratifs, Paris (Giraudon) 264 Goblet. Cleveland Museum of Art (Carter Jones, courtesy *Time*)—Bowl. Toledo Museum of Art (Carter Jones, courtesy *Time*)—Marriage beaker. Cleveland Museum of Art 264-65 Gondola. Donato Bertelli, *Le Vere Imagini . . . ,* 1578. NYPL, Prints Division 265 "La Rotonda," Vicenza (David Lees, courtesy *Time*) 266 Drawing of a palace by Jacopo Bellini. Louvre (Giraudon) 267 Hunter by Veronese. Villa Barbaro at Maser (Alinari)—Villa Foscari, "La Malcontenta" (Giuseppi Fini) 268 "Wedding at Cana" by Veronese. Louvre (Giraudon) 269 "Fête Champêtre" by Giorgione. Louvre (Studio Sun Ltd., courtesy *Life*) 270 "Triumph of Venice" by Veronese. Palazzo Ducale (Alinari) 270-71 Engraving of fire. Museo Correr 271 Detail from arch. San Marco (Alinari) 272 Doge Francesco Foscari by Lazzaro Bastiani. Museo Correr 281 "Lion of St. Mark" by Carpaccio. Detail. Palazzo Ducale 282-83 "Corpus Christi Procession" by Gentile Bellini. Gallerie dell' Accademia, Venice (Eric Schaal, courtesy *Life*) 284-85 "Healing of the Demoniac" by Carpaccio. Gallerie dell' Accademia (Foto Fiorentini) 286-87 All: Yale University Library, Rare Books (Loebel) 288 Duck-shooting in the lagoon by Carpaccio (fragment). Homeless (Courtesy Istituto Geografico de Agostini,

Novara) **288-89** Manuscript illumination attributed to Veronese's studio. Charles Magius, *Voyages et Aventures,* 1578. A.D. 134, BN, Cabinet des Estampes **289** "Banquet of Epulon" by Pozzoserrato. Detail. Treviso, Monte di Pietà (Giuseppe Fini)—Villa plan. Palladio, *I Quattro Libri dell' Architettura,* 1581. NYPL, Reserve Division **290-91** Woodcut, "Battle of Zonchio." BM **292** "Reception of an Ambassador in Cairo." School of Bellini. Louvre—"John V Palaeologus Setting Out for Venice, 1369." Florentine School. Sterling and Francine Clark Art Institute **293** Mohammed II by Gentile Bellini. NGL (Wallace Heaton) **295** Icon. Tesoro di San Marco (Millet, *Connaissance des Arts)* **296** "Portrait of a Man" by Titian. NGL (Conzett & Huber)—"La Bella" by Titian. Pitti (Mella)—Ranuccio Farnese by Titian. NGAW, Kress **297** "Fra Teodoro da Urbino as St. Dominic" by Giovanni Bellini. NGL —"Young Man in a Red Cap" by Lorenzo Lotto. Museo Correr (Giraudon) **298** Drawing by Titian. Albertina, Vienna **298-99** "The Tempest" by Giorgione. Detail. Gallerie dell' Accademia (Dmitri Kessel, courtesy *Life*) **300** "Venus Anadyomene" by Titian. Ellesmere Collection (Conzett & Huber) **301** Bronze dancer. Paduan. Louvre (Archives Photographiques)— "Venus of Urbino" by Titian. Uffizi (Scala) **302** "Abduction of the Body of St. Mark" by Tintoretto. Gallerie dell' Accademia (Eric Schaal, courtesy *Life*) **303** "The Crucifixion" by Tintoretto. Detail. Scuola di San Rocco (Eric Schaal, courtesy *Life*)

THE IMAGES
OF MAN

304 "David" by Michelangelo. Detail. Galleria dell' Accademia, Florence **306** Terence, *Comoediae,* Venice, 1497—Lorenzo de' Medici, *Canzone per andare in maschera,* Florence **306-7** Satire. A. M. Hind, *Early Italian Engraving* **307** Self-portrait by Alberti. NGAW, Kress **308** "Christ's Descent into Limbo" by Giovanni Bellini. City Art Gallery, Bristol **309** "April" by Francesco Cossa and others. Detail. Palazzo Schifanoia, Ferrara **310** Reverse of Aretino portrait medal. BN— Knife. MMA **311** Medal of Chigi. Collection of Marchese Giovanni Incisa, Rome—Aretino by Titian. The Frick Collection **312** "The Three Ages of Man." Venetian School, 16th century. Pitti (Anderson) **313** Federigo da Montefeltro probably by Berruguete. Detail. Palazzo Ducale, Urbino **314** *Il cavallo di picche* attributed to Bonifacio Bembo. Accademia Carrara, Bergamo (ENIT)—Medal of Vittorino da Feltre by Pisanello. BN (Giraudon) **315** "Young Man" by Bronzino. MMA **316** "Knight in a Landscape" by Carpaccio. Thyssen Collection, Lugano (Held) **317** Castiglione by Raphael. Louvre (Giraudon) **318** Andrea Odoni by Lorenzo Lotto. Hampton Court. Copyright reserved **319** Intarsia, probably designed by Francesco di Giorgio Martini. MMA **320** Federigo da Montefeltro by Piero della Francesca. Uffizi **329** Chess game. Jacopo de Cessolis, *Libro di Giuocho di Scacchi,* Florence, 1493 **330** Garden. *Fior di Virtù,* Venice, 1490—Terence, *Comoediae,* Venice, 1523 **331** Wedding dance. *The Life and Fables of Aesop,* Naples, 1485—Allegorical figure. *Antiquarie Prospettiche Romane,* Rome, *ca.* 1500 **332** Lorenzo de' Medici, *Canzoni a Ballo,* Florence, 1533 **333** Poet. Bernardo Bellincioni, *Rime,* Milan, 1493— Spelling lesson. *El Modo da Insegnare Compitare,* Florence, *ca.* 1500 **334** All: *Fior di Virtù,* Florence, 1491. LC, Lessing J. Rosenwald Collection **335** Courtly scene. Boccaccio, *Decamerone,* Venice, 1525— Lovers. Piccolomini, *Hystoria di Due Amanti.* **336** Peacocks. Cherubino da Spoleto, *Fior di Virtù,* Venice, 1492 **337** "Seven Liberal Arts" attributed to Botticelli. Musée Condé, Chantilly (Giraudon) **338** Gafori,

Theorica Musicae. Milan, 1510. LC—Gafori, *Theorica Musicae,* Naples, 1480 **339** Pacioli by Jaco...Bar... Galleria Nazionale, Naples (Parisio) **340** Jupiter. Detail. *De Sphaera.* Ms. A.X. 2.14, BEM (Aldo Martello Editore)—Book presentation. Ms. CL. I 147, Libreria Ariosto, Ferrara **341** Madonna by Fra Filippo Lippi. Pitti—Detail of Fra Filippo Lippi's tomb. Cathedral, Spoleto (Anderson) **342** Fracastoro attributed to Torbido. NGL—Hospital. Ms. Gaddiano 24, BFL (ENIT) **343** Rospigliosi Cup by Cellini. MMA (Courtesy Shell Oil Company)—Cellini by Vasari. Detail of "Cosimo I with Architects and Engineers." Palazzo Vecchio, Florence (Alinari)—Study for "Perseus" by Cellini. MNF (Anderson)

WOMEN OF
THE RENAISSANCE

344 Unknown woman. Anonymous. MNF (Alinari-Giraudon) **346-47** "The Adimari Wedding." Anonymous. Gallerie dell' Accademia, Florence **348** Marriage scene. Ms. Latin 3988, BN **348-49** Woman before judge. Ms. 441. The Pierpont Morgan Library. **349** Jewelry, 15th and 16th centuries. MNF (Alinari)— *Cassone.* MMA **350** Lady and poet. Cod. 763, Biblioteca Trivulziana, Milan (Emmer) **351** "Maiden's Dream" by Lorenzo Lotto. NGAW, Kress **352** "Concert at the Court of Caterina Cornaro." In the manner of Giorgione. Attingham, Shrewsbury (Courtesy The National Trust) **353** Cardinal Pietro Bembo by Titian. NGAW, Kress **354** "Portrait of a Lady" by Neroccio de' Landi. NGAW, Widener (Courtesy *Metropolitan Museum of Art Miniatures* and Book-of-the-Month Club)— Costume study by Pisanello. Detail. Musée Condé, Chantilly (Giraudon) **355** Ivory comb. MMA—Wood and stucco bust of a woman, 15th century. Anonymous. Louvre *(Realités)*—Venetian shoes. Musée de Cluny, Paris **356** Woodcuts of Negroes. Galleria Estense, Modena (Oscar Savio)—Silverware, Roman, late 16th century. MMA **357** Walnut chair, 15th century. MMA —Woman drying hair. Vecellio, *Degli habiti antichi,* Venice, 1590. NYPL, Spencer Collection **358** Garden of Love. A. M. Hind, *Early Italian Engraving* **359** Presumed portrait of Bianca Sforza attributed to Ambrogio de Predis. Amb. **360** Beatrice d'Este by Gian Cristoforo Romano. Louvre (Giraudon)—Isabella d'Este, drawing by Leonardo da Vinci. Louvre (Giraudon) **369** Garden of Delight. *De Sphaera.* Ms. A.X. 2.14, BEM (Aldo Martello Editore) **370** Family tree. *Genealogia Estense,* BEM **371** Leonora of Aragon by Francesco Laurana. Galleria Nazionale, Palermo (G. Mannino)—Francesco Gonzaga by Gian Cristoforo Romano. Museo Bardini, Florence (Alinari)—Lodovico Sforza. Cod. 2167, Biblioteca Trivulziana, Milan— Borso d'Este. *Genealogia Estense,* BEM **372** "Old Man and his Grandson" by Domenico Ghirlandaio. Louvre (Giraudon) **372-73** Child by Carlo Crivelli. Detail of "The Annunciation." NGL **373** Schoolroom. Cod. 2167, Biblioteca Trivulziana, Milan—Boy reading, by Vincenzo Foppa. By permission of the Trustees of the Wallace Collection **374** "Birth of Venus" by Botticelli. Detail. Uffizi (Anderson) **375** Simonetta Vespucci by Piero di Cosimo. Musée Condé. Chantilly **376-77** "La Primavera" by Botticelli. Uffizi (Scala) **378-79** Three pages from Venetian memento book. Yale University Library, Rare Books **379** Courtesans by Carpaccio. Museo Correr, Venice (Conzett & Huber) **380** "Mary Magdalen" by Donatello. Detail. Baptistery, Florence (Brogi) **381** Drawing by Correggio. The Pierpont Morgan Library—Old woman by Giorgione. Gallerie dell' Accademia, Venice (Conzett & Huber) **382** "Virgin Annunciate" by Antonello da Messina. Museo Nazionale, Palermo (Scala) **383** "The Annunciation" by Carlo Crivelli. NGL

THE SPREAD
OF THE RENAISSANCE

384 Azay-le-Rideau (Spirale) **386** Tomb of Henry VII and Elizabeth of York by Pietro Torrigiano. Westminster Abbey (National Buildings Record) **386-87** Luther and Melanchthon by Lucas Cranach the Younger. North Carolina Museum of Art, Kress Collection **387** Self-portrait by Dürer, 1484. Albertina, Vienna (Roger-Viollet)—Self-portrait by Dürer, 1493. Louvre (Giraudon)—Self-portrait by Dürer, 1500. Detail. Alte Pinakothek, Munich (Roger-Viollet) **388** "Venus" by Giorgione. Gemäldegalerie, Dresden (Alinari-Giraudon) —"The Rokeby Venus" by Velázquez. NGL **389** Sir Thomas More by Hans Holbein the Younger. The Frick Collection—Sir Thomas Cromwell by Hans Holbein the Younger. The Frick Collection **390** Engraving of University of Padua. G. F. Tomasini, *Gymnasium Patavinum,* Udine, 1654—Title page. Erasmus, *The Praise of Folly,* 1549. The Pierpont Morgan Library **391** Erasmus by Hans Holbein the Younger. Louvre (Giraudon) **392** Chambord (Archives Photographiques) **393** Francis I and court. Ms. 1672, Musée Condée, Chantilly (Giraudon) **394** Marguerite of Navarre and the Duchess d'Etampes. Ms. 1878, Musée Condé, Chantilly (Giraudon)—Pantagruel. *La Navigation du compagnon à la Bouteille,* Lyons, 1532 (Giraudon) **395** Marguerite of Navarre, after Corneille de Lyon. BN (Giraudon) **396** Moneylender and His Wife" by Quentin Matsys. Louvre (Giraudon) **397** Shakespeare. First folio, 1623. The Folger Shakespeare Library—The Swan Theater, after Johann de Witt. Ms. 842. Bibliotheek der Rijksuniversiteit, Utrecht **398** Thomas Howard, Earl of Arundel and Surrey, by Daniel Mytens or van Somer. By permission of His Grace, the Duke of Norfolk **399** Queen Elizabeth I and goddesses by Hans Eworth. Hampton Court. Copyright reserved **401** "Giovanni Arnolfini and His Wife" by Jan van Eyck. NGL **402** Frances I by Clouet. Louvre (Giraudon) **403** Saltcellar by Cellini. Kunsthistorisches Museum, Vienna (Bulloz) —"Mona Lisa" by Leonardo da Vinci. Louvre (Bulloz) **404-5** "Field of the Cloth of Gold," 16th century. Anonymous. Hampton Court. Copyright reserved **406-7** "Sack of Rome" probably by Pieter Brueghel the Elder. Collection of M. Destombes, Paris **408-9** Longleat by Jan Siberechts. Collection of the Marquess of Bath **409** Young man. Miniature by Nicholas Hilliard. Victoria and Albert Museum. Copyright reserved **410** View of Arco by Dürer. Louvre (Giraudon)—"The Four Witches" by Dürer. BN (Giraudon) **411** "The Nativity" by Dürer. Alte Pinakothek, Munich (Eric Schaal, courtesy *Time*) **412** "Surrender of Breda" by Velázquez. Prado, Madrid **413** "Adoration of the Shepherds" by El Greco. Prado, Madrid (Pierre Boulat, courtesy *Time*) **414-15** "Interior of the Uffizi" by Zoffany. Copyright reserved (Courtesy *Life*) **416** "The Roman Forum" by Canaletto. By gracious permission of Her Majesty Queen Elizabeth, the Queen Mother.

COLOR PHOTOGRAPHY: New York, Herbert Loebel, Geoffrey Clements; Washington, D. C., Henry C. Beville; London, Zoltan Wegner; Paris, Giraudon, Claude Michaelsides, Louis Laniepce, Albane, Bibliothèque Nationale (Service Photographique); Bergamo, Foto Wells; Florence, Scala, G. B. Pineider; Milan, Claudio Emmer, Walter Scansani; Modena, Umberto Orlandini; Siena, Foto Grassi; Vatican City, Sansaini; Venice, Foto Fiorentini.

NOTE: *Where page numbers appear in italics, it indicates that the subject is illustrated. Usually the italicized page number refers to the page on which the picture caption appears. Where the creator of a work of art is unknown, the work is listed by title.*

A

ABELARD, PETER, 31, 345, 351
ACRE, PALESTINE, 258
ADIGE (river), 277
ADIMARI WEDDING, 347
ADRIAN VI, POPE, *211,* 246
AENEAS, *172*
AESOP'S *FABLES, 331*
AISTOLF, LAWS OF, 14
ALAMANNI, LUIGI, 63
ALBERTI, LEON BATTISTA, 307, 331
  Autobiography, excerpt from, 331
  In Florence, 113
  In Mantua, 51, 80
  In Rimini, 51, 83
  In Rome, 216-17, 218
  Mentioned, 93, 97, 233, 253, 319, 339
  Quoted, 113, 125, 306
  Works,
    Tempio Malatestiano, *51, 83*
    Sant' Andrea, Church of, Mantua, 51
    Self-portrait, *307*
ALBIZZI FAMILY, 146
ALBIZZI, MASO DEGLI, 137
ALCHEMY, 191, 358
ALEANDER, GIROLAMO, 243
ALEXANDER VI, POPE, 74, *211,* 212, 219-20, 228, *239, 240, 241,* 325, 347
  Corruption of, 59, 219-20, 240, 241
  And French invasion, 365
  Mentioned, 60, 75, 141, 213, 217, 221, 309
  And Mistress (Vannozza), 219
  Patronage of, 215, 243
  Relations with the Turks, 238
ALEXANDRIA, EGYPT, 258, 303
ALFONSO OF ARAGON, KING OF NAPLES, 87, 400
ALFONSO, DUKE OF BISCEGLIE, 60, 75
ALLIANCES. *See* Diplomacy
ALUM, 138, 140, 232
AMALFI, 14
AMBASSADORS. *See* Diplomacy
AMBOISE, FRANCE, 190, 392
AMBROGIO DA MILANO, 327
AMBROSE, SAINT, 30, *36, 55,* 328
AMEDEUS, DUKE OF SAVOY. *See* Felix V, Antipope
AMMANATI, CARDINAL, 232
AMUSEMENTS, 314, 317
ANATOMY, 93, 113, 125, 186, 342
ANCONA, 232, *236,* 321, 323
ANDREW, SAINT, 231
ANGELICO, FRA, 20, 94, 95, 138, 147, 218, *236,* 249, 341
  Works,
    Adoration of the Magi (with Filippo Lippi, *155*
    Life of Saint Nicholas, (detail) *94*
    Saint Lawrence Distributing Alms, 249
ANGUISOLA FAMILY, 174

ANJOU, HOUSE OF, 86, 87, 323
ANTIOCHUS, 14
ANTONELLO DA MESSINA, 97, 99, 382
  Works,
    Saint Jerome in His Study, 99
    Virgin Annunciate, 382
APOLLO BELVEDERE. 213, 215, 216
AQUILA, 323
AQUINAS, SAINT THOMAS, 17, 55, 191, *254,* 327, 328
ARABS, INFLUENCE OF ON ITALY, 17, 18
ARAGON, HOUSE OF, 86, 87, 323
ARAGONA, TULLIA D', 356-57
ARCHITECTURE, 20, 89, 90, 93, 388
  In Florence, 19, 94-95, 113, 136
  In Rome, 218
  In Venice, 271, 288-89
ARCO, *410*
ARETINO, PIETRO, 270, 309-12, 313, 319
  La Cortigiana, 311
  Mentioned, 316, 318, 354, 368
  Quoted, 79, 309-10, 311
AREZZO, 25, 310
  San Francesco, Church of, Frescoes in, 89
  Via dell' Orto, 25
ARIADNE, *136-37*
ARIOSTO, LODOVICO, 307, 371, 395
ARISTOTLE, 6, 13, 17, 20, 31, 55, *134,* 187, 191, *254,* 315, 326-27, 389
ARMOR, *160, 206, 207*
ARNO (river), 117, 129, *131,* 149
ARQUÀ, 28
ARS NOVA, 338
ARTI. *See* Guilds
ART AND ARTISTS, 20, 54, 89-103, 113-127, 218, 387
  In Avignon, 91, 94
  In Florence, 89, 94-95, 97, 113, 126, 130, 143, 150, 151
  In Milan, 89, 180
  New social position, 89
  In Rome, 89, 91, 246
  In Venice, 89, 97, 98, 99, 113, 125, 126, 268-70, 271, 288-89, 294-303, 388
ARUNDEL, EARL OF. *See* Howard, Thomas
ARUNDEL HOUSE, 398
ASOLO, 349, 352, 353
ASSISI, 39
ASTROLOGY, 47, 102, 142, 172, 181, 182, 229, 231, 340, 342
ATTI, ISOTTA DEGLI, *83*
AUGUSTINE, SAINT, 26, 27, 28, 29, 31, *36, 135, 162,* 243, *254*
AUGUSTUS, ROMAN EMPEROR, 301
AVERROES, 28, 326
AVICENNA, 326
AVIGNON, FRANCE, 25, 94, 209
  Art in, 91, 94
  Mentioned, 26, 27, 216, 233,

236, 245
  Palace of the Popes, 32, 36, 209
  Papacy in, 45, 52-53, 209-10, 211, 233
AZAY-LE-RIDEAU, CHÂTEAU D', *385,403*

B

BACON, FRANCIS, 393
  Quoted, 386
BAGLIONI, SIMONETTO, 53
BAGLIONI FAMILY, 53, 54, 55, 73, 222
BAJAZET II, SULTAN OF TURKEY, 142, 238
BANDELLO, MATTEO, 354-55
BANDE NERE, GIOVANNI DELLE, 79, 311, 312
BANKING, *17, 133, 139,* 140, 143, 145, 146, 147
BARABALLO, *222*
BARBARI, JACOPO DE'
  Works,
    Plan of Venice, 258-59
    Portrait of Fra Luca Pacioli, *339*
BARBARIGO FAMILY, 277
BARBARO, ERMOLAO, 84
BARBARO FAMILY, 267
BARON, HANS, 58
BARTOLOMMEO, FRA, 143, 167, 341
  Portrait of Savonarola, *167*
BASINII, BASINIO
  Hesperides, 51
BASLE, COUNCIL OF, 226, 234
BASSANO, GIACOMO DA, *268*
BASTIANI, LAZZARO,
  Saint Jerome, 126
BEHAVIOR. *See* Manners
BELISARIUS, 14
BELLAY, JOACHIM DU, 31, 395, 405
BELLINCIONI, BERNARDO,
  Rime, 333
BELLINI, GENTILE, 294
  Painting by follower of, *292*
  Works,
    Corpus Christi Procession, 282
    Miracle of the Cross, 270
    Portrait of Mohammed II, *292*
BELLINI, GIOVANNI, 20, 97-98, 269, 294, 298
  Works,
    Christ's Descent into Limbo, 309
    Feast of the Gods (with Titian), *102, 103*
    Paintings in Doge's Palace, Venice, 99
    Saint Dominic, 297
    Saint Francis in Ecstasy, 98, 126
BELLINI, JACOPO
  Design for a Venetian palace, *267*
BELLINI FAMILY, 93, 269
BELTRAFFIO, GIOVANNI ANTONIO
  Drawing of Isabella of Aragon, *180*
BELVEDERE, CORTILE DEL.

See Vatican
BEMBO, PIETRO, CARDINAL, 243, 336, 350-53, 354, 391
  Gli Asolani, 351, 352
  Quoted, 373
BENCI, DONATO, 151
BENTIVOGLIO FAMILY, 41, 52, 354
BERENSON, BERNARD, Quoted, 90, 94
BERGAMINI, COUNT, 364
BERGAMO, 76, 265, 277, 280
BERNARDINO OF SIENA, SAINT, 54, *55,* 91, 213, 225
BERNINI, GIOVANNI LORENZO, 218
BERRUGUETE, PEDRO, Portrait of Federigo da Montefeltro, *312*
BERRY, DUC DE,
  Très Riches Heures of, 97
BERTOLDO, 106, 155
BETTO, BERNARDINO DI. *See* Pinturicchio
BIANCHINI, G., *340*
BIBBIENA, BERNARDO DOVIZIO DA, CARDINAL, 243
BILHERES, JEAN, CARDINAL OF SAINT DENIS, 107, 253
BLOIS, CHÂTEAU DE, 392
BOCCACCIO, GIOVANNI, *21,* 27, 28, 30, 31, 51, 309, 345, 354, 378, 393
  Decameron, 334, 341
BOIARDO, MATTEO MARIA, 371
BOLOGNA, 17, 41, 52, 58, 107, 109, 110, 171, 173, 220, 227
  San Petronio, Church of, 110
  University of, 26, 391
BONACOLSI FAMILY, 49, 80
BONAVENTURA, SAINT, *254*
BONFIGLI, BENEDETTO, 54
BOOKKEEPING, 339
BORGIA, ALFONSO. *See* Calixtus III, Pope
BORGIA APARTMENTS. *See* Vatican
BORGIA, CESARE, DUKE DE VALENTINOIS, 59-61, 74, *75,* 219-20, 325, 358, 366
  And Machiavelli, 59, 60-61, 62, 63, 74, 190, 219
  Mentioned, 48, 58, 84, 190, 211, 213, 312
BORGIA, GIOVANNI, CARDINAL, *240*
BORGIA, GIOVANNI, DUKE OF GANDIA, 59, 60, 74, *75,* 219
BORGIA, LUCREZIA, 59, 74, *102,* 220, 347, 351, 353, 366
BORGIA, RODRIGO. *See* Alexander VI, Pope
BORGIA FAMILY, 59, 213, 214, 311, 386
BORGOGNONE, AMBROGIO
  Carthusians Following Christ, (detail) *201*
BORGO SAN SEPOLCRO, 95
BOSCHETTI, ISABELLA (La Boschetta), 367, 368
BOSWELL, JAMES, 414
BOTTEGHE (workshops), 93, 186, 269
BOTTICELLI, SANDRO, 107,

122, 140-41, 155
Mentioned, 20, 93, 98, 139, 191, 348, 374
Works,
  Birth of Venus, 107, 125, (detail) *374*
  La Primavera, 139, *374*
  Pallas and the Centaur, 141
  Portrait of Giovanni di Pierfrancesco de' Medici, 99, *122*
  Portrait of Giuliano de' Medici, *141*
  Punishment of Korah, Dathan, and Abiram, 249
  Saint Augustine, 162
  Self-portrait, *249*
  Work in Sistine Chapel, 218, 246, *249*
BRACCIO DA MONTONE, *55*, 210
BRAMANTE, 110, 111, 221, 321, 364, 365, 388
  As Architect of Saint Peter's, 218, *245*
  Works,
    Design for Saint Peter's, *245*
    Logge, 253
    Tempietto, *209*
BRANCALEONI, GENTILE, 324
BRENTA (river), 265, 266, 288
BRESCIA, 265, 277, 280
BRETHREN OF THE COMMON LIFE, 390
BRUEGHEL, PIETER, THE ELDER
  Picture of the Sack of Rome, *406*
BRONZINO, IL, 143
  Portrait of a Young Man, *314*
BRUGES, BELGIUM, 400
BRUNELLESCHI, FILIPPO, 19, 89, 94, 95, 97, 121, 136, 161, 216
  Mentioned, 93, 134, 147, 158, 216, 388, 414
  Works,
    Church of San Lorenzo, Florence, 145
    Dome of Cathedral in Florence, 95, *129, 131, 153,* 245
    Foundling Hospital, Florence, 145
BRUNI, LEONARDO, 134
BRUSSELS, BELGIUM, 389
BUCENTAUR, 257, 275, 276, *287*
BUFFON, GEORGES LOUIS LECLERC DE, 31
BURGUNDY, DUCHY OF, 400
  Influence on Italy, 17
  School of art, 90, 94, 400
BURCKHARDT, JAKOB
  Quoted, 185
BUSSONE, FRANCESCO.
  See Carmagnola
BYRON, GEORGE GORDON, LORD, 279
  Quoted, 414
BYZANTIUM, 12, 13, 162
  Fall of, 138, 214, 230, 238, 257, 276
  Influence on Italian art, 17, 19, 90, 93, 94, 96, 126, 294
  Relations with Venice, 257, 281, 292, 294

C

CABOT FAMILY, 305
CADORE, HILLS OF, 266
CAESAR, JULIUS, 31, 162, *202-3,* 301, 326
CAIRO, EGYPT, 258
CALAIS, FRANCE, 404, 405
CALIGULA, ROMAN EMPEROR, 59
CALIXTUS III, POPE, 87, *211*
CAMBRAI, LEAGUE OF, 58, 265, 366
CAMBRIDGE, UNIVERSITY OF, 385
CANALETTO, ANTONIO,
  Picture of Roman Forum, *414*
CAPISTRANO, SAINT GIOVANNI DA, 227
CAPONE, AL, 59
CAPRANICA, CARDINAL, 226, 234
CAPUA, SACK OF, 60
CAPULET (CAPELETTI) FAMILY, 73
CARDE, BERNARDINO DELLA, 78
CARDS. *See* Amusements
CAREGGI, MEDICI VILLA AT, 152
CARMAGNOLA, 260, 276
CARPACCIO, VITTORE, 269, 294
  Quoted, 294
  Works,
    Courtesans, 379
    Departure of the Ambassadors, 84
    Duck Hunt, 289
    Healing of the Demoniac, 284
    Knight, 316
    Lion of Saint Mark, (detail) *281*
    Return of the Ambassadors, 260
    Saint Ursula, 270
    Young Man in a Red Cap (attributed to), *297*
CARPENTRAS, 25-26
CARRARA, 109
CARRARA, DESPOT OF PADUA, 264
CASA, GIOVANNI DELLA, 314-15, 336, 398
  Galateo, excerpts from, 336
  Quoted, 315
CASSONI, 101, 347, *348*
CASTAGNO, ANDREA DEL, 93, 155
  Shield by, *160*
CASTEL DEL MONTE, *19*
CASTIGLIONE, BALDASSARE, 314, 316-19, 337, 338, 349, 357, 385
  Book of the Courtier, 21, 316, 318, 321, 325, 328, 329, 352, 353, 398, 409, excerpts from, 334-35
  Mentioned, 322, 323, 354, 394, 395, 403
  Portrait of, *316*
  Quoted, 325-28, 334-35
  At Urbino, 321
CATHERINE OF SIENA, SAINT, 230, 236
  Canonization of, 227, *236*

CATO, 135
CAVALCABÒ FAMILY, 174
CAVALIERI, TOMMASO DE', 109
CELLINI, BENVENUTO, 101, 108, 313, *343,* 393, 403
  Autobiography, 343
  Quoted, 403
  Works,
    Gold Cup, *343*
    Perseus (study for), *343*
    Portrait medal of Cardinal Bembo, 343
    Saltcellar, 343, 393, *403*
CERVANTES, MIGUEL DE, 400
CEYLON, 258
CHAMBORD, CHÂTEAU DE, 388, 392, *393*
CHARITY, 132, 145, 382
CHARLEMAGNE, 400
CHARLES THE BOLD, DUKE OF BURGUNDY, 400
CHARLES IV, HOLY ROMAN EMPEROR, 28
CHARLES V, HOLY ROMAN EMPEROR, 183, 276, 301, 412
  And Francis I, 367, 392, 407
  Mentioned, 217, 294, 368
  Picture of coronation, *222*
  Quoted, 316
  And Sack of Rome, 22, 43, 142, 223, 238, 407
CHARLES VIII, KING OF FRANCE, *86,* 87, 181-82, *241*
  And French invasions of Italy, 22, 80, 86, 87, 365, 386, 392
CHAUCER, GEOFFREY, 172, 395
CHESS, *329,* 335
  See also Amusements
CHIGI, AGOSTINO, 222, 310, *311*
CHILDHOOD, 372-73
CHIOGGIA, BATTLE OF, 264
CHRISTIAN I, KING OF DENMARK, 50, 76
  Quoted, 178
CHRYSOLORAS, MANUEL, 135
CHURCH. *See* Roman Catholic Church
CICERO, MARCUS TULLIUS, 30, 52, 55, 134, 135, 136, 165, 214, 215, 225, 305, 362, 373, 398
CIMABUE, GIOVANNI, 35, 89, 94
  The Crucifix, (detail) *35*
CITTÀ DI CASTELLO, 325
CITY PLANNING, 93
CLASSICAL REVIVAL, 20, 21, 30-31, 51, 95, 101-2, 108, 109, *114,* 135-36, 162, 187, 214, 215, 216, 228, 318, 398
CLEMENT VII, POPE, *211, 222,* 223, 310, *311*
  And Michelangelo, 115
  Quoted, 407
  And Sack of Rome, 367, 406, 407
CLEMENT, SAINT, *254*
CLOUET, JEAN
  Portrait of Francis I, *402*
CLOVIS, 231
COLET, JOHN, 386, 390, 392
COLLEONI, BARTOLOMMEO, 76, 323

Equestrian statue of, *76,* 187
COLLEONI FAMILY, 174
COLOGNE, GERMANY, CATHEDRAL OF, 32
COLONNA, ODDONE. *See* Martin V, Pope
COLONNA, PROSPERO, CARDINAL, 228
COLONNA, VITTORIA, MARCHIONESS OF PESCARA, 347, 349, 354, 357, 358
  Quoted, 325-26
COLONNA FAMILY, 73, 209, 213, 324
COLOSSEUM. *See* Rome
COLUMBUS, CHRISTOPHER, 185, 305
COLUMELLA, 214
COMINES, PHILIPPE DE, 271, 392
  Quoted, 271
COMMERCE. *See* Trade
COMO, LAKE, 32, 265
CONDIVI, ASCANIO, 105, 106, 107, 109
CONDOTTIERI, 46, 61, 68, 76, 79, 322, 357
CONSTANTINE, ROMAN EMPEROR, 171, 231
  Donation of, 243
  Statue of at Barletta, 108
CONSTANTINOPLE, 258, 265, 266, 273, 280, 292, 294
  Fall of, 138, 214, 230, 238, 257, 276
CONTARINI, LUCREZIA, 277
COPERNICUS, NICOLAUS, 185
CORNARO, CATERINA, QUEEN OF CYPRUS, 349, 352, *353*
CORREGGIO, ANTONIO
  Drawing of a Woman, *381*
CORREGGIO FAMILY, 174
CORSIGNANO. *See* Pienza
CORYATE, THOMAS, 271
COSIMO, PIERO DI, 93, 246
  Works,
    Passage of the Red Sea, (detail) *46*
    Portrait of Simonetta Vespucci, *374*
COSSA, FRANCESCO
  Frescoes in Schifanoia Palace, (detail) *309, 371*
COUNTER REFORMATION, 23, 63, 64, 223, 280, 407
COURTESANS, 356-57, *378, 379*
  In Rome, 378
  In Venice, 263, 356, 357, 378, 379
CRAFTS, 92, 101, 130, 343, *355*
CRANACH, LUCAS, THE YOUNGER
  Luther and Melanchthon, 387
CRETE, 258, 279
CRIVELLI, CARLO, 382
  Annunciation, (detail) *372, 382*
CRIVELLI, LUCREZIA, 366
CROMWELL, SIR THOMAS, *389, 390,* 392
CRUSADES, 13, 18, 263, 292
  Third, *19*
  Fourth, 257
  Last, 50, 225, 230-32, 236
CUSA, NICHOLAS, CARDINAL OF, 324

D

DANDOLO, ADMIRAL, 261-62
DANTE ALIGHIERI, 17, 21,
  39, 58, 106, 131, 340
  On Astrology, 340
  And Beatrice, 28, 345, 381
  Divine Comedy, 31
  Mentioned, 25, 28, 29, 30, 31,
    51, 64, 233, 345, 381
  Portrait of, *21*
  Vita Nuova, 28
DARWIN, CHARLES
  Origin of Species, 189
DATINI, FRANCESCO, 209
DEMOSTHENES, 52
DESPOTISM. *See* Tyranny
DIJON, FRANCE, 400
DIODATO, 364
DIPLOMACY, 45, 46-47, 50,
  58-59, 84, 87, 134, 176, 259,
  264, 273, 332, 389
DISCOVERIES AND
  EXPLORATIONS, 143,
  305-6, 385, 393, 397,
  405, 412
DJEM, 238, *239*
DOMENICO VENEZIANO, 93
DONÀ, ERMOLAO, 277, 279
DONÀ FAMILY, 277
DONATELLO, 94, 95, 138, 155
  Mentioned, 20, 89, 90, 96, 109,
    134, 147, 414
  Works,
    David, *93*, 94-95, 100,
      136, 219
    Equestrian statue of
      Gattamelata, *47*
    Judith and Holofernes, 136, *155*
    Mary Magdalen, *381*
DORIA FAMILY, 325
DOSTOEVSKY, FEDOR
  MIKHAILOVICH, 143
DRAMA, 287, 307, 308, 371,
  396, 397
DRESS. *See* Fashions
DUBLIN, IRELAND
  Trinity College, 414
DUCCIO, AGOSTINO DI, 108
  Relief by, *51*
DUCCIO DI BUONINSEGNA,
  20, 21, 94
  Works,
    *Temptation on the Mountain
      Top*, *21*
    The Virgin in Majesty, *21*
DUPRAT, ANTOINE, *393*
DÜRER, ALBRECHT, 387,
  410, 414
  Quoted, 391, 410
  Works,
    Four Witches, *410*
    Landscape of Arco, *410*
    Nativity, *410*
    Self-portraits, *387*

E

EDUCATION, 20, 21, 51-52,
  102, 165, 314, 315, 322, 328,
  329, 333, 346, 359, 373,
  396-97
  See also Feltre, Vittorino da
EDWARD IV, KING OF
  ENGLAND, 385
ELEONORA OF PORTUGAL,
  226
ELIOT, THOMAS STEARNS, 29
ELIZABETH I, QUEEN OF
  ENGLAND, 395, 396, *398*,
  400, 409
ELIZABETH OF YORK,
  QUEEN OF ENGLAND,
  385, *386*
ENGLAND, 238, 385, 386, 392,
  393, 395, 400, 403, 405,
  408-9
  Elizabethan, 395, 397, 400, 409
ENGRAVING, 387
ERASMUS, DESIDERIUS, 385,
  386, 390, *391*, 392, 393, 394
  Praise of Folly, *391*
  Quoted, 385, 394
ESTE, ALFONSO D', DUKE OF
  FERRARA, *102*, 222, 351,
  361, 362, 363, 366, 371
ESTE, BEATRICE D', DUCHESS
  OF MILAN, 181, 353, *360*,
  361-68, 370, 371
  Birth and childhood of,
    361, 362
  Death of, 182, 366
  As Duchess of Milan, 364, 365,
    366, 371
  Engagement and marriage of,
    48, 179-80, 363-65
  Quoted, 281
  Rivalry with Isabella d'Este,
    365-66
ESTE, BIANCA D', 371
ESTE, BORSO D', DUKE OF
  FERRARA, 227, 229, 231,
  361, *371*
ESTE, ERCOLE D', DUKE OF
  FERRARA, 361-62, 363,
  370, 371
ESTE, FERRANTE D', 361, 362
ESTE, GINEVRA D', *51*
ESTE, IPPOLITO D', 361
ESTE, ISABELLA D',
  MARCHIONESS OF
  MANTUA, 52, 80, 106, 205,
  353, *360*, 361-68, *370*
  Birth and childhood of,
    361, 362
  Court of, 354, 358, 368, 378
  Engagement and marriage of,
    362-63
  Last years of, 367, 368
  Quoted, 366
  Rivalry with Beatrice d'Este,
    365-66
  In Rome, 366-68
  As Ruler of Mantua, 366, 367
ESTE, LEONELLO D', DUKE OF
  FERRARA, *122*, 361, 371
ESTE, LORENZO D', *370*
ESTE, LUCREZIA D', *370*
ESTE, NICCOLÒ III D', DUKE
  OF FERRARA, 361
ESTE, PARISINA, D', 361
ESTE, SIGISMONDO D', 361
ESTE, UGO D', 361
ESTE FAMILY, 50, 52, 222,
  361, 363
  Family Tree, *370*
ESTOUTEVILLE, GUILLAUME
  D', CARDINAL OF ROUEN,
  227, 228
ÉTAMPES, DUCHESS D', *395*
EUGENIUS IV, POPE, *210*, 211,
  214, 226, *249*
EYCK, JAN VAN, 97, 400
  Arnolfini Marriage, 400
EYCK, VAN, BROTHERS, 382

F

FACTIONALISM, 22, 41-45,
  57, 73
  In Florence, 57, 58, 73,
    132-33, 137
  In Lombardy, 169
  In Mantua, 49
  In Milan, 183
  In Perugia, 53-54, 73
  In Rome, 73
FAENZA, 366
FANO, 324
FARNESE, ALESSANDRO.
  See Paul III, Pope
FARNESE, ALESSANDRO,
  CARDINAL, 89, *240*
FARNESE, GIULIA, 240
FARNESE, OTTAVIO, *240*
FARNESE, RANUCCIO, *297*
FARNESE FAMILY, 325
FASHIONS, 328, 353, 355, 357,
  359, 379
FELIX V, ANTIPOPE, 226,
  227, 234
FELTRE, VITTORINO DA,
  51-52, 53, *314*, 315, 322,
  327, 328, 337
FERRANTE OF ARAGON,
  KING OF NAPLES, 150,
  179, 181, 203, 231, 362, 365
FERRARA, 45, 52, 265, 325,
  351, 356, 361, 362, 363,
  364, 371
  Schifanoia Palace, frescoes in,
    (detail) *309*, 371
  University of, 350, 361
FEUDALISM, 14, 102
FICINO, MARSILIO, 102, 107,
  129, 135, 139, 151, *165*, 326
FIELD OF THE CLOTH OF
  GOLD, *404*, 405, 407
FIESCHI, SAINT
  CATERINETTA, 382
FIESOLE, 162
FILARETE, ANTONIO
  Works,
    Doors of Saint Peter's, *249*
    Drawing by, *139*
    Sforzinda, 202
FILELFO, FRANCESCO, 51,
  175, 225, 243
FIOR DI VIRTÙ, 329, *330, 334*
FIORENTINO, NICCOLÒ
  Portrait medal of Pico della
    Mirandola, *162*
FIRENZUOLA, ANGELO
  Quoted, 369
FISHER, BISHOP JOHN, 386
FLANDERS, 178, 321, 397,
  398, 400
  Influence on Italy, 17, 19
  School of painting, 90, 94, 97,
    99, 267, 386-87
FLORENCE, 19, 57, 58-59, 108,
  129-43, 145, 147, 149, 150,
  153, 158, 167, 170, 176, 186,
  217, 227, 305, 321, 332, 357
  Army of, 46, 61
  Arts in, 89, 94-95, 97, 113,
    126, 130, 133-34, 136,
    137-38, 143, 150, 151
  Baptistery, *132*, 347
    Doors of, *158, 159*
  Campanile, 39
    Reliefs on, *33*, *129*, 134
  Cathedral, 95, *129, 131*, 141,
    153, 167, 245
  Cultural center of Renaissance,
    23, 89, 129, 137, 153, 187
  Decline of, 140, 142-43
  Diplomacy of, 46, 58-59, 87,
    134, 332
  Economy of, 130-33, 137,
    138, 140, 142-43, 151
  Factionalism in, 57, 58, 73,
    132-33, 137
  Foundling Hospital, 145
  Government of, 44, 58, 73,
    131, 132-33, 137, 139, 145,
    146, 147, 148, 150, 151
    Under Cosimo de' Medici,
      146-47
    Under Lorenzo de' Medici,
      58, 138-39, 148-52, 187
    Under Piero de' Medici,
      147-48
    Under Savonarola, 58, 140-42,
      167
  Humanism in, 58, 129, 134,
    135-36, 150-51, 161, 162,
    165, 187
  Individualism and freedom
    in, 57, 58, 134-35, 143, 275
  Loggia dei Lanzi, 343
  Medici Library, 187
  Medici Palace, 19, 136, 137,
    147, 155
  Mentioned, 21, 43, 44, 45, 74,
    211, 231, 232, 271, 338, 347,
    371, 374, 386, 388
  And Milan, 58, 130, 134, 135,
    136-37, 173, 174, 175, 176,
    179
  Pageantry in, 138, 147-48,
    160-61
  Palazzo della Signoria
    (Palazzo Vecchio), 108, *129,
    167*
  Patronage in, 89, 91, 133-35,
    136, 137-38, 143, 147, 150,
    151, 153, 155, 162, 165, 187
  Piazza della Signoria, 129, 134,
    136, 139, 141, 160, 305
  Piazza Santa Croce, *160*
  Pitti Palace, *131*
  Ponte Vecchio, 129
  San Lorenzo, Church of, 114,
    115, 137, 145, 147
  San Marco, Monastery of, 137,
    142, 147, 152, 326
  San Miniato al Monte, Church
    of, 137
  Santa Maria del Carmine,
    Church of, 90
    Brancacci Chapel, frescoes in,
      90, 94
  Santa Maria Novella, Church
    of, 110
  Santissima Annunziata, Church
    of, 137

Santo Spirito, Church of, 201
Struggle with Pisa, 22, 58-59, 61, 141, 142
Trade in, 131, 133, 138, 140, 143
Uffizi Gallery, *414*
University of, 150
Wars of, 22, 58, 61, 78, 130, 140, 142, 150
Wealth of, 138-39
FLORENCE, COUNCIL OF, 146
FOGLIANO, GUIDORICCIO DA, *14*
FOIX, GASTON, CARDINAL DE, 228
FOLIGNO, 41
FORNOVO, BATTLE OF, *68-69*, 80, 365
FORTIFICATIONS, *14, 69, 71, 72*
FOSCARI, DOMENICO, 276
FOSCARI, FRANCESCO, DOGE OF VENICE, 265, *272*, 273-80
Becomes Doge, 275
Character, 275, 277
Death of, 263, 279
Forced resignation of, 278, 279
Pageants of, 275-76, 277
Personal power of, 276
Quoted, 279
Rivalry with Loredan family, 263, 275, 277, 279, 280
Warnings against, 274, 275
FOSCARI, JACOPO, 263, 277, 279
FOSCARI, MARCO, 279
FOSCARI FAMILY, 267, 277
FOSSOMBRONE, 323
FRACASTORO, GIROLAMO, *342*
FRANCE, 176, 190, 238, 338, 385, 388, 392, 394, 395, 400, 403
Claims to Milan, 180-81, 182, 365
Claims to Naples, 86, 87, 181
Influence on Italy, 17, 19
Invasions of Italy, 22, 58, 68-69, 71, 80, 86, 87, 167, 181-83, 190, 205, 365, 366, 386, 387, 392
Mentioned, 43, 80, 89, 141, 167, 241, 325, 392, 393, 398, 405
FRANCESCA, PIERO DELLA, 89, 93, 95, 97, 120, 328, 371
Mentioned, 98, 221, 246, 253, 321, 326, 328
Works,
Brera Madonna, *94, 96*
Drawing by, *120*
Flagellation of Christ, 120
Portrait of Sigismondo Malatesta, *83*
Story of the True Cross, 89
Urbino diptych, 97, 99, *320*, 321, 324
FRANCIS OF ASSISI, SAINT, 98, *126*
FRANCIS I, KING OF FRANCE, *183*, 231, 343, 368, 392, *393*, 395, 400, *402*, 403
And Charles V, 367, 392, 407
Court of, 393, 395, 403
At Field of the Cloth of Gold, *404, 405*

And French invasions of Italy, 22
Patronage of, 190, 392-93, 403
Quoted, 393, 403
FRANGIPANI FAMILY, 11, 209
FRANKFURT, CONGRESS OF, 230
FREDERICK I (BARBAROSSA), HOLY ROMAN EMPEROR, 169
FREDERICK II, HOLY ROMAN EMPEROR, 18-19
FREDERICK III, HOLY ROMAN EMPEROR, 226, 230, 231, *234, 340*
FREUND, JOHN, 226
FUGGER FAMILY, 239

G

GADDI, TADDEO
Portrait of Dante, (copy) *21*
GAFORI, FRANCHINO, *338*
GALEN, 192
GALILEO, 106, 189, 391
GALLERANI, CECILIA, *122, 189, 363, 364*
GALLI, JACOPO, 107, 253
GAMA, VASCO DA, 258
GAMBLING. *See* Amusements
GAMES. *See* Amusements
GANDIA, DUKE OF. *See* Borgia, Giovanni
GARDA, LAKE, 277
GATTAMELATA, 47, 322
Equestrian statue of, *47*
GENOA, 14, 58, 169, 179, 180, 258, 259, 264, 273, 275, 280, 305
GENTILE DA FABRIANO, 100, 246
GENTLEMEN, 21, 102, 136, 314-19, 329-36, 337, 359, 398-99, 414
GEORGE III, KING OF ENGLAND, 409
GERMANY, 294, 385, 386, 387, 389, 390, 392, 400, 406, 407, 410
GENGHIS KHAN, 18
GHENT, BELGIUM, 400
GHIBELLINES, 42, 43, 73, 170, 361
GHIBERTI, LORENZO, 20, 89, 95, 134, 158
Quoted, 159
Works,
Doors of Baptistery, Florence, *158, 159*
Self-portrait, *159*
GHIRLANDAIO, DOMENICO, 106, 110, 218, 246
Works,
Portrait of Florentine merchant, *372*
Portrait of four humanists, *165*
Portrait of Poliziano and Giuliano de' Medici, *164*
GIACOMO II, KING OF CYPRUS, 352
GIBBON, EDWARD, 414

GIOCONDO, 190
GIORGIO, FRANCESCO DI, 71, 327
Fortress design by, *71*
GIORGIONE, 93, 98, 103, 126, 262, 266, 269, 294, 298
Works,
Adoration of the Shepherds, (detail) *126*
Castelfranco Madonna, 99
Fête Champêtre, 268
Portrait of Old Woman, *381*
Tempest, 103, 298
Venus, 301, 388
GIOTTO, 20, 32, 33, 39, 89, 90, 94, 106, 136, 218, 369
Works,
Campanile, Florence, *39*
Reliefs on (with Andrea Pisano), *33, 134*
Kiss of Judas, 39
Pietà, 39
GIOVANNA OF ARAGON, 362
GIOVIO, PAOLO
Quoted, 173
GOBELLINUS OF BONN, 227
GOLDEN ROSE, *241*
GONZAGA, CARLO, 51
GONZAGA, ELISABETTA, 348, 358, 363
Court of, 349, 352, 358
Quoted, 348
GONZAGA, ELEONORA, 365
GONZAGA, ERCOLE, 367, 368
GONZAGA, FEDERIGO I, MARQUIS OF MANTUA, 52
GONZAGA, FEDERIGO II, DUKE OF MANTUA, 367, 368
GONZAGA, FERRANTE, 367, 368
GONZAGA, FRANCESCO, CARDINAL, 50, *80*
GONZAGA, FRANCESCO, MARQUIS OF MANTUA, 52, *80*, 362, 363, 365, 366, 367, *371*
Quoted, 366
GONZAGA, IPPOLITA, 367
GONZAGA, LODOVICO, MARQUIS OF MANTUA, 50-52, *53, 80*
Quoted, 51
GONZAGA, MARGHERITA, 365
GONZAGA, PAOLA, 367
GONZAGA FAMILY, 49, 50-52, *53, 80*, 311, 324, 363, 367
GORIZIA, HEINRICH, COUNT OF, 229
GORKI, MAXIM
Quoted, 109
GOTHIC ART
Influence of on Italy, 19, 90, 94, 96
GOYA, FRANCISCO JOSÉ DE, 388
GOZZOLI, BENOZZO, 138, 146, 147
Journey of the Magi, 96, (detail) *139, 146, 155*
GRAND TOUR, 414
GRECO, EL, 387, 400, 412, 413
Adoration of the Shepherds, 413
GREGOROVIUS, FERDINAND
Quoted, 231
GREGORY XI, POPE, 236

GREGORY XII, POPE, 209
GROCYN, WILLIAM, 386, 390
GUARINO DA VERONA, 51
GUBBIO, 321
Palace of, (detail) *318*
GUELPHS, 42, 43, 57, 73, 170, 361
Shield of, *42*
GUICCIARDINI, FRANCESCO, 55, 143, 151
Quoted, 69, 148, 150, 151, 367
GUILDS, 43, 130-32, 397
GUILD OF SAINT LUKE. *See* Roman Academy

H

HANNIBAL, *202*
HAPSBURG FAMILY, 43
HAWKWOOD, SIR JOHN, 46, 236
HÉLOÏSE, 345
HENRY VII, KING OF ENGLAND, 385, *386*
HENRY VIII, KING OF ENGLAND, 238, 389, 390, *404, 405*, 407, 408, 409
HERODOTUS, 26
HILLIARD, NICHOLAS
Miniature by, *409*
HOHENSTAUFEN FAMILY, 42, 45
HOLBEIN, HANS, THE YOUNGER, 389
Works,
Portrait of Erasmus, *391*
Portrait of Sir Thomas Cromwell, *389*
Portrait of Sir Thomas More, *389*
HOLY ROMAN EMPERORS, 16, 42, 45, 169-70, 171, 180
HOLY ROMAN EMPIRE, 16, 41-42, 57, 412
HOMER, 30, 52, 202, 214, 328
HORACE, 17, 63
HOWARD, THOMAS, EARL OF ARUNDEL, *398*
HUMANISM AND HUMANISTS, 20, 102, 162, 307, 309, 328, 338, 393, 410
In Florence, 58, 129, 134, 135-36, 151, 161, 162, 165
In Rome, 213-15, 233, 243
Search for manuscripts, 214
Spread of, 386, 389-90
HUTTEN, ULRICH VON, 390

I

IMPERIA OF ROME, 356
INCISA, 25
INDRE (river), 385
INDULGENCES, SALE OF, 223, 239, 241
INGHIRAMI, TOMMASO, *243*
INNOCENT IV, POPE,
Decretals on marriage, illustration from, *348*

INNOCENT VIII, POPE, *210*, 241, 332, 356
ISABELLA OF ARAGON, DUCHESS OF MILAN, 180, 181, 362, 364-65
ISABELLA OF VALOIS, 171
ISCHIA, BATTLE OF, 86
ISFAHAN, 258
ISLAM, 11, 12, 17
ITALY
  Balance of power in, 46, 50, 84, 87, 324
  Burgundian influence on, 17
  Byzantine influence on, 17, 19, 90, 93, 94, 96, 126, 294
  During Middle Ages, 16, 19-20
  First to grow rich on commerce, 397
  Flemish influence on, 17, 19
  French influence on, 17, 19
  French invasions of, 22, 58, 68-69, 71, 80, 86, 87, 167, 181-83, 190, 205, 365, 366, 386, 387, 392
  Mentioned, 43, 80, 89, 141, 241, 325, 392, 403
  Gothic influence on, 19, 90, 94, 96
  Influence on rest of Europe, 386, 387-89, 396, 397, 398-99, 400, 409, 414
  Map of, *9*
  States of, 41, 42, 43, 45, 57-58, 64, 265

J

JAMES I, KING OF SCOTLAND, 226, 227
JEROME, SAINT, 55, *99, 126, 249*
JERUSALEM, 19
JESUITS. See Society of Jesus
JEWELRY, 101, 263, *348*, 353, 364, 371
  See also Crafts
JEWS, 262
JOAN OF ARC, SAINT, 227
JOANNA, QUEEN OF NAPLES, 76, 236
JOHN II, KING OF FRANCE, 28
JOHN VII, POPE, *213*
JOHN XXIII, ANTIPOPE, *210*
JOHN, SAINT, *303*
JOHNSON, SAMUEL
  Quoted, 414
JONSON, BEN, 400
JOUFFROY, CARDINAL OF ARRAS, 227
JUBILEE YEARS, 213, 400
JULIAN CHOIR, 338
JULIUS II, POPE, 47, 58, 142, *210*, 212, 217, *218*, 220-21, 241, *243*, 254, 340
  And Michelangelo, 105, 109, 110, 115, 117, 221
  Patronage of, 221, 246, 254
  Tomb of, 109, 110, 115, 117, *220*, 221
  Works of, 215, 218, 245, 253

JUSTINIAN, LAWS OF, 17, 18
JUSTUS OF GHENT, 328
JUVENAL, 63

K

KEMAL ALI (CHMALI), *291*
KEMPIS, THOMAS À, 390
KORAN, THE, 294

L

LADISLAS, KING OF HUNGARY AND BOHEMIA,
  Letter from Aeneas Silvius (Pope Pius II), excerpts from, 333
LADISLAS, KING OF NAPLES, 210
LAFRÉRY, ANTOINE
  Print by, *213*
LA GIOCOSA, 53
LANDINO, CRISTOFORO, *53*, 326
LANDINO, FRANCESCO, 338
LANDSCAPE PAINTING, 96-98, 99, 113, 126
LANDUCCI
  Quoted, 129
LANGLAND, WILLIAM, 395
LAOCOÖN, 111, 213, *215*, 246
LA PLÉIADE, 395
LAURANA, LUCIANO, 327
LAWRENCE, SAINT, *249*
LAZZARO, MAESTRO, 326
LEFÈVRE D'ÉTAPLES, JACQUES, 390
LEO X, POPE, *165*, 190, *210*, 221-22, 223, 241, 246, 310, 367
  Letter from father, excerpts from, 332
  Mentioned, 142, 164, 211, 217, 243, 352, 357
  Quoted, 190
LEONARDO DA VINCI, 97, 100, 185-92, 193-200
  Background, 185
  Character, 185, 186, 187, 188, 189, 191-92
  Divine Proportion, 188
  In France, 190-91, 392, 403
  And Lodovico Sforza, 89, 187, 188, 189, 190
  Mentioned, 20, 48, 55, 93, 98, 102, 139, 143, 339
  As Military engineer, 71, 72
  In Milan, 48, 89, 179, 180, 187-90, 359, 364, 365
  Notebooks, 72, 189-90, 191, 193
    Excerpts and drawings from, 193-200
  Quoted, 122, 186-92, 193-99
  In Rome, 190, 249
  Scientific interests, 23, 98, 186-87, 188, 189, 190, 191-92, 193-200

Universality, 337
  Works,
    Annunciation, 197
    Battle of Anghiari, 108, 109, 190, 195
    Drawings, 65, 72, 97, 120, 193-200
    Designs for fortifications and weapons, 71, 72
    Last Supper, 190, 403
    Mona Lisa, 103, 190, 197, *403*
    Portrait of Cecilia Gallerani, *122*, 189
    Portrait of Isabella d'Este, *360*
    Saint Jerome, 249
    Self-portrait, *184*, 190-91
    Sforza Monument, *183*, 187, 188, 190, 197
    Trivulzio Monument, 190
    Virgin of the Rocks, 103
  Youth of, 185-87
LEONORA OF ARAGON, DUCHESS OF FERRARA, 217, 218, 362, 371
  Portraits of, *218, 370, 371*
  Quoted, 362, 365
LIBRARIES, 187, 214-15
LIMBOURG BROTHERS
  Très Riches Heures of the Duc de Berry, 97
LINACRE, THOMAS, 386, 390
LIPPI, FRA FILIPPO, 20, 138, 147, *341*, 354
  Works,
    Adoration of the Magi (with Fra Angelico), *155*
    Madonna and Child, 341
LIVY, 30, 55, 64, 225, 326
LOCHES, CASTLE OF, 183, 366
LODI, 41, 45
LODI, LEAGUE OF, 84, 277
LOIRE (river), CHÂTEAUX ON, 388, 392, 403
LOMBARDO, TULLIO, 368
LOMBARDY, 43, 45, 58, 169, 173, 183, 385
LONDON, ENGLAND, 389
  Lombard Street, 15
  Westminster Abbey
    Tomb of Henry VII, 385, *386*
LONGLEAT HOUSE, *409*
LOREDAN, FRANCESCO, 277
LOREDAN, JACOPO, 263, 279
LOREDAN, PIETRO, 274, 275
LOREDAN FAMILY, 275, 277, 279, 280
LORENZETTI, AMBROGIO, 94, 100
  Effects of Good Government, 13
LORRAINE, CLAUDE, 388
LOTTO, LORENZO
  Works,
    Maiden's Dream, 350
    Portrait of Andrea Odoni, *318*
    Young Man in a Red Cap (attributed to), *297*
LOUIS XI, KING OF FRANCE, 147, 232
LOUIS XII, KING OF FRANCE, 22, 181, 182, 392, 403
LUCCA, 130
LUCRETIUS, 214, 238
LUTHER, MARTIN, 106, 185, 223, 238, 241, 382, 386, *387*, 391, 392, 410

M

MACHIAVELLI, BERNARDO, 58
MACHIAVELLI, NICCOLÒ, 22, 23, 55, 57-64, 65-72, 139, 143, 151, 152, 355, 409
  Background, 57, 58, 62
  Cesare Borgia his hero, 59, 60-61, 62, 63, 74, 190, 219
  Character, 61-64
  Diplomatic career, 58-61, 62
  Letters and verses of, 61, 62, 309
  Opinion of man, 313
  Portrait of, *56*
  Quoted, 68, 72, 145, 146, 147-48, 151, 152
  Religious beliefs, 62, 64
  On Statecraft, 63, 64, 65-67
  On War, 61, 65, 68-69, 72, 323
  On Weapons and Fortifications, 65, 71, 72
  Works,
    Art of War, 61
    Discourses on the First Ten Books of Livy, 61, 65, excerpts from, 67
    History of Florence, 61
    The Prince, 61, 62-64, 65, 74, 190, excerpts from, 66-67
MADRID, SPAIN, 389, 400
  Escorial Palace, 412
MAGGI, CARLO, 289
MAGGI FAMILY, 289
MALATESTA, GIOVANNI, 82
MALATESTA, PAOLO, 82
MALATESTA, ROBERTO, *46*, 324, 325
MALATESTA, SIGISMONDO PANDOLFO, 51, 82-83, 203, 231, 322, 323-24
  Enmity with Federigo da Montefeltro, 322, 323-24
  Pius II's opinion of, 82, 83, 227
MALATESTA FAMILY, 82, 83, 324
MAN, 21, 305-19, 329-36, 337
  Pico della Mirandola on dignity of, 162, 330
MANDEVILLE, BERNARD, 305
MANFREDI, ASTORRE, 60, 75
MANNERS, 21, 313-19, 321, 329, 332, 334-35, 336
  Books on, 329, 398
MANTEGNA, ANDREA, 20, 51, 80, 92, 96, 109, 387, 410
  Works,
    Frescoes in Camera degli Sposi, Mantua, 51, *53, 80*
    Madonna of Victory, 80
MANTUA, 45, 49-52, 80, 305, 311, 321, 322, 354, 363, 364, 366, 367, 368
  Castello, 49, 51
  Palace of Bonacolsi, 49
  Piazza Sordello, 49
  Sant' Andrea, Church of, 51
MANTUA, CONGRESS OF, 50, 230-31, *236*
MANUTIUS, ALDUS, 267, 307, 352
  Aldine Classics, 267
MARGUERITE OF NAVARRE,

393, *395, 403*
MARIGNANO, BATTLE OF, *183*
MARIUS, 187
MARLOWE, CHRISTOPHER, 393, 400
MARK, SAINT, *303*
Theft of relics of, 14
MARRIAGE, 347-49, 373, 381
Diplomatic, 171, 202-3, 324, 347
MARTIN V, POPE, 45, 210-11
MARTINI, SIMONE, 36, 94
Works,
Guidoriccio da Fogliano, 14
Illustration in a manuscript on Virgil, *23*
Portrait of Laura, 32, 36
Three Saints, 36
MARTYR, PETER (Pietro Martire Vermigli), 392
MARY, THE VIRGIN, 382
MARY MAGDALEN, 381
MARY STUART, QUEEN OF SCOTS, 403
MASACCIO, 89, 90, 94, 96, 135, 136, 246
Frescoes in Church of Santa Maria del Carmine, Florence, *90, 94*
MASER
Frescoes in Villa Barbaro at, *267*
MASQUES. See Drama
MATARAZZO, FRANCESCO, 53
MATHEMATICS, 95, 120, 121, 188, 253, 328, 339
MATSYS, QUENTIN, 397
The Moneylender and His Wife, 397
MAULDE LA CLAVIÈRE, R. DE, 57
MAXIMILIAN I, HOLY ROMAN EMPEROR, 183, 190, 203, 205, 365
MEDICI, CATHERINE DE', 62, 403
MEDICI, CLARICE DE'. See Orsini, Clarice
MEDICI, COSIMO DE', 137, 139, 146-47, 148, *155,* 227, 274
Friendship with Federigo da Montefeltro, 175-76
Friendship with Francesco Sforza, 147, 175
Patronage of, 137-38, 139, 147, 155
Quoted, 146, 147
Statesmanship, 146, 147
MEDICI, GIOVANNI DE'. See Leo X, Pope
MEDICI, GIOVANNI DI BICCI DE', 137, 145-46
MEDICI, GIOVANNI DI PIERFRANCESCO DE', 99, *122*
MEDICI, GIULIANO DE' (Brother of Lorenzo), *141,* 149, 165, 374
MEDICI, GIULIANO DE' (Son of Lorenzo), *164,* 249
MEDICI, GIULIO DE'. See Clement VII, Pope
MEDICI, LORENZO DE' (The Magnificent), 106, 137, 138,

141, 145-52, *155,* 187, 188
Birth of, 139
Canzoni, 148, 161, 307
Illustrations from, *307, 332*
Character of, 147-48, 151
Death of, 152, 153, 167
Humanism of, 151, 162
Letter to son, excerpts from, 332
Marriage of, 147, 148
Mentioned, 21, 165, 181, 187, 324, 325, 327, 359
Patronage of, 138, 150, 151, 152, 155, 161, 162
Pazzi conspiracy, 141, 148-50, 165
Quoted, 148, 150-51, 374
Rule of, 58, 138-39, 148-52, 187
And Savonarola, 129, 151, 152
Statesmanship of, 139, 150, 181
Writings of, 148, 346
MEDICI, LORENZO DI PIERFRANCESCO DE', 107, 139
MEDICI, PIERO DE' (Son of Cosimo), 137, 147-48, *155*
MEDICI, PIERO DE' (Son of Lorenzo), 58, 107, 141, 152, 155
MEDICI FAMILY, 19, 44, 58, 63, 73, 99, 133, 137, 139, 151, 176, 186, 187, 356, 386
Exile and return of, 58, 61, 141, 142, 152, 167
Origins, 145, 313
Patronage of, 135, 137-38, 139, 153, 155, 165, 187
Rise to power, 145-46
And Savonarola, 141-42
Tombs of. See Florence, San Lorenzo, Church of.
MEDICINE, 186, 342
See also Syphilis
MELANCHTHON, PHILIPP SCHWARZERT, *387,* 392
MELOZZO DA FORLÌ, 321
Sixtus IV Receiving Platina, 243
MEMMO, MARIN, 279
MERCENARIES. See Condottieri
METALWORK. See Crafts
MICHAEL, ARCHANGEL, 36, 294
MICHELANGELO BUONAR-ROTI, 100, 105-12, *113, 114,* 115
As Architect of Saint Peter's, 218, 245, 407
Birth, 106
Character, 93, 105-6, 117, 139
Early life in Florence, 106-7, 111, 155
Friendship with Vittoria Colonna, 354
Interest in antiquity, 109
Letter of, 110
Mentioned, 20, 89, 98, 136, 139, 141, 143, 158, 190, 191, 233, 347, 386, 392
Nudes of, 93, 95, *114,* 125
Poetry of, 112, 354
Portrait bust of, *105*
Quoted, 105, 107, 220, 245, 253, 294, 343
Relationship with Julius II, 105, 109, 110, 115, 117, 221
In Rome, 107, 109, 190

Sculpture of, 100, 117
Works,
Adam, 219
Bacchus, 106, 107, 109
Battle of Cascina (cartoon), 106, 107, 108, 109, 110, 190
Campidoglio, 222
Captives, 111, *117*
David, 107-8, 109, 115, 136, *305*
Drawings, *113, 114*
Hercules, 393
The Holy Family (Doni tondo), 110
Julius II, statue of, 110
Julius II, tomb of, 109, 110, 115, 117, 221, *220*
Last Judgment, 106, 111, 246
Medici tombs, 111, *114,* 115
Moses, 220
Pietà (Saint Peter's), 107, *253*
Rape of Dejanira (Battle of the Centaurs), 106, 109
River God, 114
Rondanini Pietà, 117
Saint Matthew, 109
Sistine ceiling, 110-11, *114, 115, 117,* 218, 246
MICHELINO, DOMENICO DI
Allegory of the Divine Comedy, (detail) *153*
MICHELOZZO DI BARTO-LOMMEO, 147
MIDDLE AGES, 11-20, 90, 308-9, 313
MILAN, 21, 28, 43, 45, 50, 58, 146, 169-83, 188, 201-7, 265, 273, 305, 321, 322, 323, 324, 339, 368, 371
Armor industry of, 206, 207
Arts in, 89, 190
Castello, *170, 177, 179,* 305
Cathedral, 48, *169,* 201
Convento delle Grazie, 354
Diplomacy of, 46, 87, 176
Factionalism in, 183
And Florence, 58, 130, 134, 135, 136-37, 173, 174, 175, 176, 179
French claims to, 180-81, 182, 365
And French invasions of Italy, 43, 182, 183, 190, 403
Government of,
Under Filippo Maria Visconti, 174-76
Under Francesco Sforza, 176-77
Under Galeazzo Maria Sforza, 177-79
Under Gian Galeazzo Visconti, 58, 170-74
Under Gian Maria Visconti, 174
Under Lodovico Sforza, 89, 179-83
Leonardo in, 48, 89, 179, 180, 187-90, 359, 364, 365
Pageantry in, 177-78, 179-80, 181, 205, 207, 364, 365
Patronage in, 23, 89, 91
Plan of, *170*
Santa Maria delle Grazie, 366
Struggle with Venice, 50, 174, 180, 273
War, 22
Wealth of, 177-78, 180

MILITARY CAMPAIGNS. See War
MINCIO (river), 49
MINO DA FIESOLE, 246
MIRANDOLA, 162
MISSAGLIA FAMILY, 206, 207
MOCENIGO, TOMMASO, DOGE OF VENICE, 273, 274, 275
MOHAMMED II, SULTAN OF TURKEY, 230, 231, *292, 294*
MOLINELLA, BATTLE OF, 323
MONACO, LORENZO, 100
MONASTIC LIFE, 308, 341
MONFERRATO, 368
MONTAGUE (MONTECCHI) FAMILY, 73
MONTAIGNE, MICHEL DE, 31, *327,* 393, 400
MONTEFELTRO, FEDERIGO DA, DUKE OF URBINO, 21, *53,* 99, 228, *312, 320,* 321-28
Accomplishments, 321-22
Art collection, 325
Background, 321-22
Becomes Duke, 325
Character, 322-23, 325, 326, 327, 328
As Condottiere, 211-12, 322, 323, 324, 325
Court of, 325, 327
Death of, 325
Distinctions, 312, 324, 385
Education, 52, 322
Enmity with Sigismondo Malatesta, 322, 323-24
Friendship with Francesco Sforza, 175-76
Library of, 312, 326, 328
Marriage, 322, 324
Palaces of, 318, 327
Patronage of, 326, 327, 328, 400
Quoted, 322
Statesmanship, 321-22, 323, 324
MONTEFELTRO, GUIDO-BALDO DA, DUKE OF URBINO, 325, *339,* 363
MONTEFELTRO, GUIDO-BALDO II DA, DUKE OF URBINO, *314*
MONTEFELTRO, ODDAN-TONIO DA, DUKE OF URBINO, 322, 323
MONTEFELTRO FAMILY, 46, 52, 321, 322, 324
MONTEMASSI, 14
MONTPELIER, UNIVERSITY OF, 26
MORALITY, 48, 59, 185, 308-9, 312-13, 341
MORE, SIR THOMAS, *389,* 390, 392
Quoted, 389, 405
MORO, CRISTOFORO, DOGE OF VENICE, 232, *236*
MORONE, DOMENICO
Works,
Expulsion of the Bonacolsi from Mantua, (detail) *80*
Picture of a tournament, *260*
MOSES, *220, 249*
MOUNTJOY, LORD, 386
MULAZZANO, BATTLE OF, 324

MURANO, 263, 266, 281
MUSIC, 90, 178, 268, 317, 328, 335, 338, 371
MYTENS, DANIEL, 398
Portrait of Thomas Howard, Earl of Arundel, 398
MYTHOLOGY, CLASSICAL, 101-3

N

NAPLES, 43, 45, 58, 71, 86, 87, 91, 147, 176, 181, 182, 273, 294, 305, 322, 323, 324, 362, 364, 400
Castel Nuovo, 86
French claims to, 86, 87, 181
Invasion of, 182, 365, 386
War, 22
NAPOLEON BONAPARTE, 169, 174, 399
NARNI, ERASMO DA. See Gattamelata
NATURE, INTEREST IN, 27, 97, 98, 126, 186, 229
NASI, BARTOLOMMEA DE', 151
NAUPLIA, GREECE, 277
NAVARRE, CHARLES OF, 355
NEGROLI FAMILY, 206, 207
NEOPLATONISM, 97, 102, 107, 111
NEPOTISM, 59, 217, 219-20, 226, 240, 241, 324
NERONI FAMILY, 137
NETHERLANDS, THE, 385, 386, 392
NEWTON, SIR ISAAC, 185
NEW WORLD. See Discoveries
NICHOLAS V, POPE, 147, 211, 212, 214-18, 222, 230, 243, 245, 249
Chapel of, 249
NICODEMUS, 303
NUDE, THE, 113, 125, 294, 388
Michelangelo's, 93, 95, 114, 125
Titian's, 301
NUREMBERG, GERMANY, 387, 410

O

ODDI FAMILY, 53, 54, 73
ODONI, ANDREA, 318
OGNIBENE, 51
ORCAGNA, 94
ORLEANS, LOUIS, DUKE OF. See Louis XII
ORSEOLO, PIETRO, DOGE OF VENICE, 257
ORSINI, CLARICE, 148, 165
ORSINI FAMILY, 73, 147, 209, 213, 219, 325
ORVIETO, 36, 42, 43, 44, 52
Cathedral, 11
OXFORD, UNIVERSITY OF, 326, 389
OVID, 17, 102, 191

P

PACIOLI, FRA LUCA, 188, 339, 341
PADUA, 45, 265, 274, 382, 386, 391
Sant' Antonio, Church of, 47
Scrovegni Chapel, frescoes in, 39
University of, 389, 390, 391
PAINTING, 89-90, 93-94
In Avignon, 91, 94
Burgundian School, 90, 94, 400
Byzantine art, 17, 90, 93, 94, 96, 126, 294
Flemish School, 90, 94, 97, 99, 267, 386-87
In Florence, 94, 95, 97, 126, 130, 136, 137-38, 143
Gothic art, 19, 90, 94, 96
Landscapes. See Landscape
Nudes. See Nude, The
Oil, 97, 99, 267, 294
Portraits. See Portraiture
Religious, 90-91, 96
In Rome, 91
Sienese School, 21, 94, 209
Umbrian School, 98
In Venice, 267, 294-303
PAGEANTRY, 48, 101, 308
In Florence, 138, 147-48, 160-61
In Milan, 177-78, 179-80, 181, 205, 207, 364, 365
In Rome, 217, 222
In Venice, 76, 99, 257, 260, 268-69, 275-76, 277, 281, 283, 284, 287, 288, 289, 347, 357
PALAEOLOGUS, JOHN, BYZANTINE EMPEROR, 276, 292
PALAEOLOGUS, THOMAS, DESPOT OF MOREA, 231, 276
PALEOLOGA, MARGHERITA, 368
PALLADIO, ANDREA, 266, 271, 288, 388
Works,
La Malcontenta, 267
La Rotonda, 265
Villa Trissina, 289
PALLADIUS, 31
PANDOLFINI, AGNOLO, 373
PAPACY, 45, 209-24, 233-46, 332, 386, 407
Absence in Avignon, 45, 52-53, 209-10, 211, 233
Conflict with Holy Roman Empire, 16, 41-42, 57
Corruption of, 59, 64, 213, 217, 219-20, 223, 238, 240, 241, 324, 407
During Great Schism, 52, 53, 210, 211
During Middle Ages, 16
Increasing worldliness and temporality, 211, 212, 220, 238, 324, 325
Patronage of arts, 91, 115, 212, 218-19, 221, 243, 245, 246, 254
Patronage of humanism, 213-15

Relations with Turks, 231, 238
Return to Rome, 53, 211, 213, 245
And Savonarola, 141
Threats to, 222-23, 230-31, 238, 391-92
Wealth of, 209, 212
PAPAL STATES, 45, 52-53, 58, 59, 60, 211
PARENTUCELLI, TOMMASO. See Nicholas V, Pope
PARIS, FRANCE, 345, 389, 390, 393, 400, 403
PARMA, 179, 305
PARTHENON, THE, 114
PASQUINO, STATUE OF, 109, 310
PASTI, MATTEO DE'
Portrait medal by, 83
PATER, WALTER
Quoted, 268
PATRONAGE, 21, 48, 49, 76, 83, 100-1, 188
Of Artists, 89, 91-92, 218
In Florence, 89, 91, 133-35, 136, 137-38, 139, 143, 147, 150, 151, 153, 155, 162, 165, 187
In France, 190, 392-93, 403
Of Humanists, 213-15
In Mantua, 50, 51, 80
In Milan, 23, 89, 91
In Rome, 89, 91, 115, 212, 214-15, 218-19, 221, 243, 245, 246, 254
In Urbino, 326, 327, 328, 400
In Venice, 89, 91
PAUL II, POPE, 210, 241, 245, 324
PAUL III, POPE, 47, 211, 240, 246
Quoted, 313, 343
PAUL IV, POPE, 64
PAUL, SAINT, 28
PAVIA, 45, 172, 174, 177, 183, 364, 365
Battle of, 183, 392
Castello, 364
Certosa of, 48, 175, 201, 203, 388
Library of, 326, 364
University of, 175
PAZZI, FRANCESCO DE', 149
PAZZI, JACOPO DE', 149
PAZZI CONSPIRACY, 133, 137-39, 141, 148-50, 151, 165, 217, 325
PAZZI FAMILY, 73, 133, 137, 148-49, 150, 152
PECKHAM, ARCHBISHOP JOHN, 253
PERSPECTIVE, 93, 94, 95, 96, 97, 120, 121, 158, 253, 298, 339
PERUGIA, 42, 44, 49, 52, 53-54, 58, 173, 220, 305, 310, 381
Arts in, 54
Cathedral of, 54
Emblem of, 55
Factionalism in, 53-54, 73
Palazzo dei Priori, 53
Piazza, 53, 54
PERUGINO, 54, 98, 218, 221, 246
PESARO, 323
PESARO, JACOPO, 239
PESARO FAMILY, PALACE OF, 262

PESCARA, MARCHIONESS OF. See Colonna, Vittoria
PESCARA, MARQUIS OF, 347
PETER, SAINT, 239, 249
PETRACCO, ELETTA, 25, 26
PETRACCO, GHERARDO, 25, 26, 27
PETRACCO, SER, 25, 26
PETRARCA, FRANCESCA, 27, 28
PETRARCA, GIOVANNI, 27
PETRARCH, (FRANCESCO PETRARCA), 17, 24, 25-32, 36, 234, 378, 381
And Boccaccio, 28, 30, 31
Character of, 26, 31-32
Crowned poet laureate, 27, 222
Death of, 28
Drawing by, 21
First humanist, 31
Grandchildren, 28
And Laura, 26, 27, 28-30, 32, 36, 345, 381
Mentioned, 21, 23, 51, 64, 214, 225, 229, 233, 309, 350, 378
Poetry of, 29-30
Quoted, 25-32, 36
Travels of, 26-28
Works, 26-28
Letter to Posterity, 31
Life of Julius Caesar, 28
On His Own Ignorance and That of Many Others, 28
Rime in Vita e Morte di Madonna Laura, 29
Secretum, 27, 29, 31
Triumphs, 30
Youth of, 25-26
PETRONIUS, 309
PETRUCCI, ALFONSO, CARDINAL, 222
PETRUCCI, OTTAVIANO DE', 338
PHIDIAS, 36
PHILIP II, KING OF FRANCE, 19
PHILIP II, KING OF SPAIN, 301, 412
PIATTI, 326
PIAVE (river), 265
PICASSO, PABLO, 55
PICCININO, NICCOLÒ, 46, 55
PICCOLOMINI, AENEAS SILVIUS. See Pius II, Pope
PICCOLOMINI, ANTONIO, 226
PICCOLOMINI, FRANCESCO. See Pius III, Pope
PICCOLOMINI LIBRARY, SIENA, 234
PICO DELLA MIRANDOLA, GIOVANNI, 51, 102, 135, 151, 162, 329, 391
On Astrology, 340
Dignity of Man, 162, excerpts from, 330
Quoted, 102, 306
And Savonarola, 129, 140, 162
PIENZA, 225, 230
Cathedral of, 230
PIETRO, SANO DI,
San Bernardino Preaching, 55
PILGRIMAGES, 14, 212-13, 262-63
PINTURICCHIO, 98, 234, 236

Borgia Apartments, 234, 246
Piccolomini Library frescoes, *234, 236*
Sistine Chapel frescoes, 218, 246
PISA, 14, 36, 45, 130, 150, 173
  Struggle with Florence, 22, 58-59, 61, 141, 142
  Struggle with Milan, 58
PISANELLO, 99, 122, 246, 355
  Works,
  Drawing of a girl, *355*
  Portrait of Gian Galeazzo Visconti, *171*
  Portrait of Ginevra d'Este, *51*
  Portrait medal of Filippo Maria Visconti, *176*
  Portrait medal of Leonello d'Este, *122*
  Portrait medal of Niccolò Piccinino, *46*
  Portrait medal of Vittorino da Feltre, *314*
  Saint George and the Princess of Trebizond, (detail) *82*
PISANO, ANDREA, 20, 33, 89
  Reliefs on Campanile, Florence (with Giotto), *33, 134*
PISTOIA, 45
PISTOIA, GIOVANNI DA
  Michelangelo sonnet to, 112
PIUS II, POPE, *211*, 225-32, 234-37, 324
  Becomes Pope, 226, 228
  Canonization of Saint Catherine of Siena, 227, *236*
  Character, 225, 226, 228, 229, 231, 232
  Commentaries, 226-28, 229
  And Congress of Mantua, 50, 230-31, 236
  At Council of Basle, 226, 234
  Crowned poet, 226, *234*
  Death of, 232
  Envoy to Emperor Frederick III, 226, 234
  As Humanist, 226, 228
  And Last crusade, 225, 230-32, 236
  Letter to King of Hungary and Bohemia on education, excerpts from, 333
  Mentioned, 212, 233, 238, 241, 309, 326
  Nepotism of, 226
  Portrait of grandniece, *354*
  Quoted, 82, 83, 214, 226-32, 234
  On Sigismondo Malatesta, 82, 83, 227
  Struggle with Turks, 230-32
  Travels, 226, 228, 229
  Welcomes skull of Saint Andrew, 231
  Writings of, 226, 227, 228, 229
  Youth of, 225-26
PIUS III, POPE, *211*, 226
PIZZICOLLI, CIRIACO DE', 216
PLAGUE, 13, 27, 44, 58, 381
  In Ferrara, 351
  In Florence, 140, 158
  In Mantua, 50, 80
  In Perugia, 54
  In Venice, 303
PLATINA, 51, *243*

PLATO, 20, 31, 55, 122, 129, *134*, 162, 165, 187, 254, 309, 314, 315, 389
PLATONIC ACADEMY, 129, 135, 150-51, 162, 187
PLAUTUS, 307, 311
PLETHO, GEMISTUS, 83
PLINY THE ELDER, 21, 215
PLOTINUS, *155*
PLUTARCH, 55
PO (river), 169, 273, 361
POETRY, 29-30, 112, 135, 165, 308, 354, 371, 403
POGGIO BRACCIOLINI, 134, 151, 214, 243, 326
  Quoted, 316
POITIERS, DIANE DE, 403
POLE, REGINALD, CARDINAL, 390
POLIZIANO, ANGELO, 51, 129, 151, *164*, 165, 243, 374, 410
POLLAIUOLO, ANTONIO, 20, 97, 253, 324, 387
  Works,
  Hercules and Antaeus, 101
  Metamorphosis of Daphne (with Piero Pollaiuolo), *102*
  Portrait of a man, 99
  Romulus and Remus, *215*
  Tomb of Sixtus IV, (details) *253*
POLLAIUOLO, PIERO
  Portrait of Galeazzo Maria Sforza, *179*
POLO, MARCO, 18, *23*, 258, 305
POLYCLITUS, 114
PONTORMO, JACOPO DA, 143
POPES. *See* Papacy
PORTRAITURE, 99, 122, 267, 270, 297
POZZOSERRATO
  Banquet of Epulon, 289
PORTUGAL, PRINCE OF, 275
POUSSIN, NICOLAS, 387-88
PRAGMATIC SANCTION OF BOURGES, 238
PRATO, 61, 62
PRAXITELES, 36
PREDIS, AMBROGIO DE
  Works,
  Portrait of Bianca Sforza, *359*
  Portrait of Massimiliano Sforza, *204*
PRINTING, 20, 49, 80, 188, 267
PROUST, MARCEL, 143
  Quoted, 106
PTOLEMY, 328
PUNISHMENTS, *45, 49, 82*, 260
PYTHAGORAS, 186

Q

QUINTILIAN, 214

R

RABELAIS, FRANÇOIS, 393-95, 400

RAGUSA, 258
RAPHAEL, 49, 54, 186, 220, 221, *222*, 236, 246, 253, 254
  As Architect of Saint Peter's, 218, 245
  Mentioned, 93, 98, 100, 111, 190, 191, 234, 321
  Works,
  Deposition, (sketch for) *55*
  Disputation on the Sacrament, 254
  Logge, 246, 253
  Madonna of the Chair, 414
  Mass of Bolsena, (details) *220*, 254
  Portrait of Castiglione, *316*
  Portrait of Leo X, (detail) *165*
  Portrait of Tommaso Inghirami, *243*
  School of Athens, 111, *254*
  Stanza of Heliodorus, (cartoon for) *218*
RASIGLIA, PIETRO, 41
RASIGLIA FAMILY, 41
RATISBON, DIET OF, 226, 230
RAVENNA, 277
REFORMATION, THE, 23, 185, 223, 238, 386, 390, 391, 399
  In England, 238, 395, 405
  In Germany, 410
  Influence on art, 387
RELIGION, 54, 212-13
  In Florence, 140-41, 167
  Image of Mary, 382
  In Middle Ages, 12-13
REMBRANDT VAN RIJN, 185, 388
REMUS, *215*
RENAISSANCE, 20-23, 55, 187-88
  In England, 386, 395-96, 408-9
  In France, 388, 392-93, 394-95, 403
  In Germany, 410
  Image of Man, 305-9, 313, 318-19, 329-36, 337
  Individualism of, 143, 306-7, 337
  Interest in Nature, 27, 97, 98, 126, 186, 229
  In Spain, 412
  Search for truth, 22-23, 396-97
  Spread of, 23, 385-414
  See also Classical Revival
RENOIR, PIERRE AUGUSTE, 388
REPUBLIC OF SAINT MARK.
  See Venice
REUCHLIN, JOHANN, 390
REYNOLDS, SIR JOSHUA, 388
RHODES, KNIGHTS OF, *239*
RICCIO, ANDREA, 101
RICHARD I, KING OF ENGLAND, *19*
RIMINI, 51, 82-83, 324
  Sant' Andrea, Church of, 51
  Tempio Malatestiano (Church of San Francesco), *51*, 83
RIMINI, FRANCESCA DA, 82
ROBBIA, LUCA DELLA, 95, 101, 147
ROBERTI, ERCOLE DE', 363
ROMAGNA, 61, 74, 175, 219, 324

ROMAN ACADEMY, 218
ROMAN CATHOLIC CHURCH
  During Middle Ages, 12, 14, 15
  Wealth of, 15, 41, 211
  See also Papacy
ROMANINO, IL, 76
ROMANO, GIAN CRISTO-FORO, 364
  Bust of Beatrice d'Este, *360*, 364
ROMANO, GIULIO, 311, 368
ROME, 11, 19, 23, 73, 209-23, *233*, 305, 324, 325, *406*, *414*
  Appian Way, 382
  Arch of Constantine, 215, *249*
  Arch of Titus, 216
  Arts in, 89, 91, 246
  Baths of Caracalla, 228
  Baths of Diocletian, 233
  Baths of Trajan, 215, 253
  Borghese Gallery, 55
  Campidoglio, Piazza del, *222*
  Campus Martius, 310
  Capitoline Hill, 27, 222
  Castel Sant' Angelo, 209, 216, *217*, 358, *406*, *407*
  Circus Maximus, 216
  Colosseum, 11, 215-16, 228, 233, 245
  Column of Marcus Aurelius, 233
  Column of Trajan, 233
  Corruption in, 59
  During Counter Reformation, 407
  Courtesans in, 378
  Forum, 11, 216, *217*, 228, *414*
  Golden House of Nero, 253
  During Great Schism, 52-53, 210-11
  Humanism in, 213-15, 233, 243
  Loggia della Benedizione, 228
  Mausoleum of Hadrian, 217, 246
  Mentioned, 21, 48, 107, 147, 171, 265, 271, 321, 322, 332, 386, 400, 405
  Pageantry in, 217, 222
  Palatine Hill, 215, 245
  Palazzo Colonna, 367
  Palazzo San Marco, 245
  Pantheon, *233*, 245
  During Papacy's Absence in Avignon, 52-53, 210-11
  Patronage in, 89, 91, 115, 212, 214-15, 218-19, 221, 243, 245, 246, 254
  Piazza Navona, 60, 218, 310
  Quirinal Hill, *233*
  Restoration of, 210, 211, 212, 213, 216-17, 218, 223, 245
  Ruins of, 11, 95, 215-16, *217*, 228, 233, 245, *414*
  Sack of, 22, 43, 142, 211, 217, 222, 223, 238, 367, *406*, 407
  Saint John Lateran, Palace of, 216
  Saint Peter's. *See* Vatican
  San Pietro in Vincoli, Church of, 221
  Santo Spirito, Hospital of, *218*
  Septimius Severus, Palace of, *215*
  Sistine Chapel. *See* Vatican

Statue of Marcus Aurelius, 233
Tempietto of Bramante, *209*
Temple of Castor and Pollux, 11
Temple of Venus, 216
Theater of Marcellus, 245
University of, 215
Vatican. *See* Vatican
Via Giulia, 213
War, 22
Wolf of the Capitoline, *215*
ROMULUS, *215*
RONSARD, PIERRE DE, 395, 403
ROSSELLI, COSIMO, 218, 246
ROSSELLI, DOMENICO, 327
ROSSELLINO, BERNARDO, 216-17, 230
ROVERE, FRANCESCO MARIA DELLA, 348
ROVERE, GIULIANO DELLA.
  See Julius II, Pope
RUBENS, PETER PAUL, 388
RUCELLAI, ANNIBALE, 336
RUCELLAI FAMILY, 19
RUSKIN, JOHN
  Quoted, 379

S

SADOLETO, JACOPO, 243
SAINT DENIS, CARDINAL OF.
  See Bilheres, Jean
SAINT GALL, SWITZERLAND, 214
SALAI, GIACOMO, 188
SALERNO, 346
SALONIKA, GREECE, 276, 280
SALUTATI, COLUCCIO, 55, 134, *135*
SALVIATI, ARCHBISHOP, 149
SALVIATI FAMILY, 149
SANGALLO, ANTONIO DA, 245
SANGALLO, GIULIANO DA,
  Letter to from Michelangelo, 110
SAN LEO, FORTRESS OF, *41*
SAN MARINO, 41, 51, 321
SANSEVERINO, GALEAZZO DI, 364
SANSOVINO, JACOPO, 271
SARPI, FRA PIETRO, 260
SARTO, ANDREA DEL, 143
SASSOFORTE, 14
SAVONAROLA, FRA
  GIROLAMO, 107, 129, 140-42, 151, 152, 162, *167*, 341
  Book of Revelations, *142*
  Death of, 129, *167*
  Mentioned, 58, 91, 106-7, 132, 139, 213, 223
  Quoted, 152, *167*
  Tract against astrologers, *142*
SAVOY, BLANCHE OF, 171
SAVOY, HOUSE OF, 170
SCHISM, THE GREAT, 45, 52, 53, 210-11
SCULPTURE, 90, 100, 117, 136
  In Florence, 89, 95, 106, 133-34, 136, 138
  Michelangelo's, 100, 106-11, 114, 115, 117, 136, 220-21,

253, *305*
SEMPLICIANUS, 14
SENECA, 17, 328
SENIGALLIA, 324
SETTE, GUIDO, 25, 26
SFORZA, ALESSANDRO, 324
SFORZA, ANNA, 363, 366
SFORZA, BATTISTA, DUCHESS OF URBINO, 99, 324
SFORZA, BIANCA, *359*
SFORZA, BIANCA MARIA, 183, 190, 203
SFORZA, CATERINA, 75, 357-58
SFORZA, FRANCESCO, 170, 175-77, 179, 201, *202-3*, 232
  Becomes Duke, 176-77
  Character, 175
  As Condottiere, 46, 175, 211
  Friendship with Cosimo de' Medici, 147, 175
  Friendship with Federigo da Montefeltro, 175-76
  Statue of, *183*, 187, 188, 190, 197
SFORZA, FRANCESCO (Son of Gian Galeazzo), 181, 182
SFORZA, FRANCESCO (Son of Lodovico), 365
SFORZA, GALEAZZO MARIA, DUKE OF MILAN, 177-78, *179*, 190, 201, 203
  Quoted, 178
  Wife of (Bona of Savoy), 178, *179*, 203
SFORZA, GIAN GALEAZZO, DUKE OF MILAN, 179, *180*, 181, 182, 362, 364, 365
SFORZA, LODOVICO IL MORO, DUKE OF MILAN, 152, 170, 179-83, 190, 205, 338, 362, 363, 371
  Becomes Duke, 365
  Birth of, 177
  Character, 180, 188
  Court of, 89, 364
  Death of, 183, 366
  Diplomacy of, 180-82
  Emblem of, *180*
  And French invasions, 182, 183, 190, 205, 365
  And Leonardo da Vinci, 89, 187-90
  Marriage and relationship with wife, Beatrice d'Este, 48, 179-80, 207, 363-65, 366
  Patronage of, 48-49, 188
SFORZA, MASSIMILIANO, DUKE OF MILAN, 181, 183, *204, 205*, 365, *373*
SFORZA, MUZIO ATTENDOLO, 175, 202
SFORZA FAMILY, 50, 177, 180, 183, 192, 202-3, 274, 313, 323, 324, 364, 365, 366
SFORZIAD, THE, 202
SFORZINDA, 202
SHAKESPEARE, WILLIAM, 73, 185, 393, *397*, 400, 408
  Quoted, 73, 405, 409
SICILY, 18, 171, 172
SIDON, PHOENICIA, 258
SIENA, *13*, 14, 42, 44, 58, 78, 130, 173, 225, 241, 321, 382
  Arts in, 21, 94, 209
  Palazzo Pubblico, fresco in, *14*
  Piccolomini Library, frescoes

in, *234, 236*
SIGISMUND, HOLY ROMAN EMPEROR, 226
SIGNORELLI, LUCA, 20, 125, 218, 221, 246
  Drawing by, *125*
SIMONETTA, CECCO, 179
SIMONY, 59, 228, 239, 241
SIMPLICIANUS, SAINT, 31
SISTINE CHAPEL. *See* Vatican
SISTINE CHOIR, 338
SIXTUS IV, POPE, 148, *210*, 211, 217-18, *243*, 260, *254*, 325
  Corruption of, 217, 241, 325
  Patronage of, 218, 243
  And Pazzi conspiracy, 148, 149, 150, 325
  Quoted, 241
  Tomb of, (details) *253*
  Works of, 215, 216, 245, 246
SLAVERY, 14, 263, 356
SOCIETY OF JESUS, 63, 223
SODOMA, 221, 246
SOLAROLO, 368
SOLOMON, 31, 328
SOUTHAMPTON, ENGLAND, 258
SOZZINI, 225
SPAIN, 238, 294, 321, 325, 371, 386, 388, 395, 400, 403, 405, 406, 412
SPENSER, EDMUND, 107, 395, 400
SPERONI, 395
SQUARCIALUPI, ANTONIO, 151
SQUARCIALUPI CODEX, 338
SQUARCIONE, FRANCESCO, 92
STARKEY, THOMAS, 390
STATECRAFT, 57, 65-67
STATES OF THE CHURCH.
  See Papal States
STORY OF TWO LOVERS, THE, 334
STROZZI, ERCOLE, 350-51
STROZZI FAMILY, 19, 356
SUETONIUS, 55
SUMATRA, 258
SUPERSTITIONS, 342
SWAN THEATER, LONDON, *397*
SWISS GUARDS, *218, 254*
SWITZERLAND, 385
SYMONDS, JOHN ADDINGTON, 62, 112
SYPHILIS, 342, 378

T

TACITUS, 326
TALAMONE, HARBOR OF, 234
TAROCCHI CARDS, *314*
TASSO, TORQUATO, 307
TEODORO, FRA, *297*
TERENCE, 31, *307*, 311, *330*, 362
TEXTILES, 80, 131, 138, 140, *263*
THEATER. *See* Drama
THEBAID, THE, 126

THEODORE, SAINT, 260
THEOLOGY, 55, 103
THREE AGES OF MAN, THE, *312*
TIEPOLO, GIOVANNI BATTISTA, 266
TINTORETTO, 93, 98, 266, 269, 303, 387, 412, 413
  Works,
    Crucifixion, (detail) *303*
    Paradise, 270
    Stealing the Body of Saint Mark, 303
TITIAN, 98, *268*, 269, 294, 298, 301, 312
  Mentioned, 99, 103, 266, 270, 297, 318, 381, 387, 388, 412
  Quoted, 350
  Works,
    Alexander VI Presents Pesaro to Saint Peter, 239
    Diana and Actaeon, 125
    Drawing of two figures, 298
    Feast of the Gods (with Giovanni Bellini), *102*, 103
    Il Bravo, 48
    Paul III and His Grandsons, 240
    Portrait of Aretino, *311*
    Portrait of a lady, *297*
    Portrait of a nobleman, *297*
    Portrait of Pietro Bembo, *353*
    Portrait of Ranuccio Farnese, *297*
    Venus Anadyomene, *301*
    Venus of Urbino, *301*, 388, *414*
TITO, SANTI DI
  Portrait of Machiavelli, *56*
TIVOLI, 209, 228
TOLEDO, SPAIN, 412, 413
TOLFA, 138, 140, 232
TOLSTOY, LEO, 109
TORRIGIANO, PIETRO, 385, 386
  Tomb of Henry VII, 385, *386*
TORSO BELVEDERE, 109
TOURNEUR, CYRIL, 396
TOURNAMENTS
  In Florence, 147-48, *160*
  In Venice, *260*
  See also Pageantry
TRADE, 17, 397
  During Middle Ages, 12, 13, 14-15, 17
  In Florence, 131, 133, 138, 140, 143
  Importance of, 397
  In Mantua, 50
  In Milan, 207
  In Venice, 14, 258-59, 262, 263, 264-65, 266, 273, 274, 281, 284, 292
TRAINI, FRANCESCO
  Triumph of Death, 45
TRENT, COUNCIL OF, 223, 368
TREVISO, 265, 277
TRIESTE, 265
TRIPLE ALLIANCE, 181
TRIVULZIO, GIAN GIACOMO, 190
TURA, COSIMO, 371
TURKS, 13, 18, 150, 227, 266, 292, 324
  Capture of Constantinople, 138, 230, 238, 257

Crusades against, 230-32, 236, 239
Relations with Papacy, 231, 238
Struggle with Venice, 265, 266, 273, 276, 281, 292, 324
TYRANNY, 44, *45*, 47, 48, 82-83
TYRE, PHOENICIA, 258

U

UBERTI, FAZIO DEGLI, *233*
UCCELLO, PAOLO, 93, 95, 97, 120, 321
Works,
Drawing by, *120*
Mosaic design by, *120, 275*
Rout of San Romano, 78
Saint George and the Dragon, 96, 97
UDINE, GIOVANNI DA, *253*
UNIVERSITIES, 26, 150, 175, 215, 340, 350, 389, 390, 391, 400
URBAN II, POPE, 230
URBAN VI, POPE, 236
URBINO, 52, 219, 312, 316, 321-28
Court of, *325*, 327, 328, 329, 339, 349, 352
Palace of, 318, *326*, 327, 400

V

VALLA, LORENZO, 214, 243, 309
VALOIS, HOUSE OF, 403
VARESE, 172
VASARI, GIORGIO, 89, 93, 105, 107, 117, *297*, 298, 327
On Correggio, 381
On Filarete, 202
On Fra Angelico, 249
On Giotto, 33
On Michelangelo, 89, 108, 386
On Petrarch, 36
On Raphael, 220
On Simone Martini, 36
On Titian, 297
Portrait of Cellini, *343*
VATICAN, 213, 219, 246-55
Borgia apartments, 234, 246
Cortile del Belvedere, 246, 318
Library, 213, 214, 215, *218*, 246, 309, 312, 326, 328
Logge, 246, 253
Museum, 215
Palace, 215, 216, 219, *406*
Saint Peter's, *213*, 218-19, 245, 246, 324, 406, 407
Dome of, *245*, 407
Doors of, *249*
Excavations under, 213
Plans for new basilica, 19, 216-17, 245
Sistine Chapel, 106, 110-11, *114*, 115, 117, 218, *246*, 249
Stanze, 111, *218*, 220, 221,

222, 246, *254*
Treasures of, 213, 219, 246-55
VAUCLUSE, FRANCE, 26, 27, 28
Fountain of, *21, 26*
VEGA, LOPE DA, 400
VELÁZQUEZ, DIEGO, 388, 400, 412, 413
Works,
Rokeby Venus, 388
Surrender of Breda, 413
VENICE, 21, *23*, 43, 45, 147, 169, 170, 173, 175, 176, 227, 257-303, 305, 321, 322, 352, 353, 363, 387
Archivio Centrale, 259
Aretino in, 312
Army, 46, 76
Arsenal, 257-58, *259*, 284, 291
Arts in, 89, 97, 98, 99, 113, 125, 126, 267, 268-70, 271, 288, 294-303, 388
Attitude toward Church, 260
Bronze horses, *23, 257*, 283
Building, 271, 283
Byzantine influence on, 257, 281, 292, 294
Campanile, *281*
Campo Santi Giovanni e Paolo, 76
Clock tower, *257*
Country life, 265, 266, 267, 288, 289
Courtesans in, 263, 356, 357, 378, 379
And Crusades, 231, 232, 257, 263
Decline, 267-68, 270-71
Diplomacy of, 46, 47, 50, 84, 87, 182, 259, 264, 273, 276, 277
Doge's Palace, 260, *270, 281*, 282-83, 347
Frescoes in, 99, 268, 269, 294
Hall of the Great Council, *270*, 275
Doges, 257, 260, 273-80, 283
Frari, Church of the, *259, 279*
Gambling in, 314
Golden Book (Libro d'Oro), 76, 261
Government, 257, 259-61, 274-75, 280, 314, 347
Grand Canal, *258*, 271, *284*, 287, 288
Industry, 263, *264, 266*, 267, 281
Inland expansion, 45, 174, 180, 264-66, 273-74, 276, 277, 280, 324
Isolation, 58, 264
League of Cambrai against, 58, 265, 366
Lido, 276
Lido, Porto di, *257*
Lion of Saint Mark, 260, *281, 283*
Lion's Mouth, 259, *260*
Marriage to the Sea, 257, 287
Navy, 257, 258, 284, 291, 292
Pageantry in, 76, 99, 257, *260*, 268-69, 275-76, 277, 281, 283, 284, 287, 288, *289*, 347, 357
Patronage, 89, 91
Piazza San Marco, *257*, 282-83, 305

Piazzetta, 99, 257, 271
Plan of, *258-59*
Rialto, 262, 284, 288, 298, 301
Rialto Bridge, *258*, 275, *284*
Riva degli Schiavoni, 262
Saint Mark's Cathedral, *23, 32, 281*, 282-83, 292, 294
Mosaics in, *120*, 275
Sculpture detail from, *270*
San Pantaleon, Church of, 275
School of Saint Mark, 303
School of Saint Rocco, 303
Shipbuilding. *See* Venice, Arsenal
Slave trade, 14, 263
Struggle with Milan, 50, 174, 180, 273
Struggle with the Turks, 265, 266, 273, 276, 281, 292, 324
Supremacy of the State, 84, 258, 259-62, 275, 280
Trade and Wealth, 14, 258-59, 262, 263, 264-65, 266, 273, 274, 281, 284, 288, 291, 292
Villas, *265, 266, 267*, 288, *289*
Wars, 258, 263, 264, 265, 276, 277
Women in, 263, 353
VENTOUX, MONT, 26
VERGIL, POLYDORE, 385
VERONA, 45, 73, 265, 274
VERONESE, PAOLO, 266, 267, 269
Works,
Allegory of Venice, *270*
Fresco at Maser, *267*
Maggi estate, *289*
Self-portrait, *268*
Wedding at Cana, (detail) *268*
VERROCCHIO, ANDREA DEL, 20, 100, 185, 186, 187, 246
Works,
Baptism of Christ, 186
Bust of Lorenzo de' Medici, *145*
Equestrian statue of Colleoni, *76*, 187
VERSAILLES, FRANCE, 403
VESPASIANO DA BISTICCI, 312, 328
Quoted, 323, 326, 327, 328
VESPUCCI, AMERIGO, 374
VESPUCCI, SIMONETTA, *374*, 381
VICENZA, 265, 274
VILLON, FRANÇOIS, 345
VIRGIL, *23*, 27, 30, 52, 109, 126, 225, 305, 362
VISCONTI, BERNABÒ, 171-72, 176, 236
VISCONTI, BIANCA MARIA, 176, 202, 203
VISCONTI, CATERINA, 172
VISCONTI, FILIPPO MARIA, DUKE OF MILAN, 170, 174-75, *176*, 277
VISCONTI, GALEAZZO II, 171
VISCONTI, GIAN GALEAZZO, DUKE OF MILAN, 58, 134, 170-74
Building projects, 171, 201
Character, 171, 172, 173
Death of, 58, 134, 136, 173, 174
Library of, 364
Marriage, 171, 172

Rivalry with Florence, 58, 134, 173
Success of his policies, 172, 173, 174
VISCONTI, GIAN MARIA, DUKE OF MILAN, 174, 355
VISCONTI FAMILY, 28, 48, 147, 170-71, 177, 180, 201, 202, 273, 274, 364
Family tree, *172*, 173
VITELLESCHI, BISHOP, 211
VITERBO, 305
VITRUVIUS, 388
Treatise on Architecture, 195, 214
VIVARINI, ANTONIO, 275
VOLTERRA, 324

W

WAR, 22, 42, 43, 45, 46, 58, 323, 325, 350, 357, 385
Florentine, 22, 58, 61, 78, 130, 140, 142, 150
Machiavelli on, 61, 65, 68-69, 72, 323
In Middle Ages, 14, 15, 16
Perugian, 53-54
Venetian, 258, 263, 264, 265, 276, 277
WARS OF THE ROSES, 231, 396
WATT, JAMES, 94
WEAPONS, 65, 68, 69, *71, 72, 75*, 76, 291, 325
WEBSTER, JOHN, 396
Quoted, 41
WEYDEN, ROGIER VAN DER, 400
WHITE COMPANY, THE, 46
WILSON, RICHARD, 388
WITT, JOHANN DE, 388
Sketch of Swan Theater, London, *397*
WOLSEY, THOMAS, CARDINAL, 389
WOMEN, 263, 345-59, 369-82
Courtesans. *See* Courtesans
Dowries, 346, 348, 381
Education of, 52, 346
Fashions. *See* Fashions
Marriages, 347
See also Marriage
New Position of, 328, 346, 348-49, 369
Salons, 349-50, 358, 378
Sheltered lives, 346-47
WYCLIFFE, JOHN, 395

Z

ZARA, DALMATIA, 258
ZOFFANY, JOHN, *414*
ZONCHIO, BATTLE OF, *291*